PROPHET AGAINST SLAVERY

BENJAMIN LAY: A GRAPHIC NOVEL

BEACON PRESS
BOSTON

Beacon Press
Boston, Massachusetts
www.beacon.org

Beacon Press books
are published under the auspices of
the Unitarian Universalist Association of Congregations.

Printed in Canada

24 23 22 21 8 7 6 5 4 3 2 1

This book is printed on acid-free paper that meets the uncoated paper ANSI/NISO specifications for permanence as revised in 1992.

Library of Congress Cataloging-in-Publication Data

Names: Rediker, Marcus, author. | Lester, David, illustrator.
Title: Prophet against slavery : Benjamin Lay: a graphic novel / David Lester, Marcus Rediker.
Description: Boston : Beacon Press, [2021]
Identifiers: LCCN 2021012708 (print) | LCCN 2021012709 (ebook) | ISBN 9780807081792 (trade paperback ; acid-free paper) | ISBN 9780807081808 (ebook)
Subjects: LCSH: Lay, Benjamin, 1677–1759—Comic books, strips, etc. | Abolitionists—United States—Biography—Comic books, strips, etc. | Quakers—Comic books, strips, etc. | Dwarfs (Persons)—Comic books, strips, etc. | Antislavery movements—United States—History—18th century—Comic books, strips, etc. | Graphic novels.
Classification: LCC E446 .R44 2021 (print) | LCC E446 (ebook) | DDC 326/.8092 [B]—dc23
LC record available at https://lccn.loc.gov/2021012708
LC ebook record available at https://lccn.loc.gov/2021012709

CONTENTS

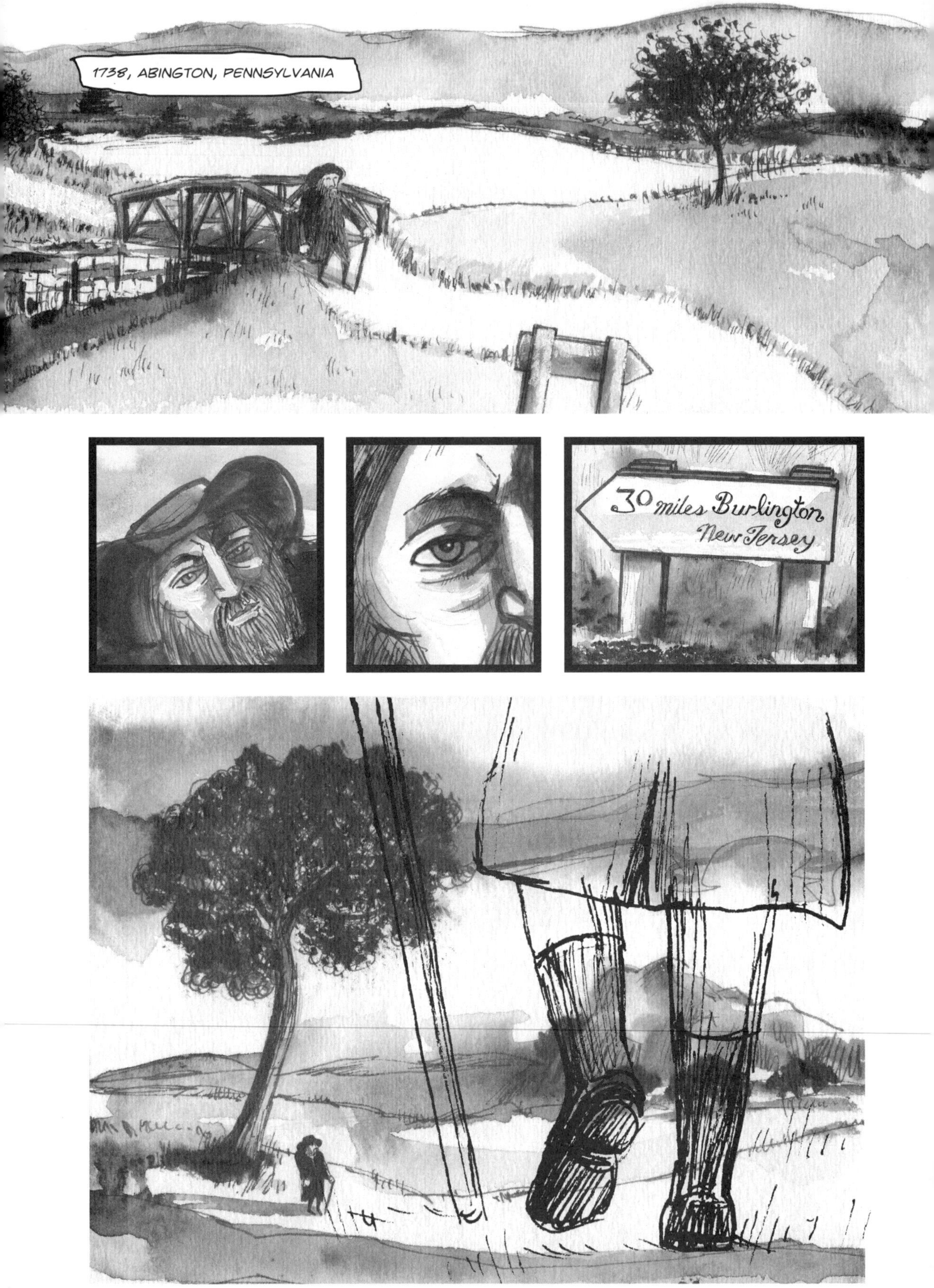
1738, ABINGTON, PENNSYLVANIA
30 miles Burlington
New Jersey

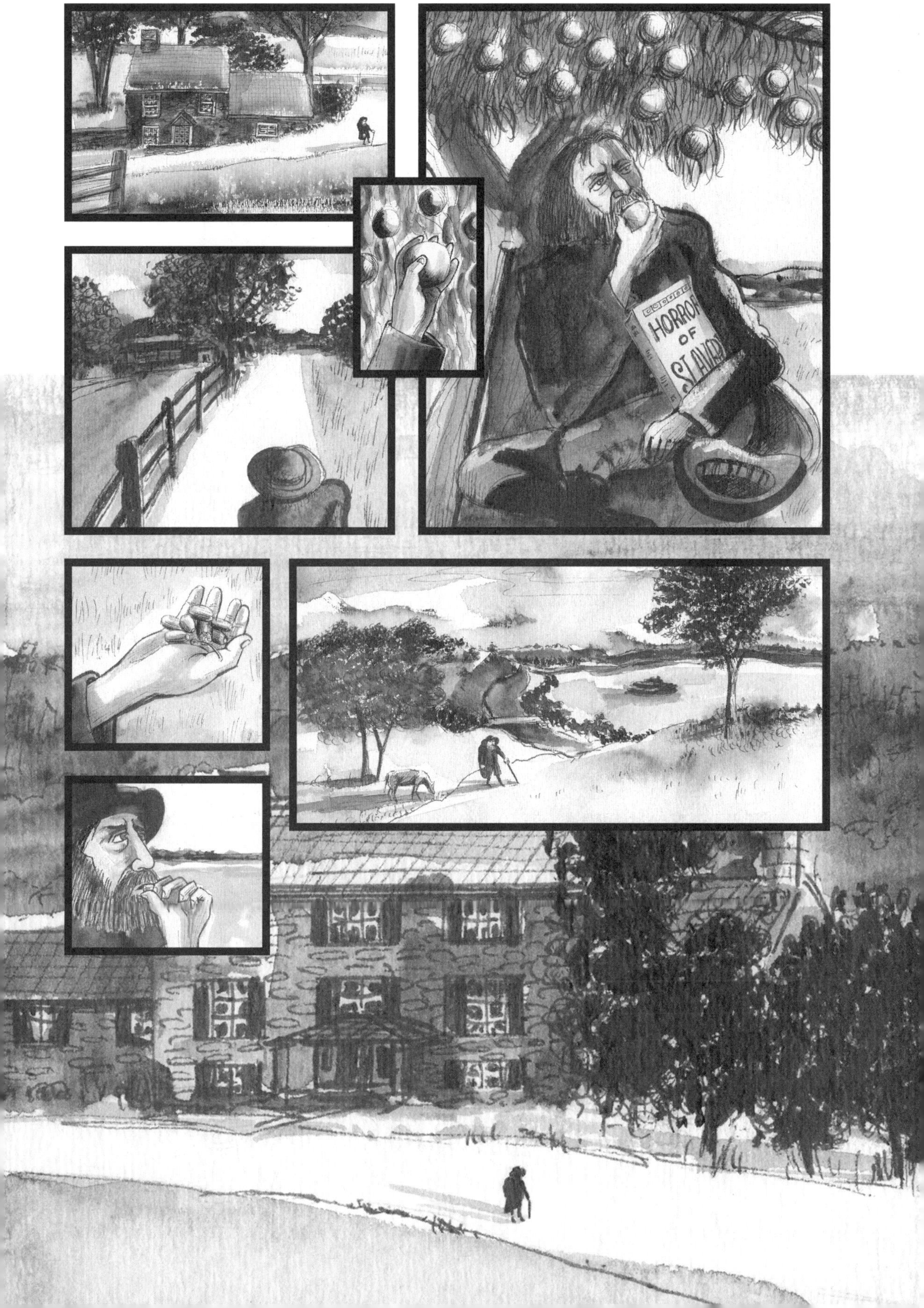
HORROR
OF
SLAV

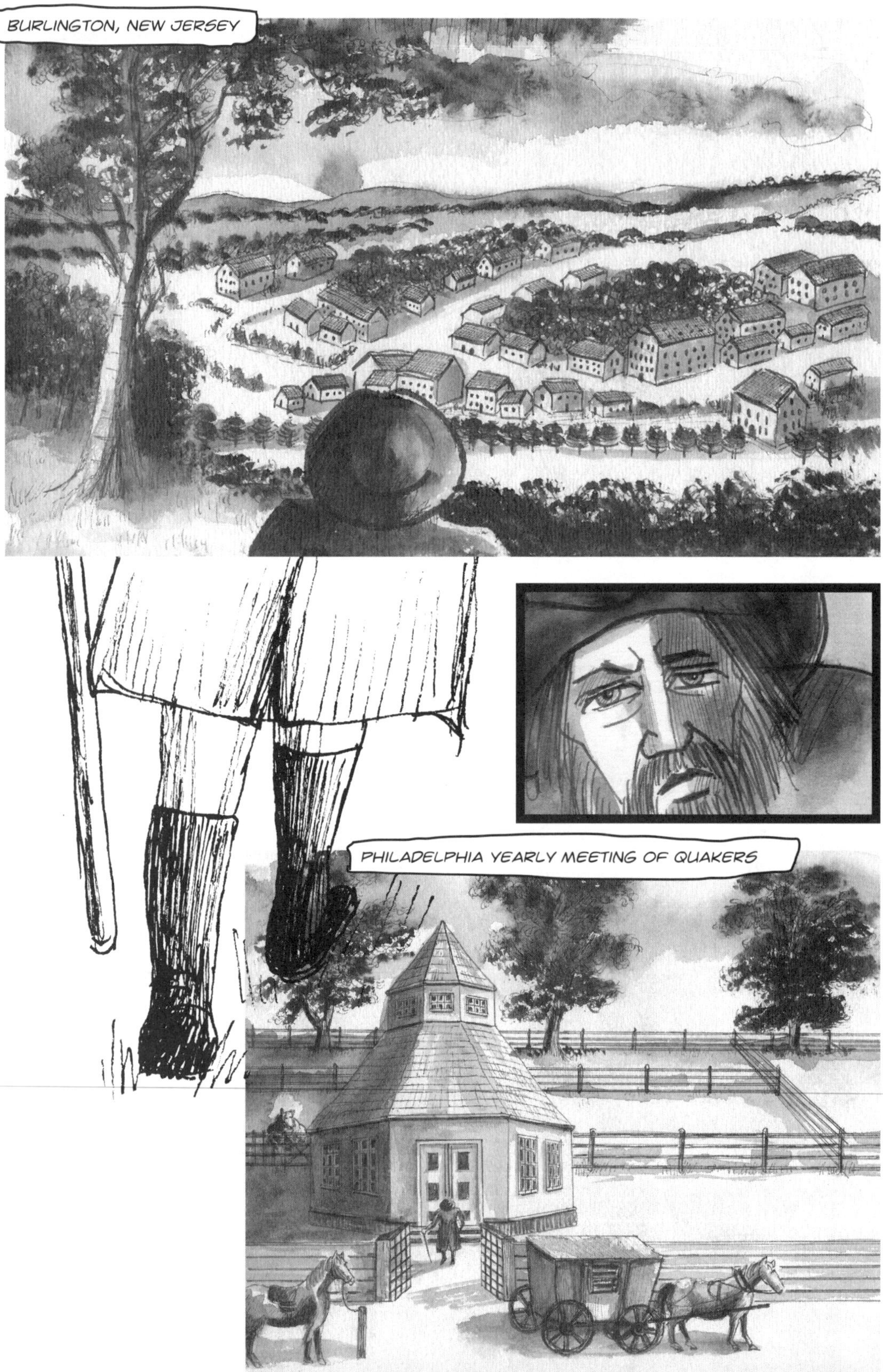
BURLINGTON, NEW JERSEY
PHILADELPHIA YEARLY MEETING OF QUAKERS

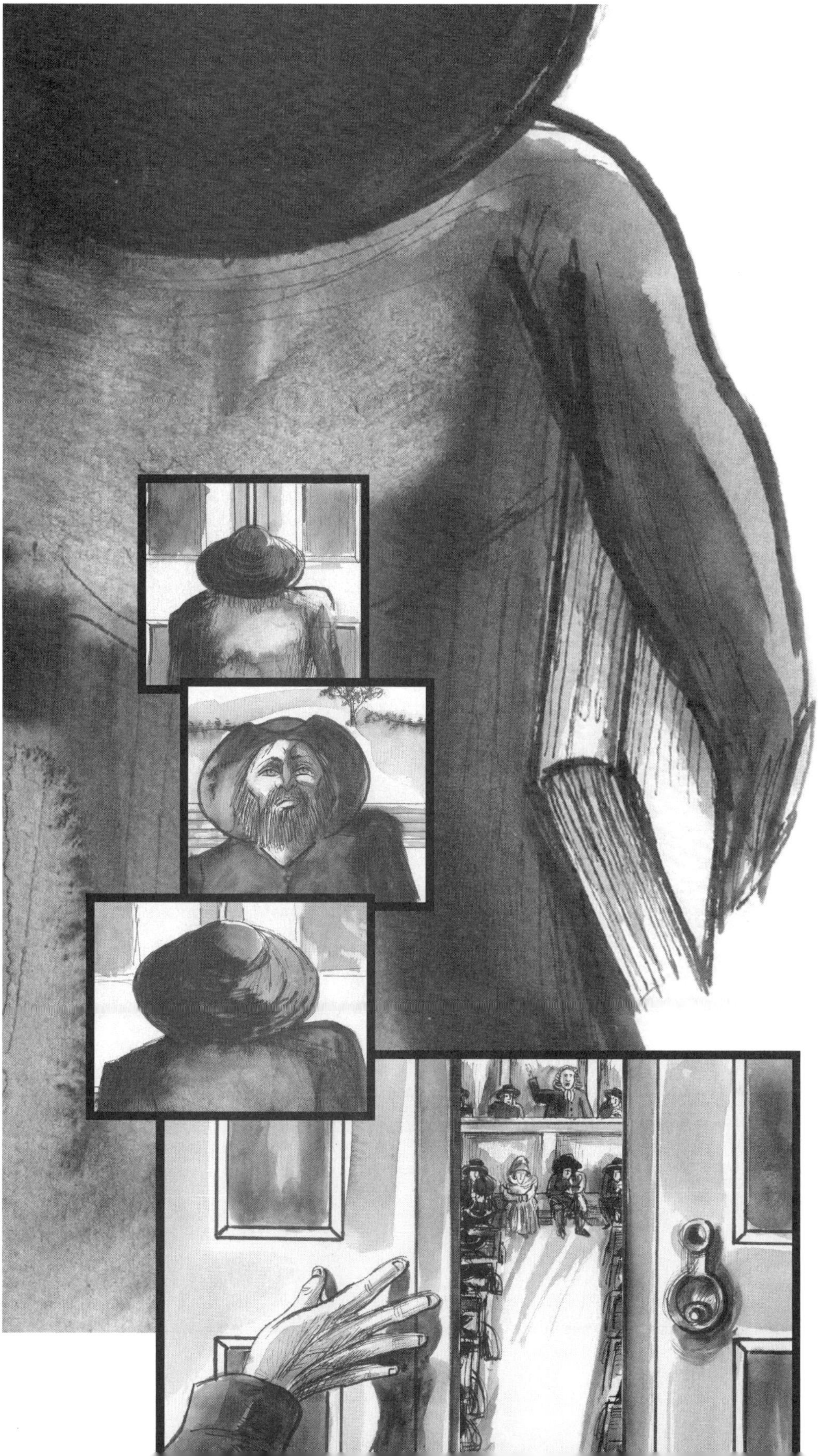

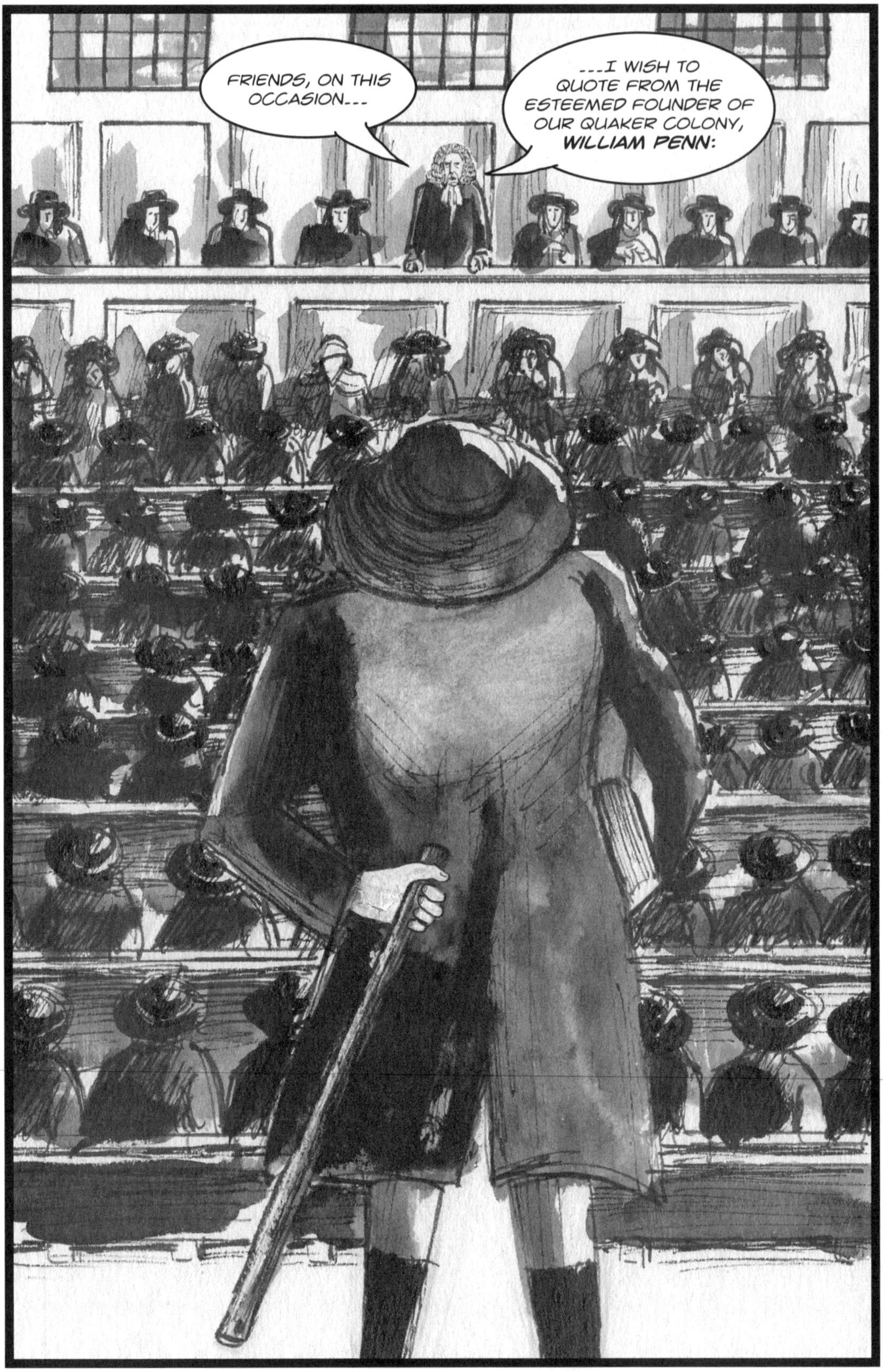
FRIENDS, ON THIS OCCASION---
---I WISH TO QUOTE FROM THE ESTEEMED FOUNDER OF OUR QUAKER COLONY, **WILLIAM PENN:**

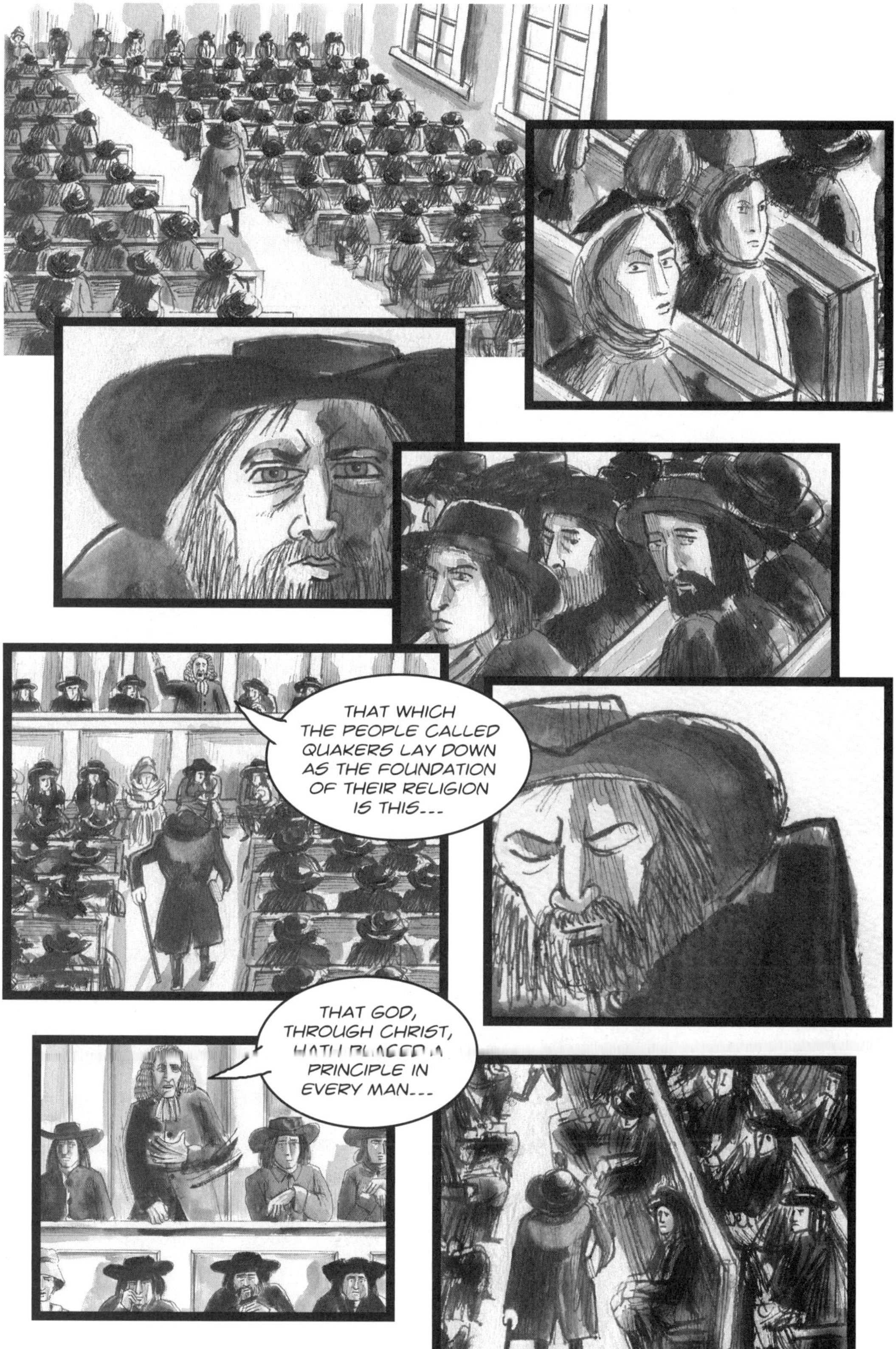
THAT WHICH THE PEOPLE CALLED QUAKERS LAY DOWN AS THE FOUNDATION OF THEIR RELIGION IS THIS---
THAT GOD, THROUGH CHRIST, HATH PLACED A PRINCIPLE IN EVERY MAN---

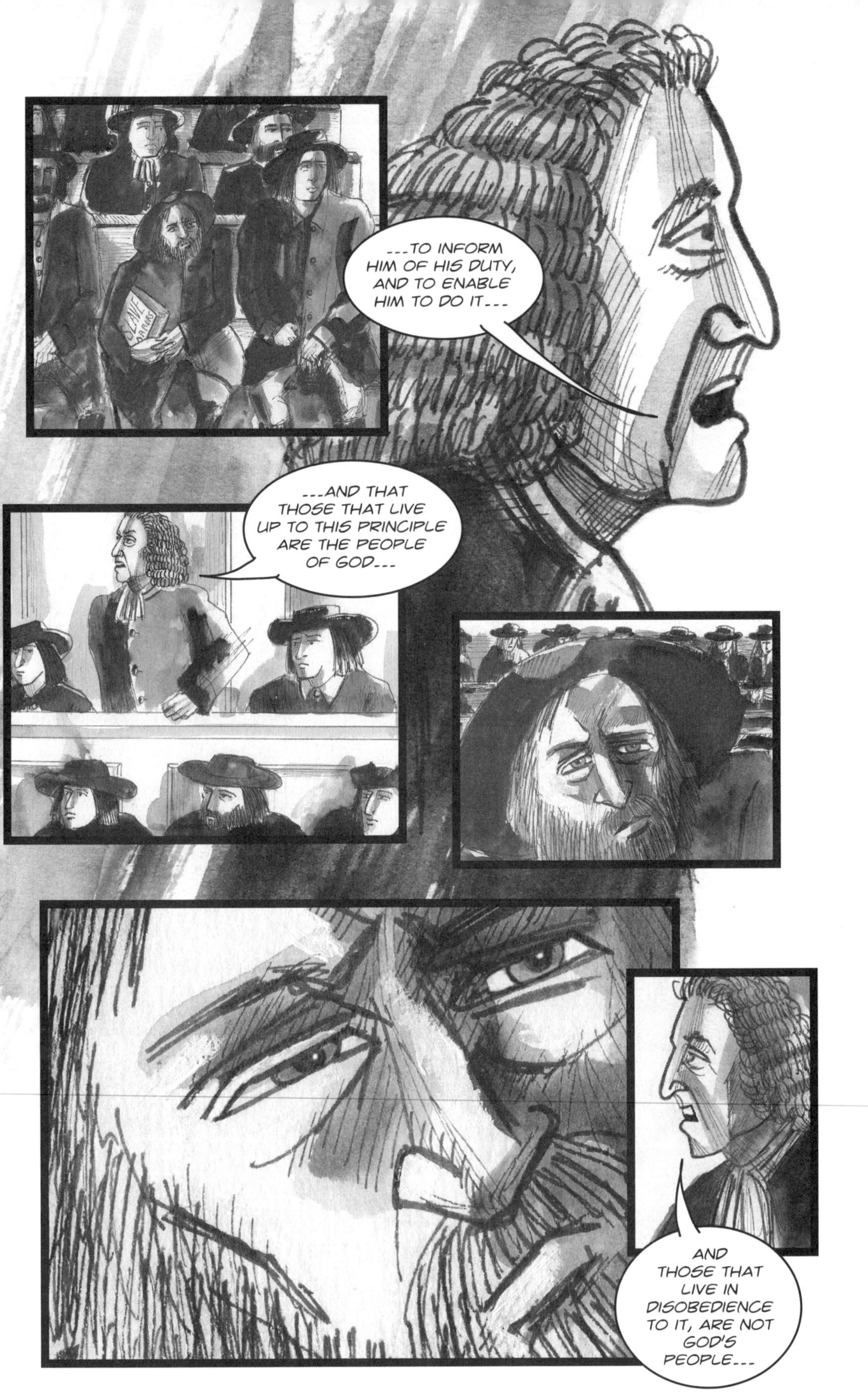

---TO INFORM HIM OF HIS DUTY, AND TO ENABLE HIM TO DO IT---
---AND THAT THOSE THAT LIVE UP TO THIS PRINCIPLE ARE THE PEOPLE OF GOD---
AND THOSE THAT LIVE IN DISOBEDIENCE TO IT, ARE NOT GOD'S PEOPLE---

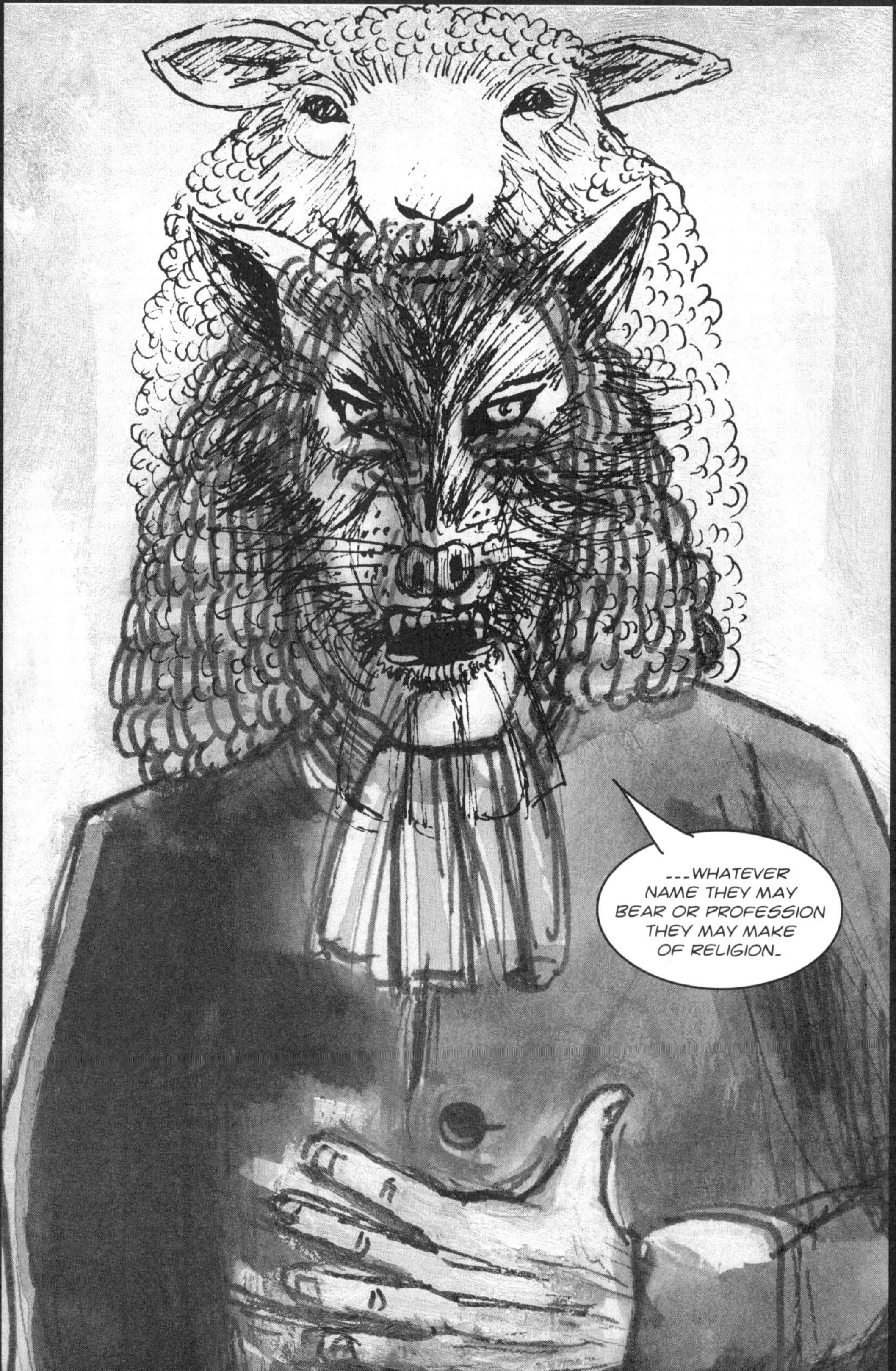
---WHATEVER NAME THEY MAY BEAR OR PROFESSION THEY MAY MAKE OF RELIGION-

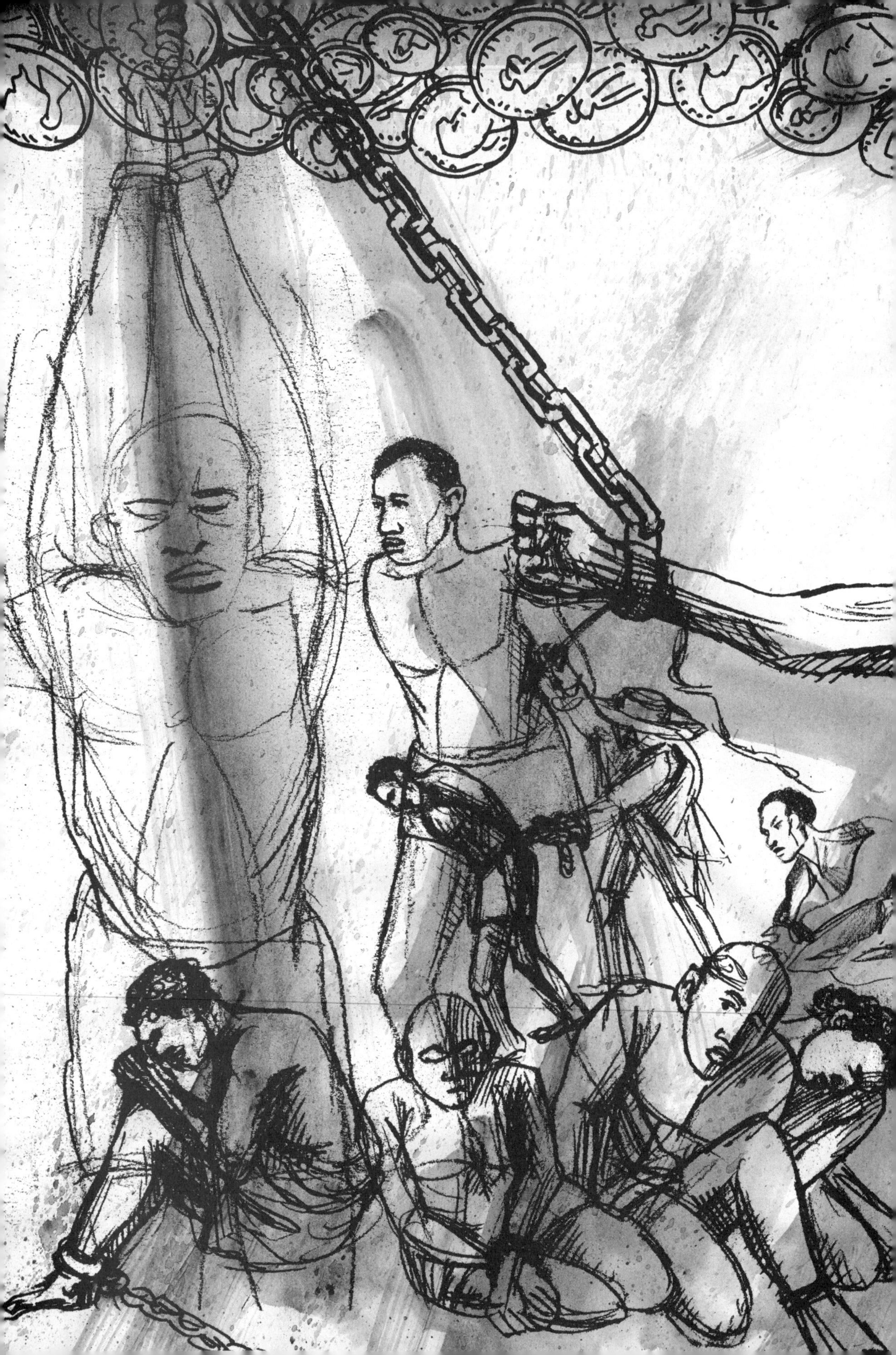

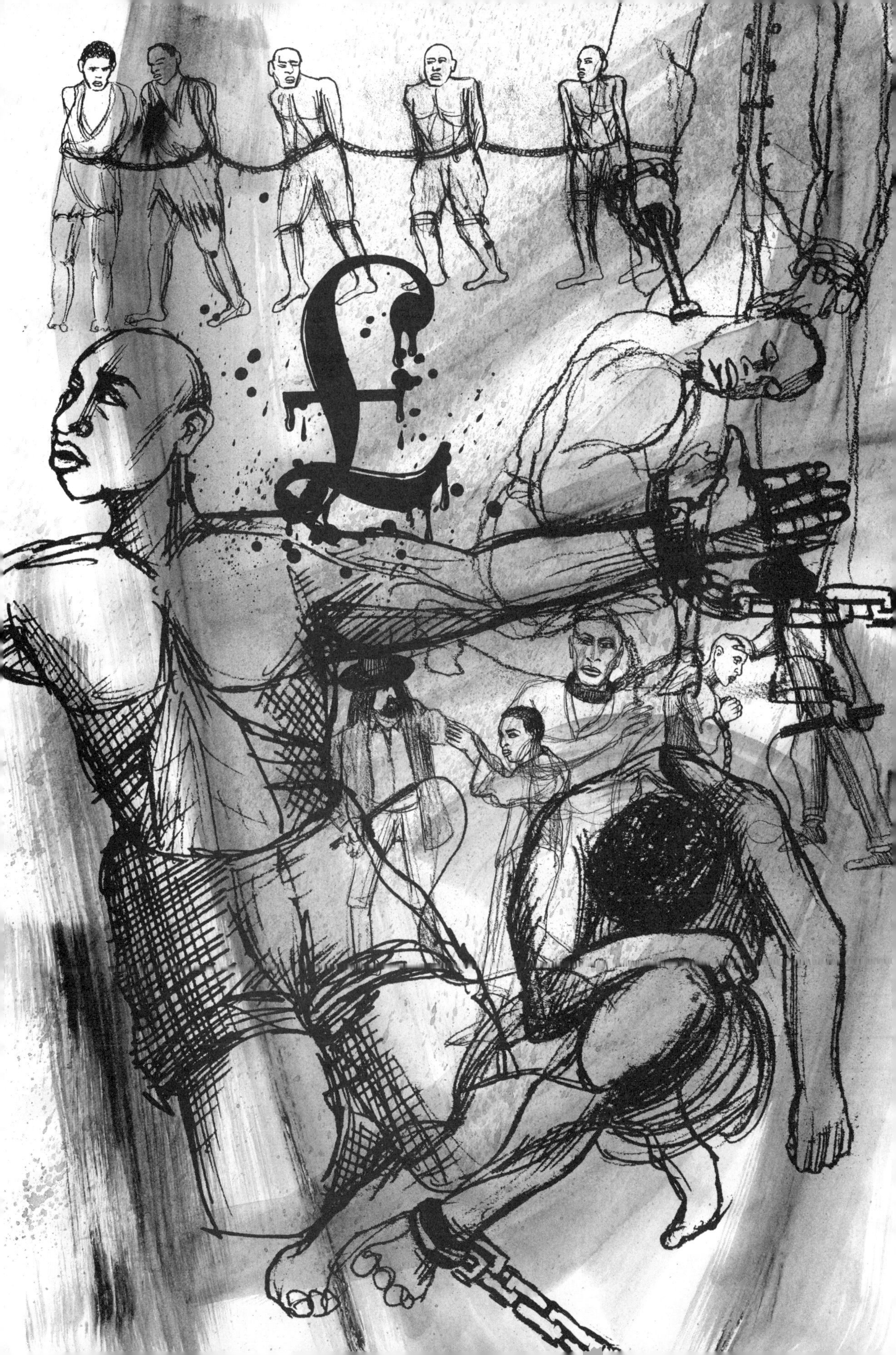

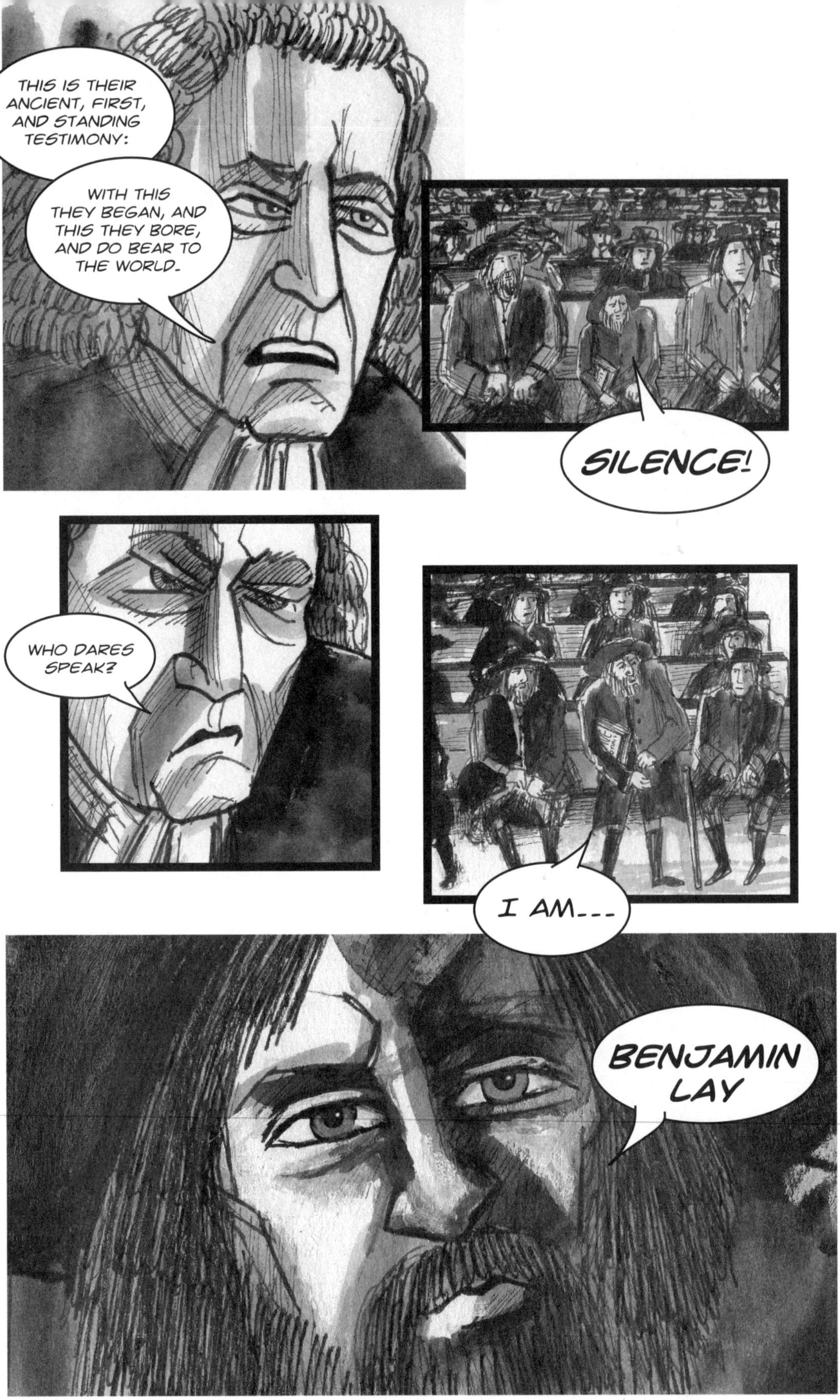
THIS IS THEIR ANCIENT, FIRST, AND STANDING TESTIMONY:
WITH THIS THEY BEGAN, AND THIS THEY BORE, AND DO BEAR TO THE WORLD.
SILENCE!
WHO DARES SPEAK?
I AM...
BENJAMIN LAY

AND I AM HERE TO TELL YOU...

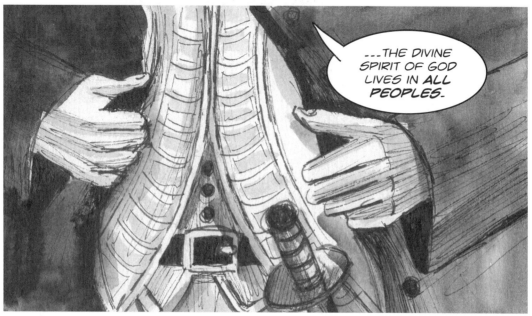

...THE DIVINE SPIRIT OF GOD LIVES IN *ALL* PEOPLES.

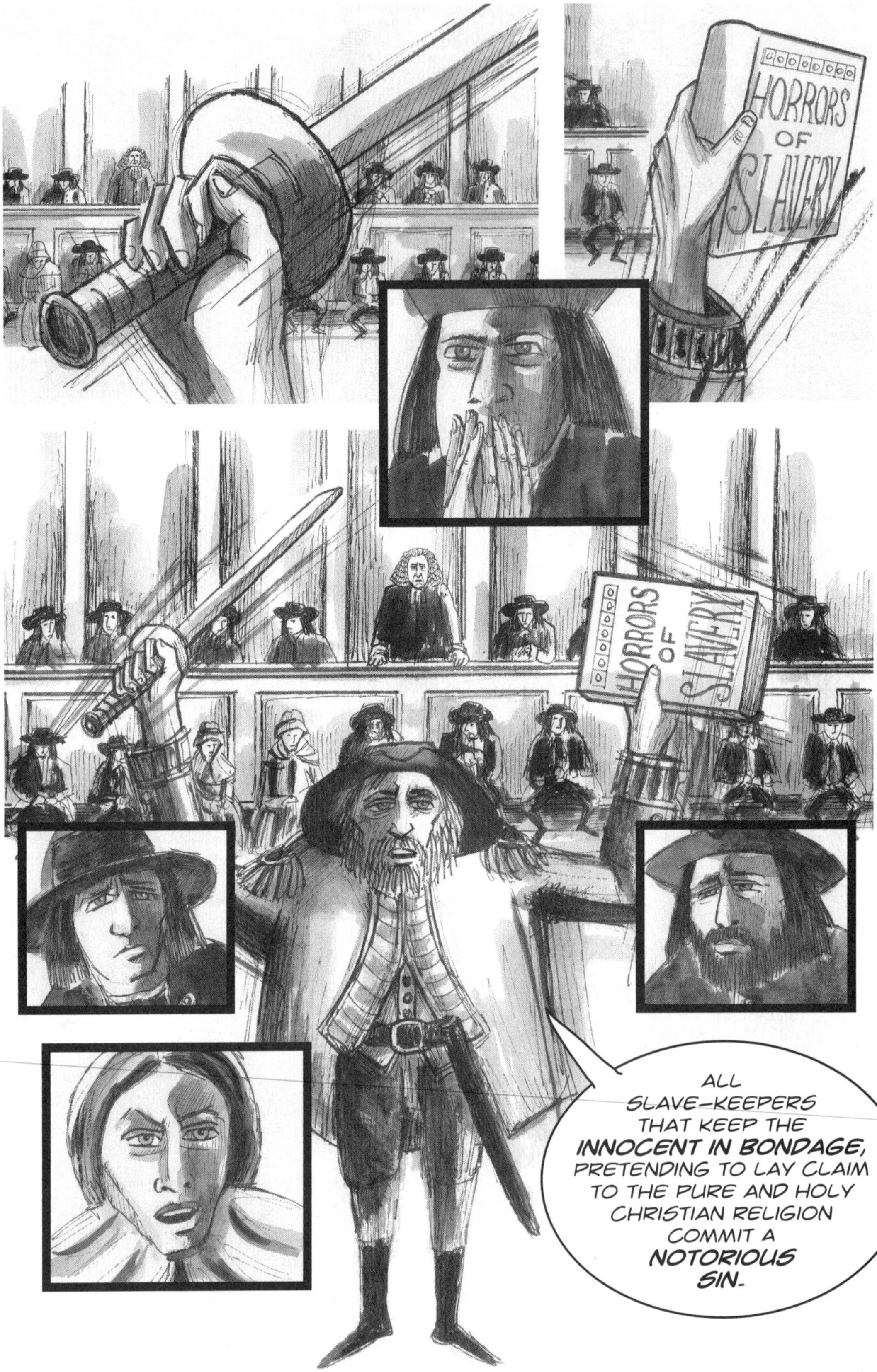
HORRORS OF SLAVERY
HORRORS OF SLAVERY
ALL SLAVE-KEEPERS THAT KEEP THE INNOCENT IN BONDAGE, PRETENDING TO LAY CLAIM TO THE PURE AND HOLY CHRISTIAN RELIGION COMMIT A NOTORIOUS SIN.

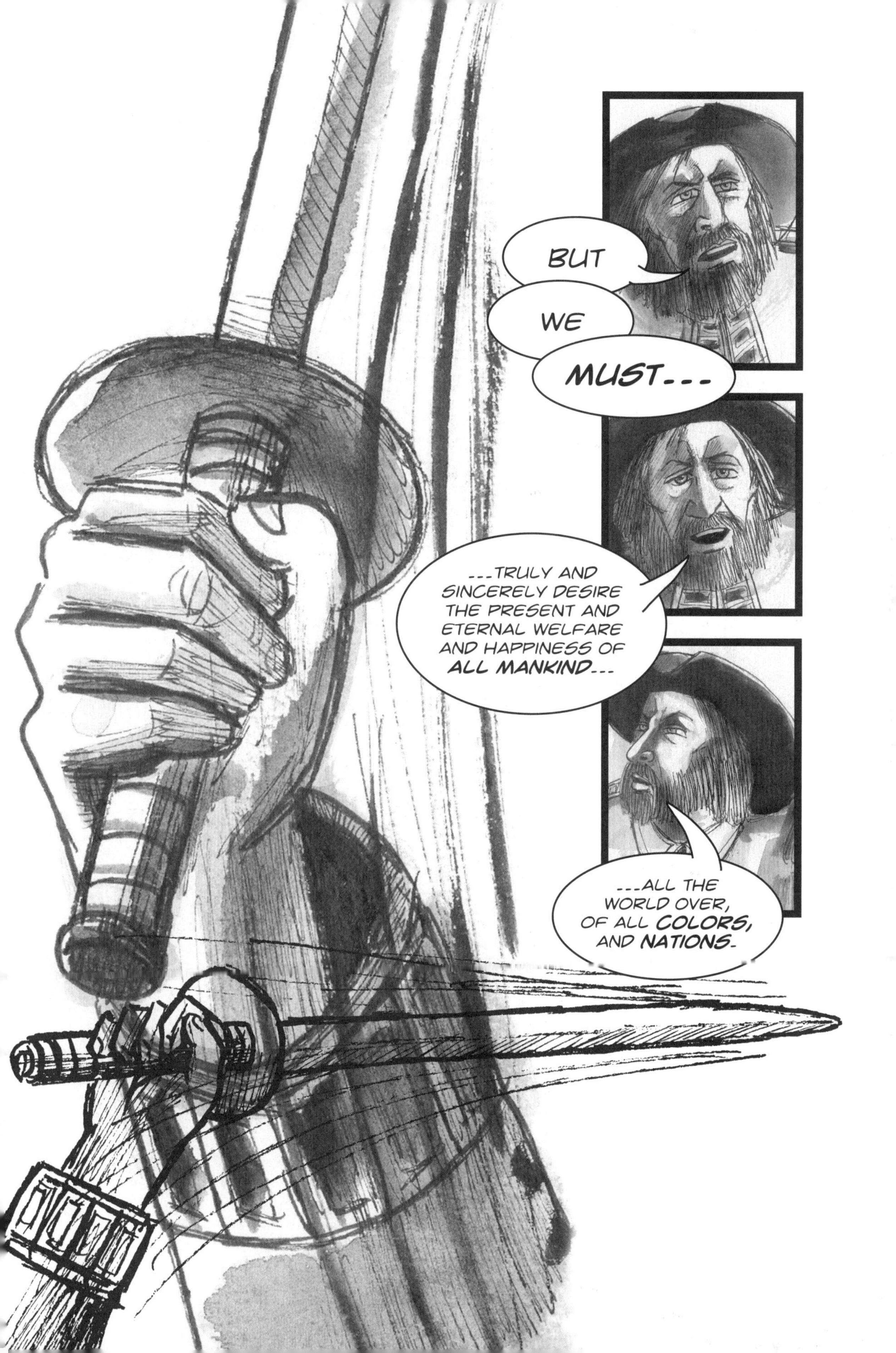
BUT
WE
MUST---
---TRULY AND SINCERELY DESIRE THE PRESENT AND ETERNAL WELFARE AND HAPPINESS OF ALL MANKIND---
---ALL THE WORLD OVER, OF ALL COLORS, AND NATIONS-

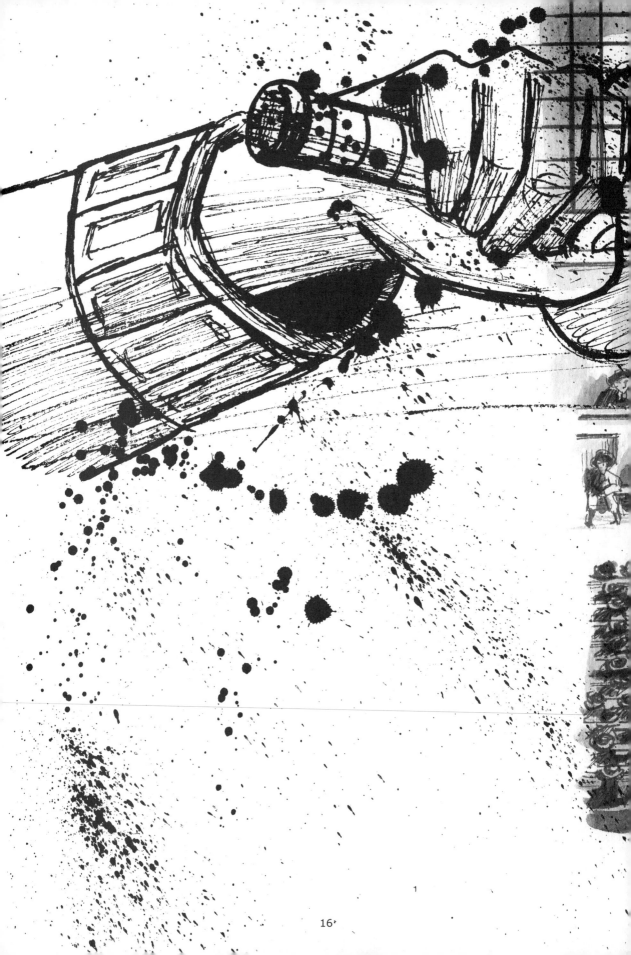

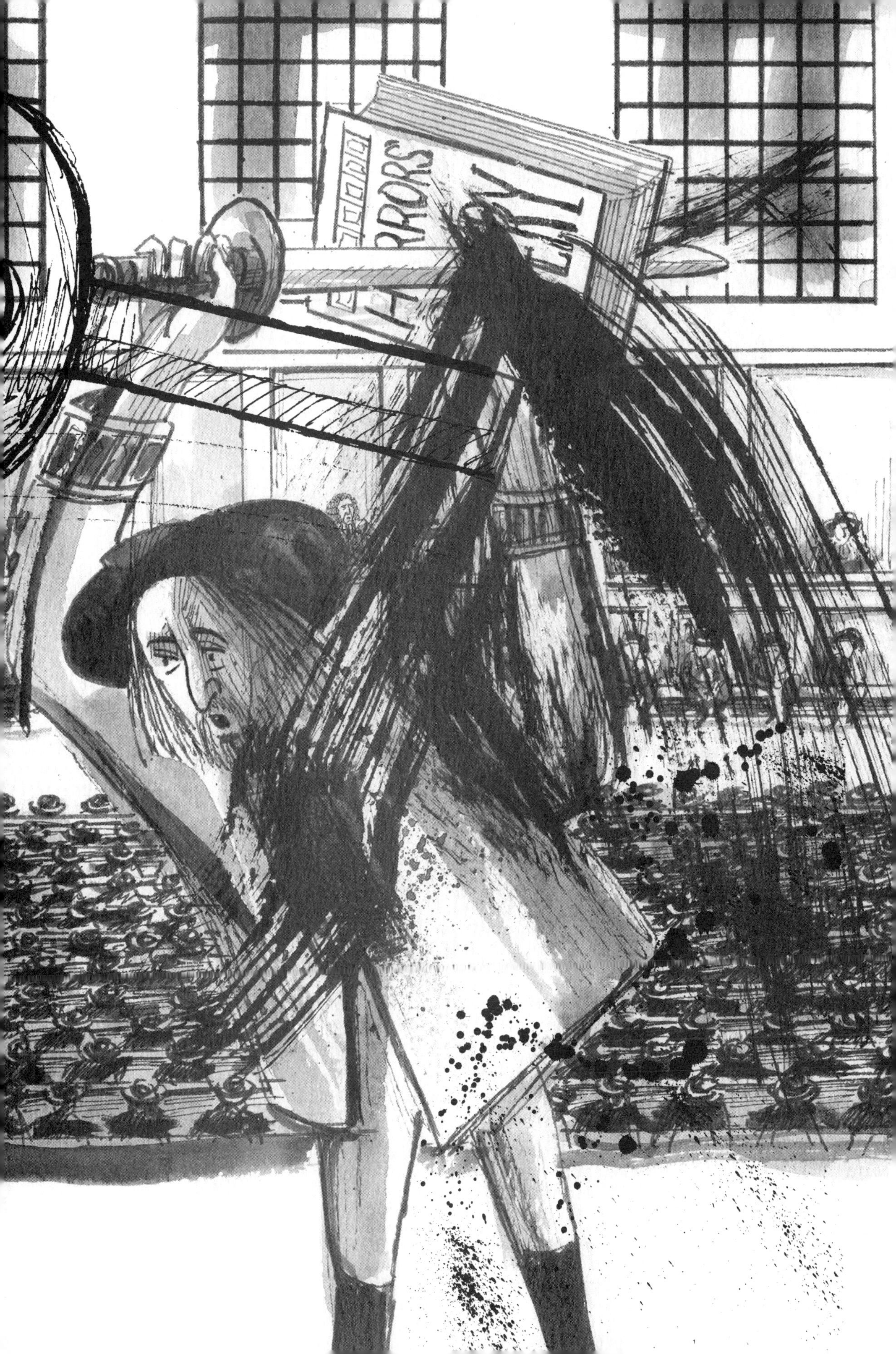

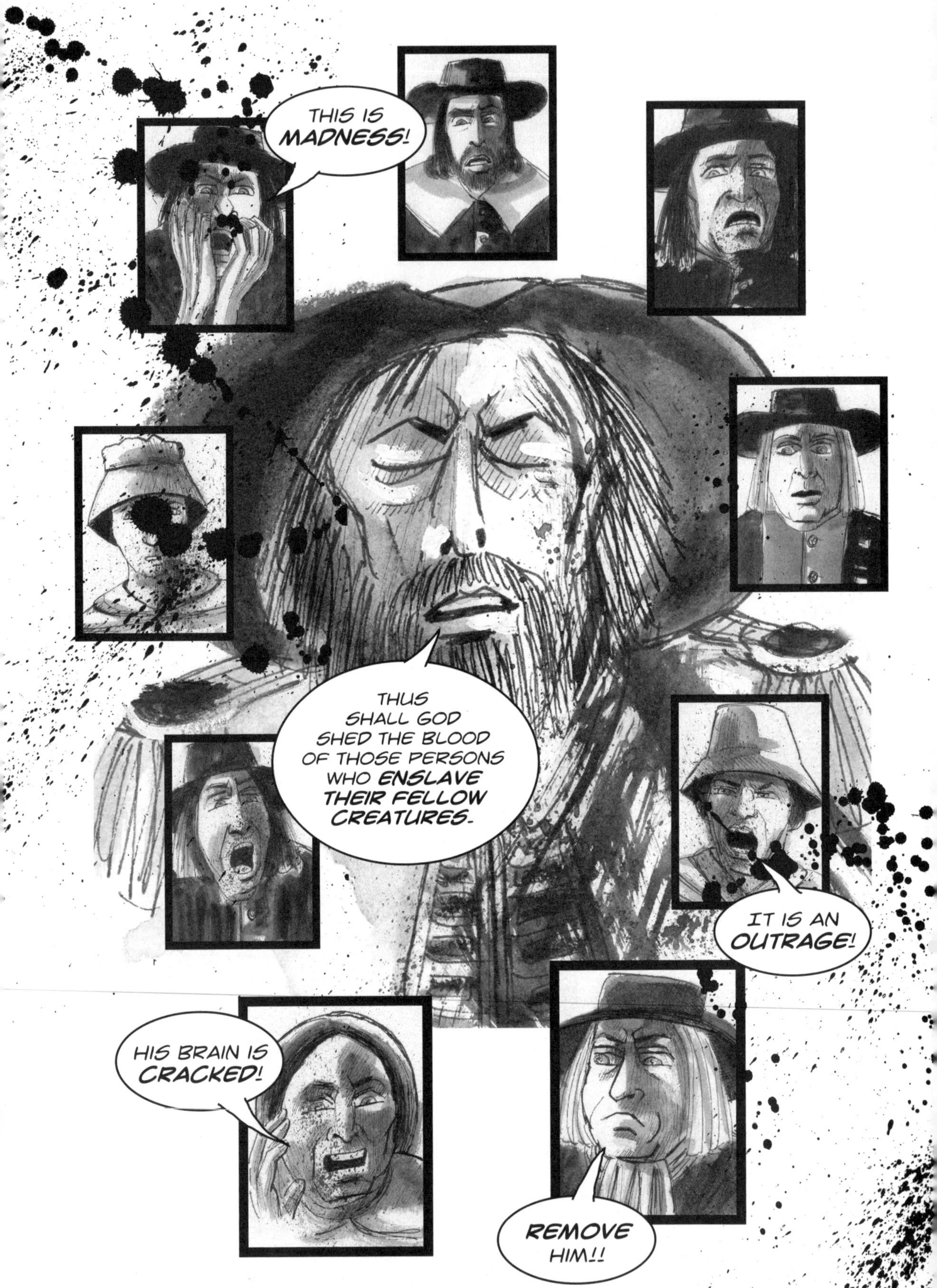
THIS IS MADNESS!
THUS SHALL GOD SHED THE BLOOD OF THOSE PERSONS WHO ENSLAVE THEIR FELLOW CREATURES.
IT IS AN OUTRAGE!
HIS BRAIN IS CRACKED!
REMOVE HIM!!

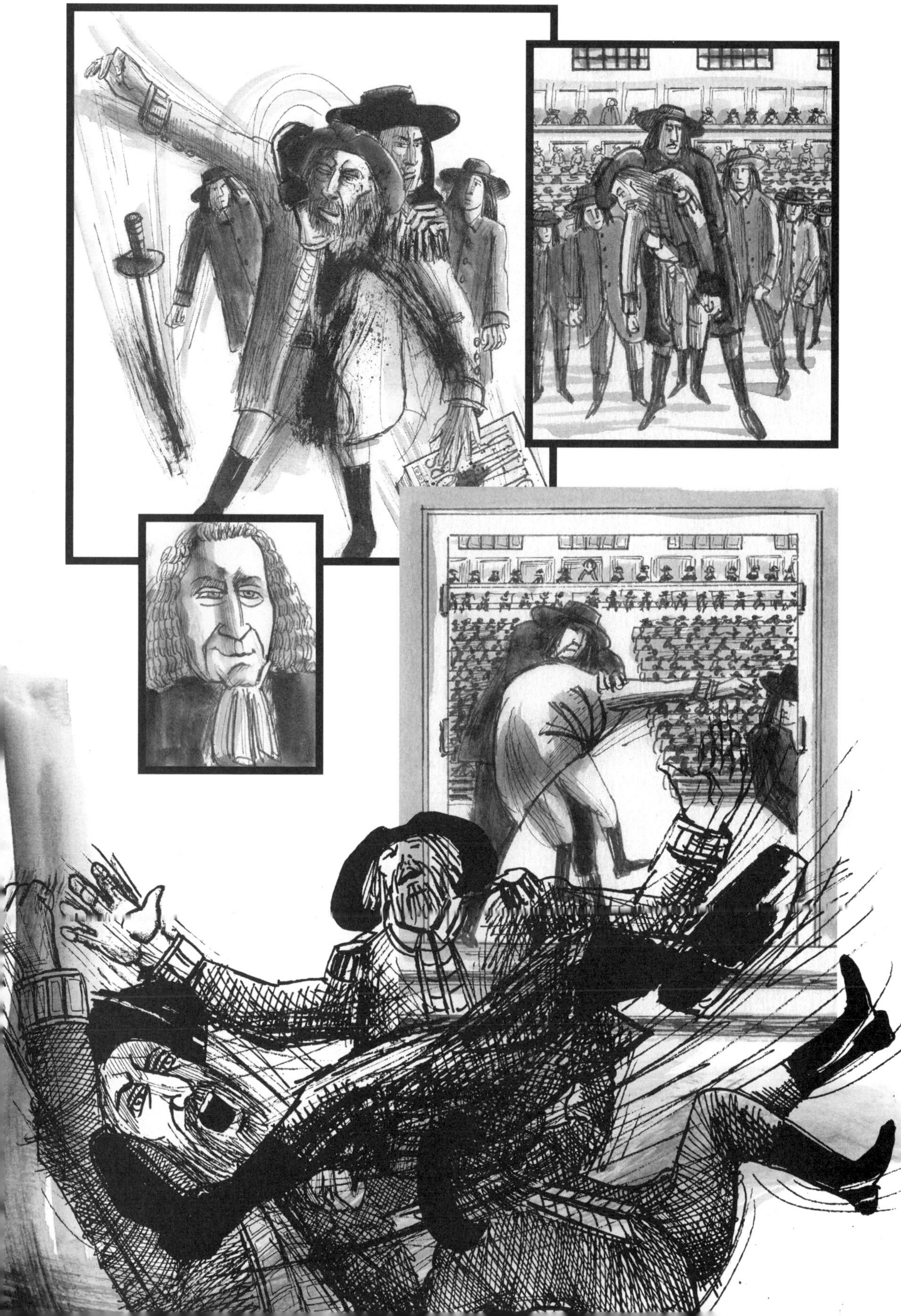

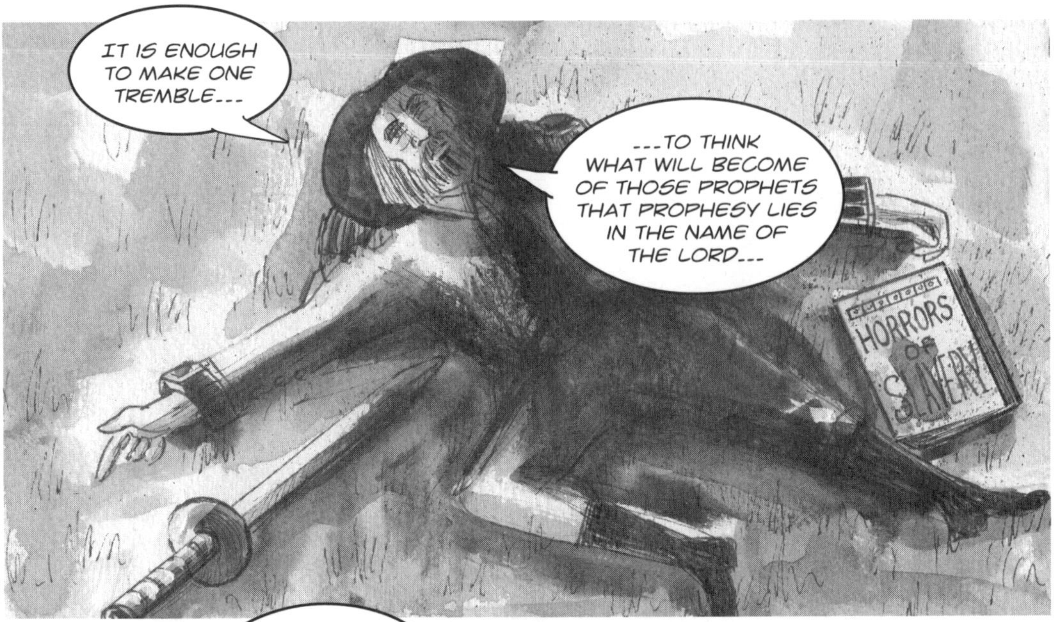
IT IS ENOUGH TO MAKE ONE TREMBLE---
---TO THINK WHAT WILL BECOME OF THOSE PROPHETS THAT PROPHESY LIES IN THE NAME OF THE LORD---
HORRORS OF SLAVERY

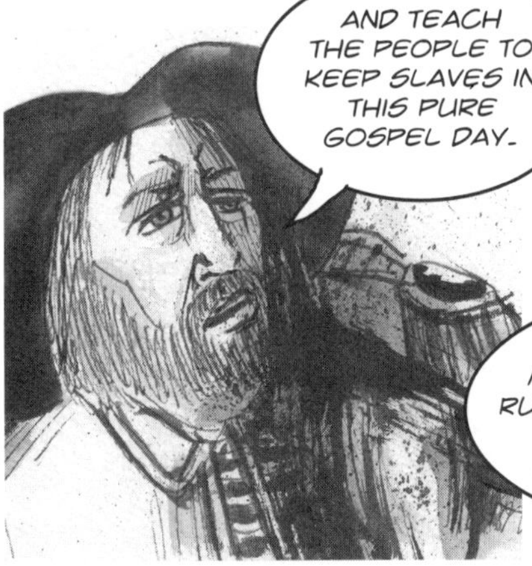
AND TEACH THE PEOPLE TO KEEP SLAVES IN THIS PURE GOSPEL DAY.

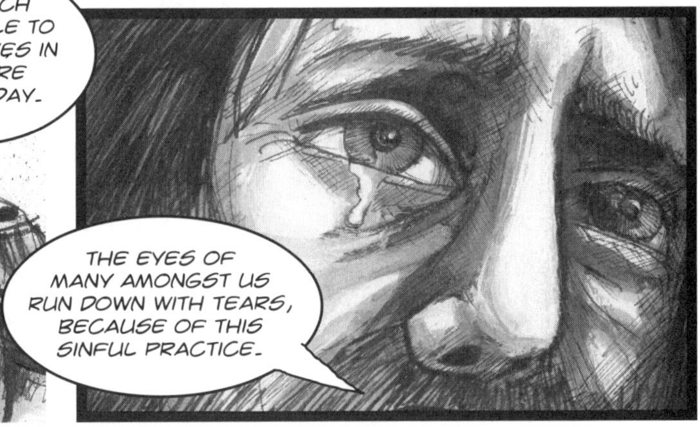
THE EYES OF MANY AMONGST US RUN DOWN WITH TEARS, BECAUSE OF THIS SINFUL PRACTICE.

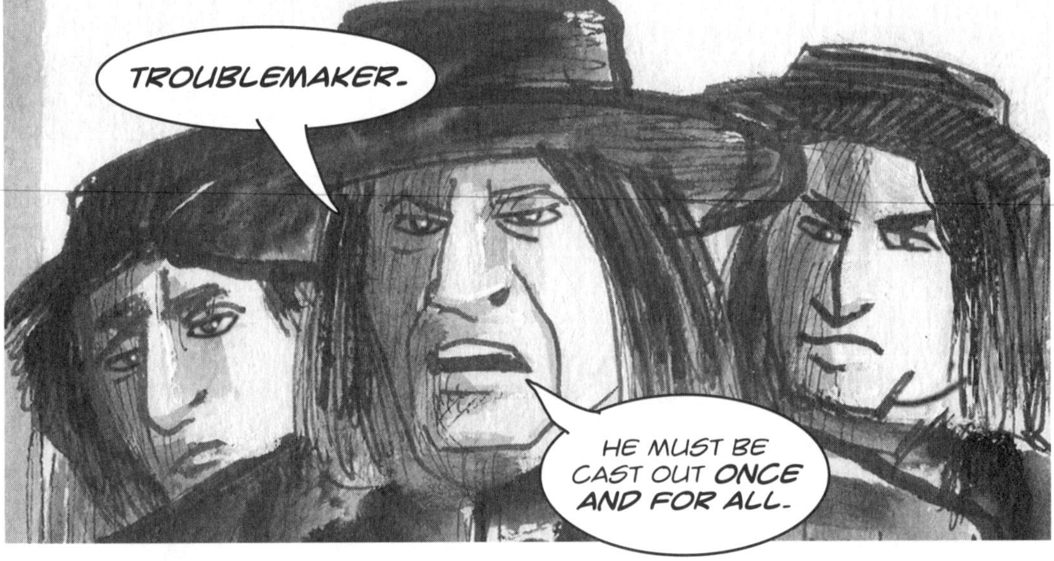
TROUBLEMAKER.
HE MUST BE CAST OUT ONCE AND FOR ALL.

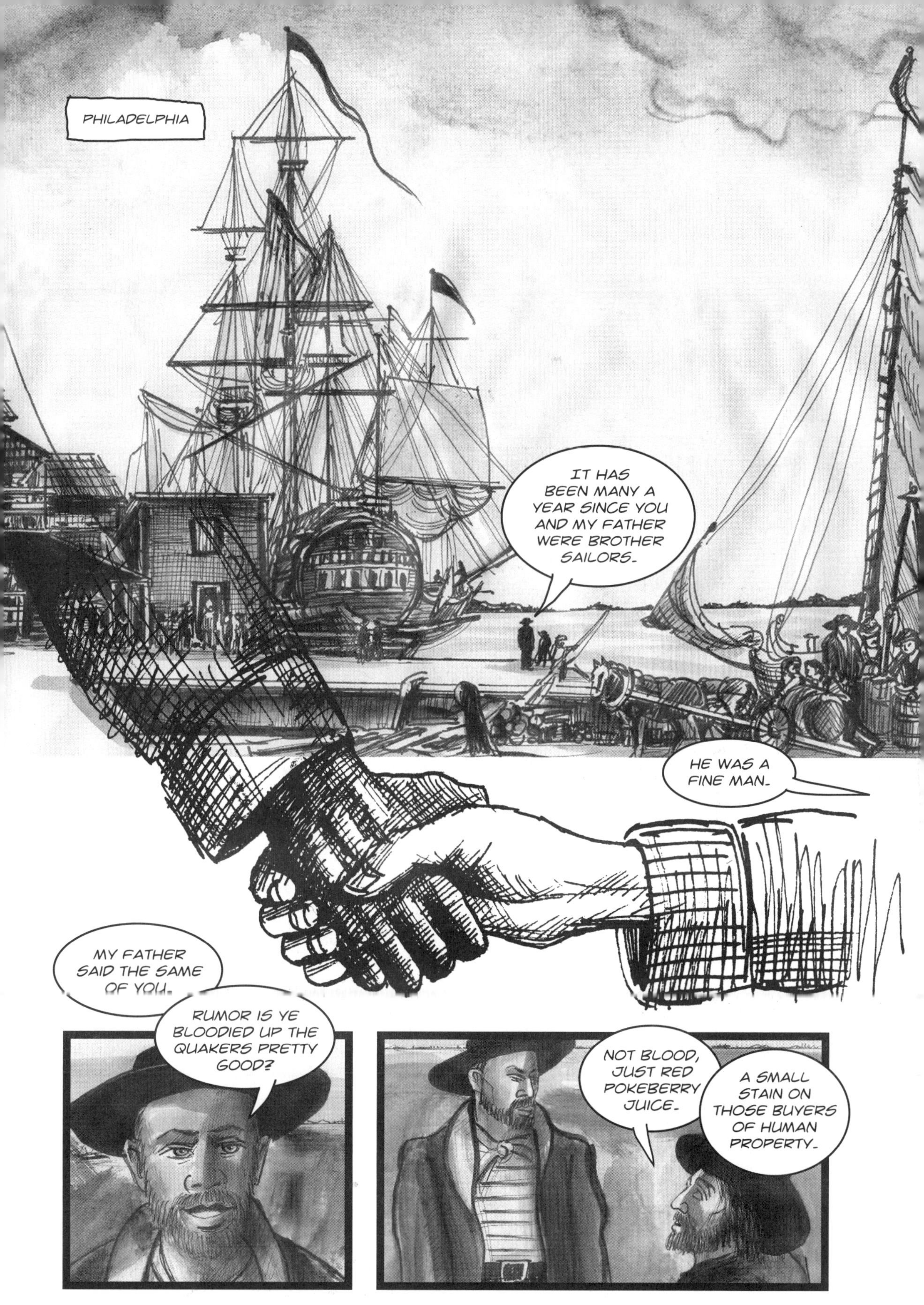
PHILADELPHIA
IT HAS BEEN MANY A YEAR SINCE YOU AND MY FATHER WERE BROTHER SAILORS.
HE WAS A FINE MAN.
MY FATHER SAID THE SAME OF YOU.
RUMOR IS YE BLOODIED UP THE QUAKERS PRETTY GOOD?
NOT BLOOD, JUST RED POKEBERRY JUICE.
A SMALL STAIN ON THOSE BUYERS OF HUMAN PROPERTY.

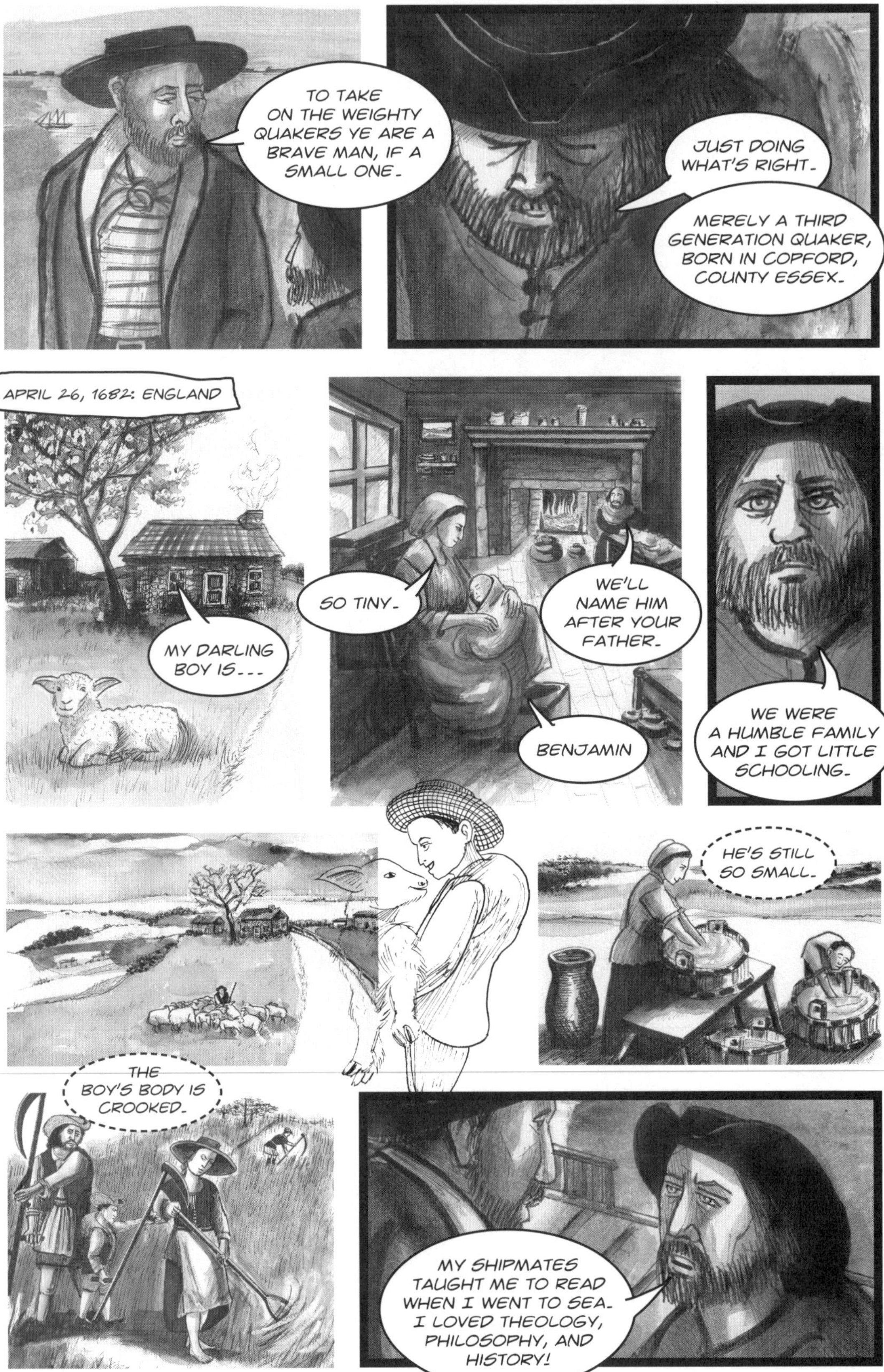
TO TAKE ON THE WEIGHTY QUAKERS YE ARE A BRAVE MAN, IF A SMALL ONE.
JUST DOING WHAT'S RIGHT.
MERELY A THIRD GENERATION QUAKER, BORN IN COPFORD, COUNTY ESSEX.
APRIL 26, 1682: ENGLAND
MY DARLING BOY IS...
SO TINY.
WE'LL NAME HIM AFTER YOUR FATHER.
BENJAMIN
WE WERE A HUMBLE FAMILY AND I GOT LITTLE SCHOOLING.
HE'S STILL SO SMALL.
THE BOY'S BODY IS CROOKED.
MY SHIPMATES TAUGHT ME TO READ WHEN I WENT TO SEA. I LOVED THEOLOGY, PHILOSOPHY, AND HISTORY!

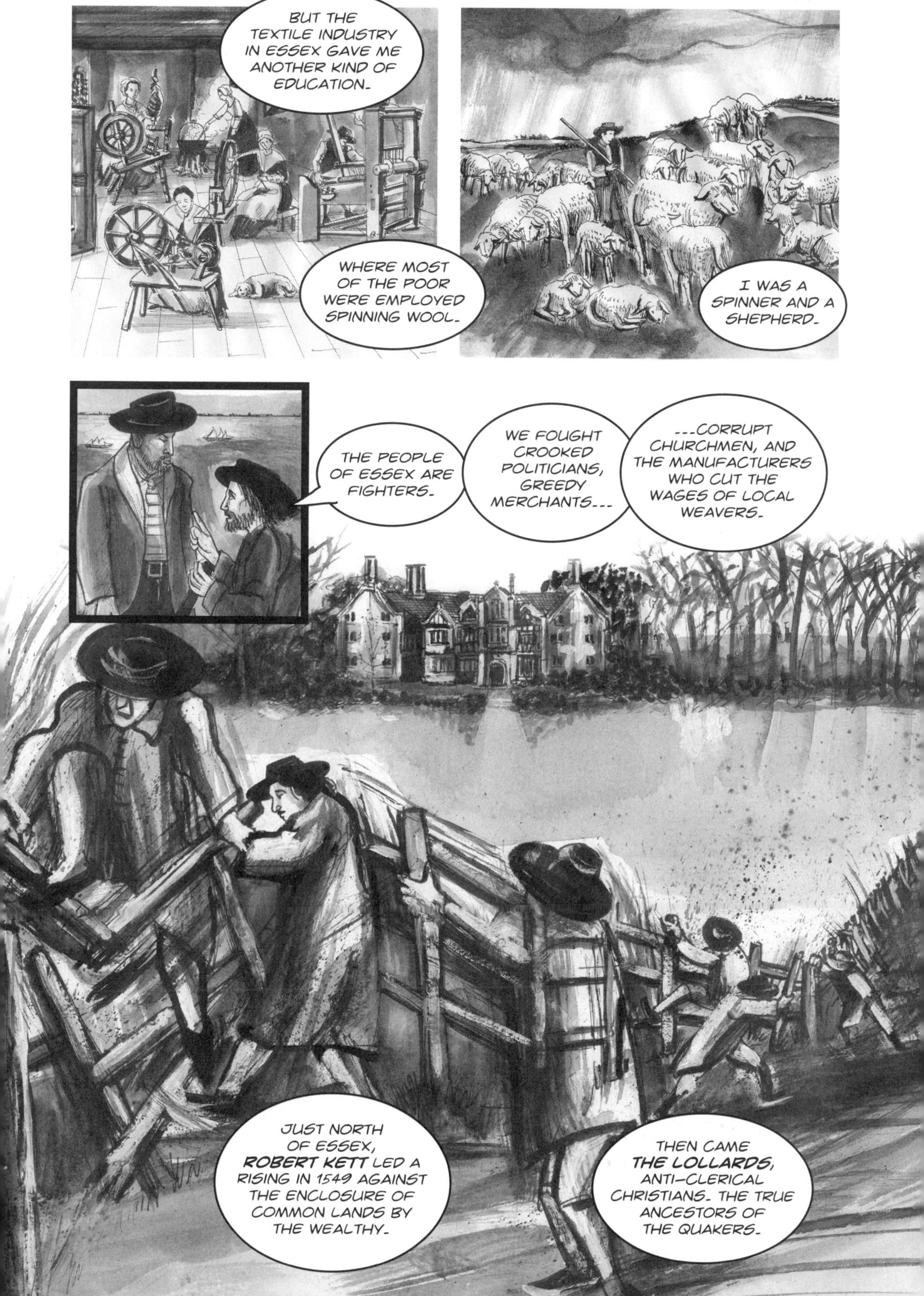
BUT THE TEXTILE INDUSTRY IN ESSEX GAVE ME ANOTHER KIND OF EDUCATION.
WHERE MOST OF THE POOR WERE EMPLOYED SPINNING WOOL.
I WAS A SPINNER AND A SHEPHERD.
THE PEOPLE OF ESSEX ARE FIGHTERS.
WE FOUGHT CROOKED POLITICIANS, GREEDY MERCHANTS...
...CORRUPT CHURCHMEN, AND THE MANUFACTURERS WHO CUT THE WAGES OF LOCAL WEAVERS.
JUST NORTH OF ESSEX, **ROBERT KETT** LED A RISING IN 1549 AGAINST THE ENCLOSURE OF COMMON LANDS BY THE WEALTHY.
THEN CAME **THE LOLLARDS**, ANTI-CLERICAL CHRISTIANS. THE TRUE ANCESTORS OF THE QUAKERS.

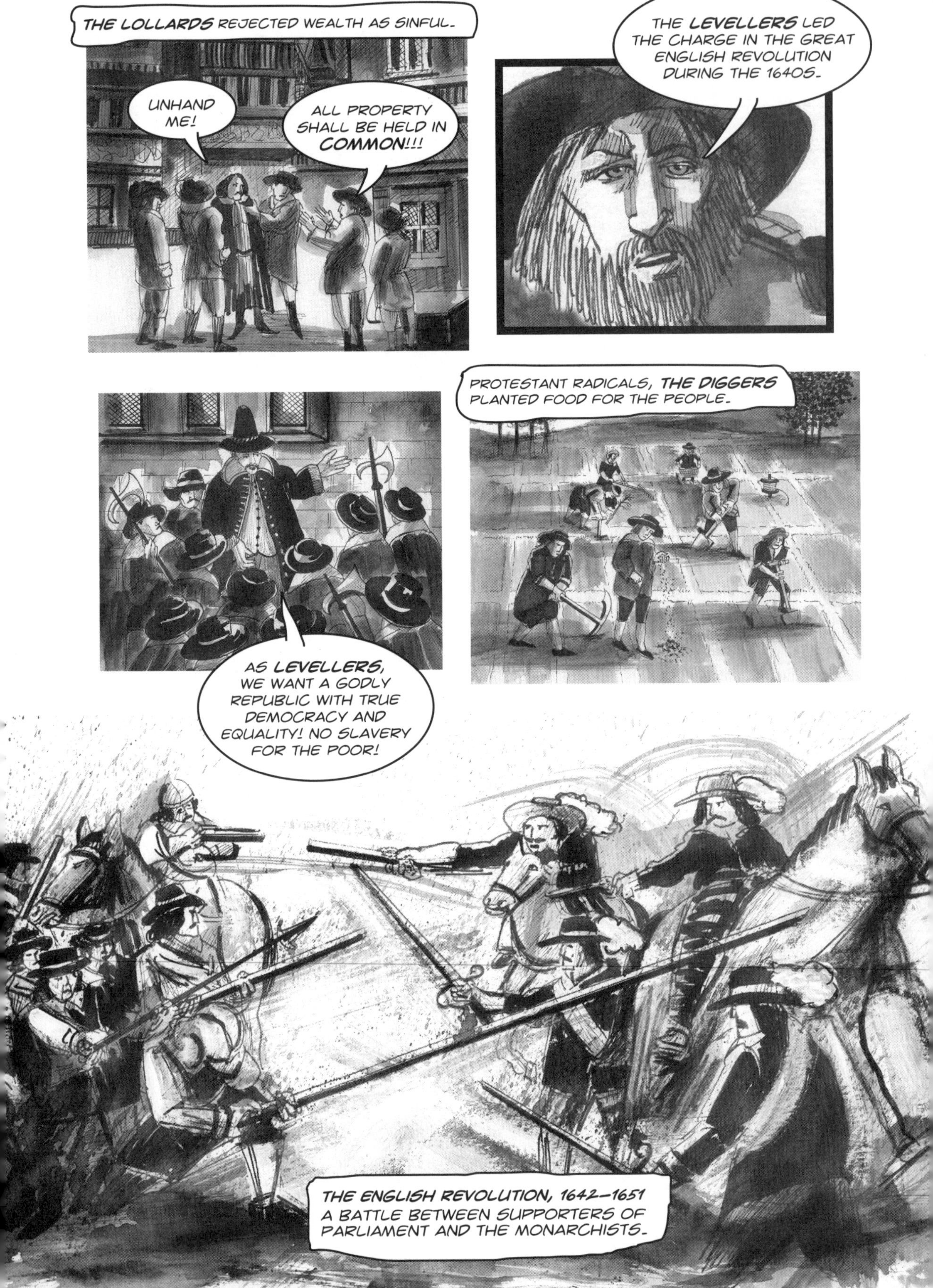
THE LOLLARDS REJECTED WEALTH AS SINFUL.
UNHAND ME!
ALL PROPERTY SHALL BE HELD IN COMMON!!!
THE LEVELLERS LED THE CHARGE IN THE GREAT ENGLISH REVOLUTION DURING THE 1640S.
AS LEVELLERS, WE WANT A GODLY REPUBLIC WITH TRUE DEMOCRACY AND EQUALITY! NO SLAVERY FOR THE POOR!
PROTESTANT RADICALS, THE DIGGERS PLANTED FOOD FOR THE PEOPLE.
THE ENGLISH REVOLUTION, 1642–1651
A BATTLE BETWEEN SUPPORTERS OF PARLIAMENT AND THE MONARCHISTS.

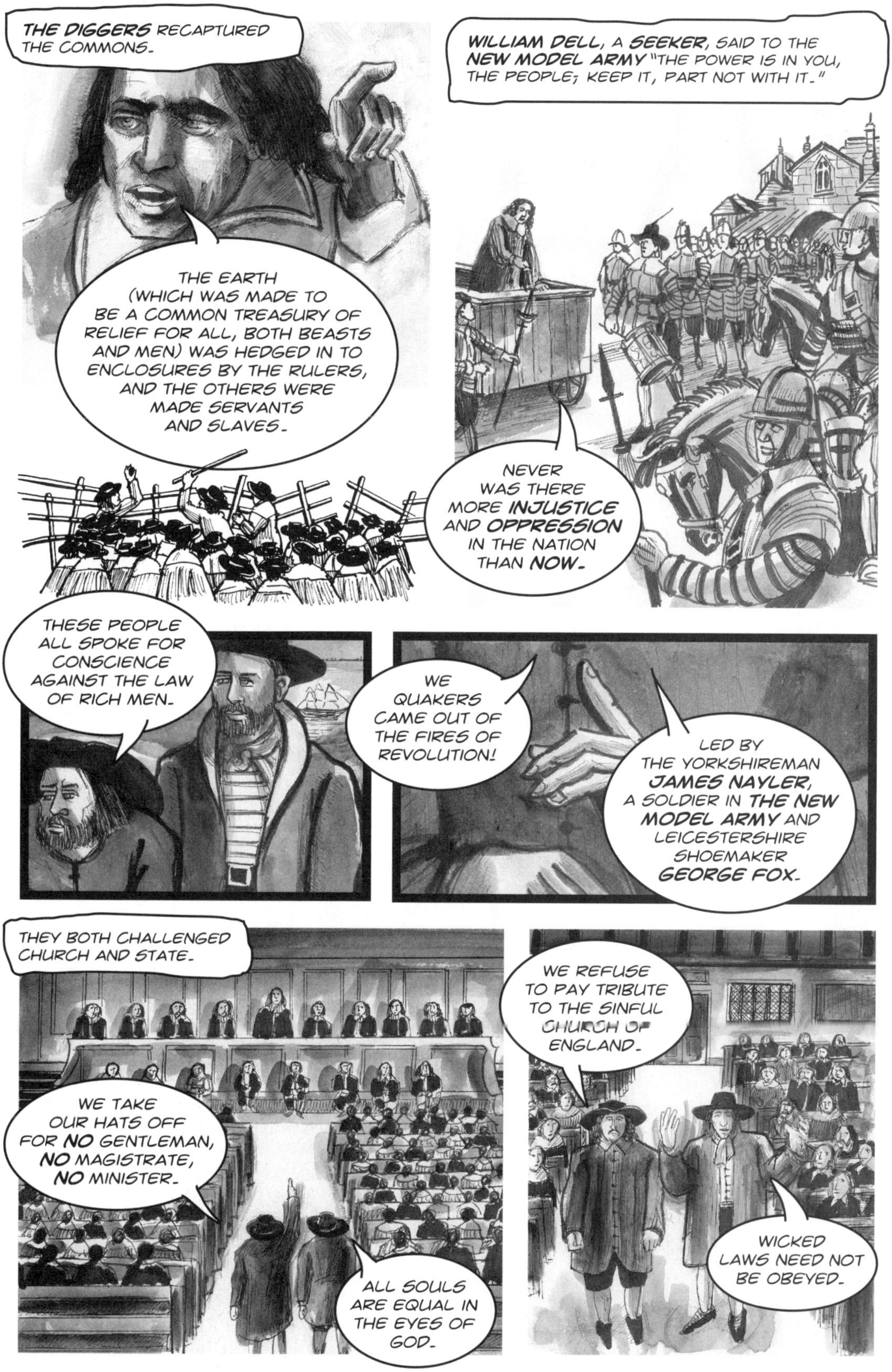
THE DIGGERS RECAPTURED THE COMMONS.
THE EARTH (WHICH WAS MADE TO BE A COMMON TREASURY OF RELIEF FOR ALL, BOTH BEASTS AND MEN) WAS HEDGED IN TO ENCLOSURES BY THE RULERS, AND THE OTHERS WERE MADE SERVANTS AND SLAVES.
WILLIAM DELL, A SEEKER, SAID TO THE NEW MODEL ARMY "THE POWER IS IN YOU, THE PEOPLE; KEEP IT, PART NOT WITH IT."
NEVER WAS THERE MORE INJUSTICE AND OPPRESSION IN THE NATION THAN NOW.
THESE PEOPLE ALL SPOKE FOR CONSCIENCE AGAINST THE LAW OF RICH MEN.
WE QUAKERS CAME OUT OF THE FIRES OF REVOLUTION!
LED BY THE YORKSHIREMAN JAMES NAYLER, A SOLDIER IN THE NEW MODEL ARMY AND LEICESTERSHIRE SHOEMAKER GEORGE FOX.
THEY BOTH CHALLENGED CHURCH AND STATE.
WE TAKE OUR HATS OFF FOR NO GENTLEMAN, NO MAGISTRATE, NO MINISTER.
ALL SOULS ARE EQUAL IN THE EYES OF GOD.
WE REFUSE TO PAY TRIBUTE TO THE SINFUL CHURCH OF ENGLAND.
WICKED LAWS NEED NOT BE OBEYED.

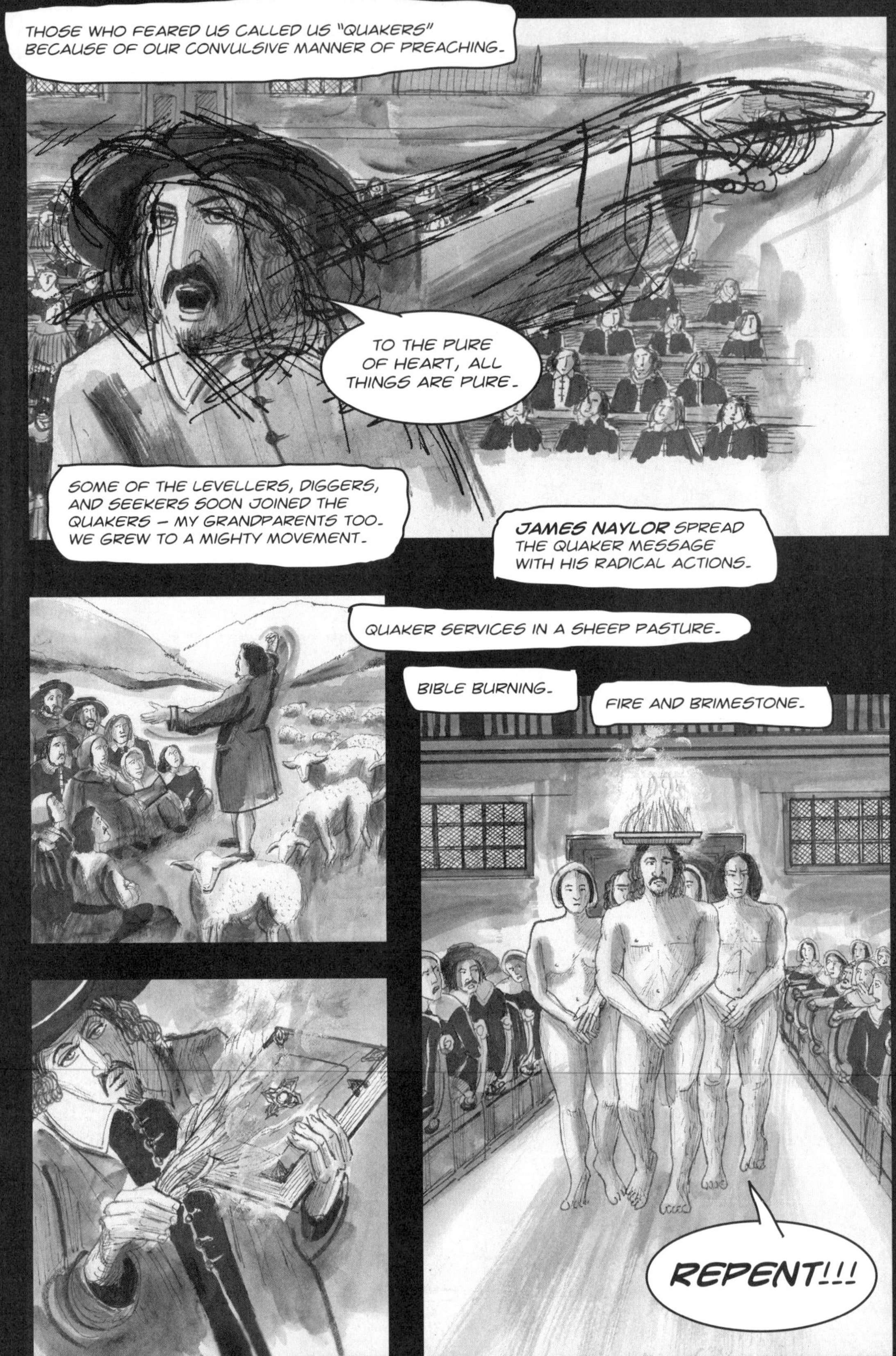
THOSE WHO FEARED US CALLED US "QUAKERS" BECAUSE OF OUR CONVULSIVE MANNER OF PREACHING.
TO THE PURE OF HEART, ALL THINGS ARE PURE.
SOME OF THE LEVELLERS, DIGGERS, AND SEEKERS SOON JOINED THE QUAKERS – MY GRANDPARENTS TOO. WE GREW TO A MIGHTY MOVEMENT.
JAMES NAYLOR SPREAD THE QUAKER MESSAGE WITH HIS RADICAL ACTIONS.
QUAKER SERVICES IN A SHEEP PASTURE.
BIBLE BURNING.
FIRE AND BRIMSTONE.
REPENT!!!

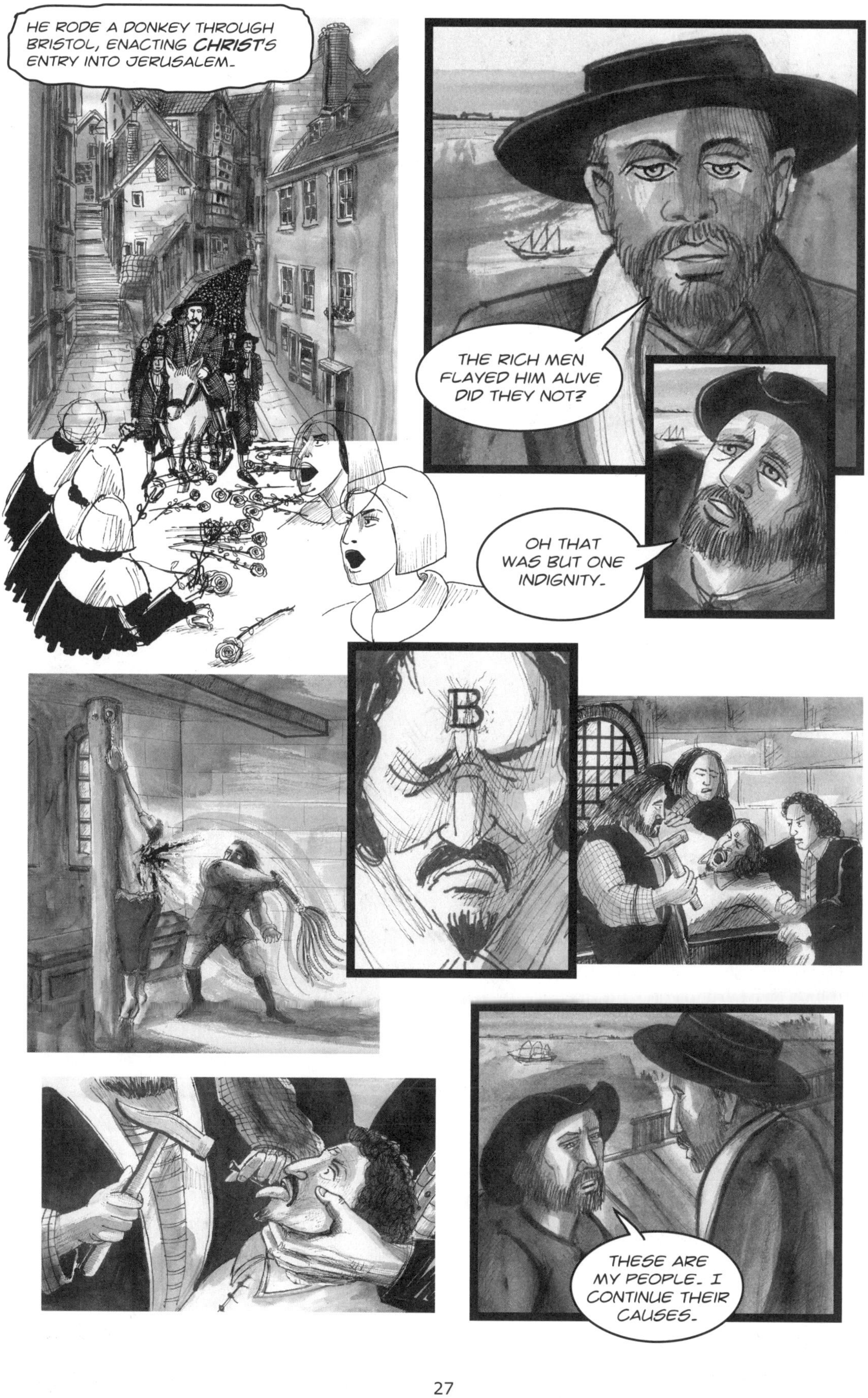
HE RODE A DONKEY THROUGH BRISTOL, ENACTING CHRIST'S ENTRY INTO JERUSALEM.
THE RICH MEN FLAYED HIM ALIVE DID THEY NOT?
OH THAT WAS BUT ONE INDIGNITY.
B
THESE ARE MY PEOPLE. I CONTINUE THEIR CAUSES.

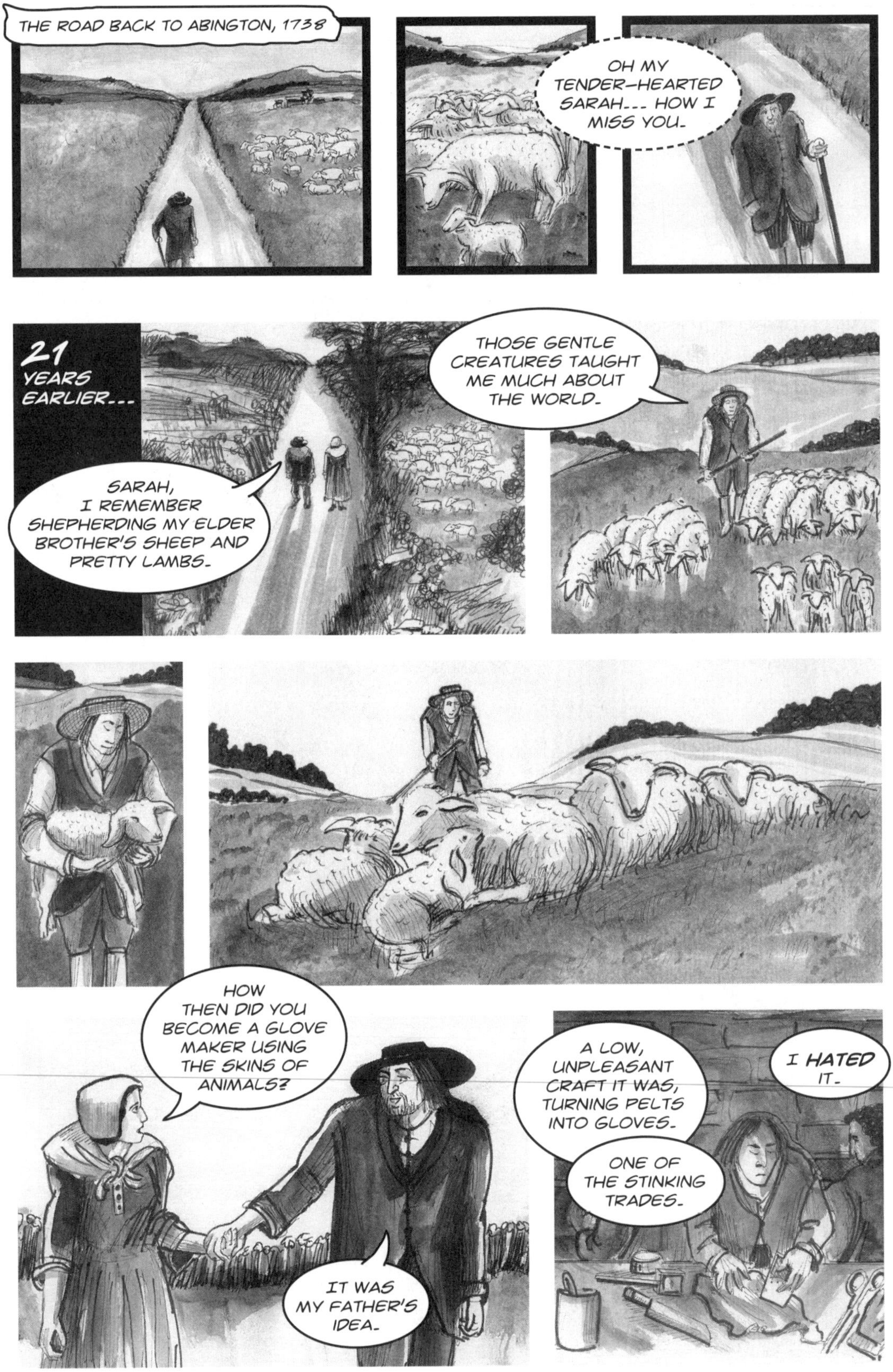
THE ROAD BACK TO ABINGTON, 1738
OH MY TENDER-HEARTED SARAH... HOW I MISS YOU.
21 YEARS EARLIER...
SARAH, I REMEMBER SHEPHERDING MY ELDER BROTHER'S SHEEP AND PRETTY LAMBS.
THOSE GENTLE CREATURES TAUGHT ME MUCH ABOUT THE WORLD.
HOW THEN DID YOU BECOME A GLOVE MAKER USING THE SKINS OF ANIMALS?
IT WAS MY FATHER'S IDEA.
A LOW, UNPLEASANT CRAFT IT WAS, TURNING PELTS INTO GLOVES.
ONE OF THE STINKING TRADES.
I HATED IT.

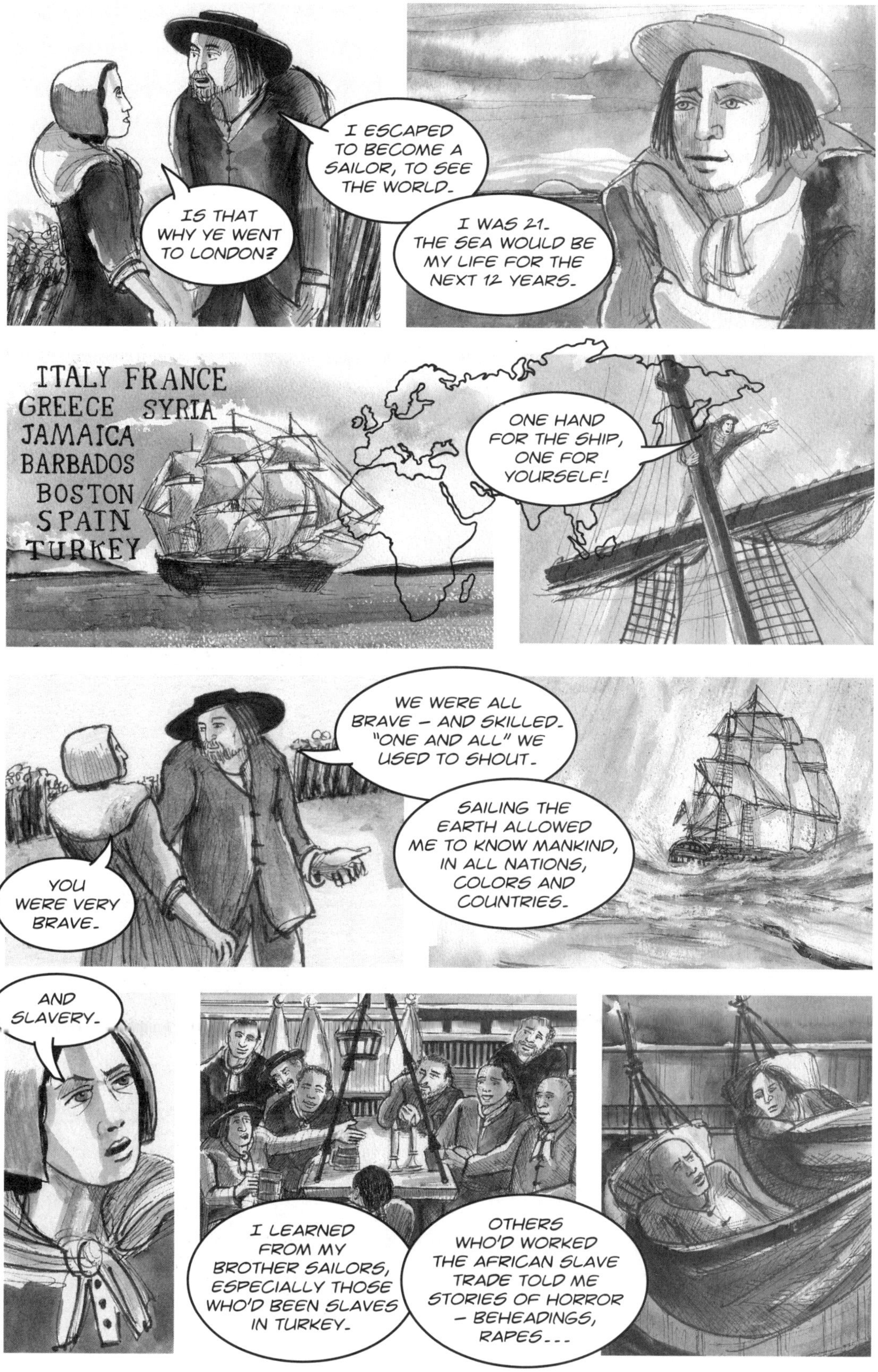
I ESCAPED TO BECOME A SAILOR, TO SEE THE WORLD.
IS THAT WHY YE WENT TO LONDON?
I WAS 21. THE SEA WOULD BE MY LIFE FOR THE NEXT 12 YEARS.
ITALY FRANCE GREECE SYRIA JAMAICA BARBADOS BOSTON SPAIN TURKEY
ONE HAND FOR THE SHIP, ONE FOR YOURSELF!
YOU WERE VERY BRAVE.
WE WERE ALL BRAVE – AND SKILLED. "ONE AND ALL" WE USED TO SHOUT.
SAILING THE EARTH ALLOWED ME TO KNOW MANKIND, IN ALL NATIONS, COLORS AND COUNTRIES.
AND SLAVERY.
I LEARNED FROM MY BROTHER SAILORS, ESPECIALLY THOSE WHO'D BEEN SLAVES IN TURKEY.
OTHERS WHO'D WORKED THE AFRICAN SLAVE TRADE TOLD ME STORIES OF HORROR – BEHEADINGS, RAPES...

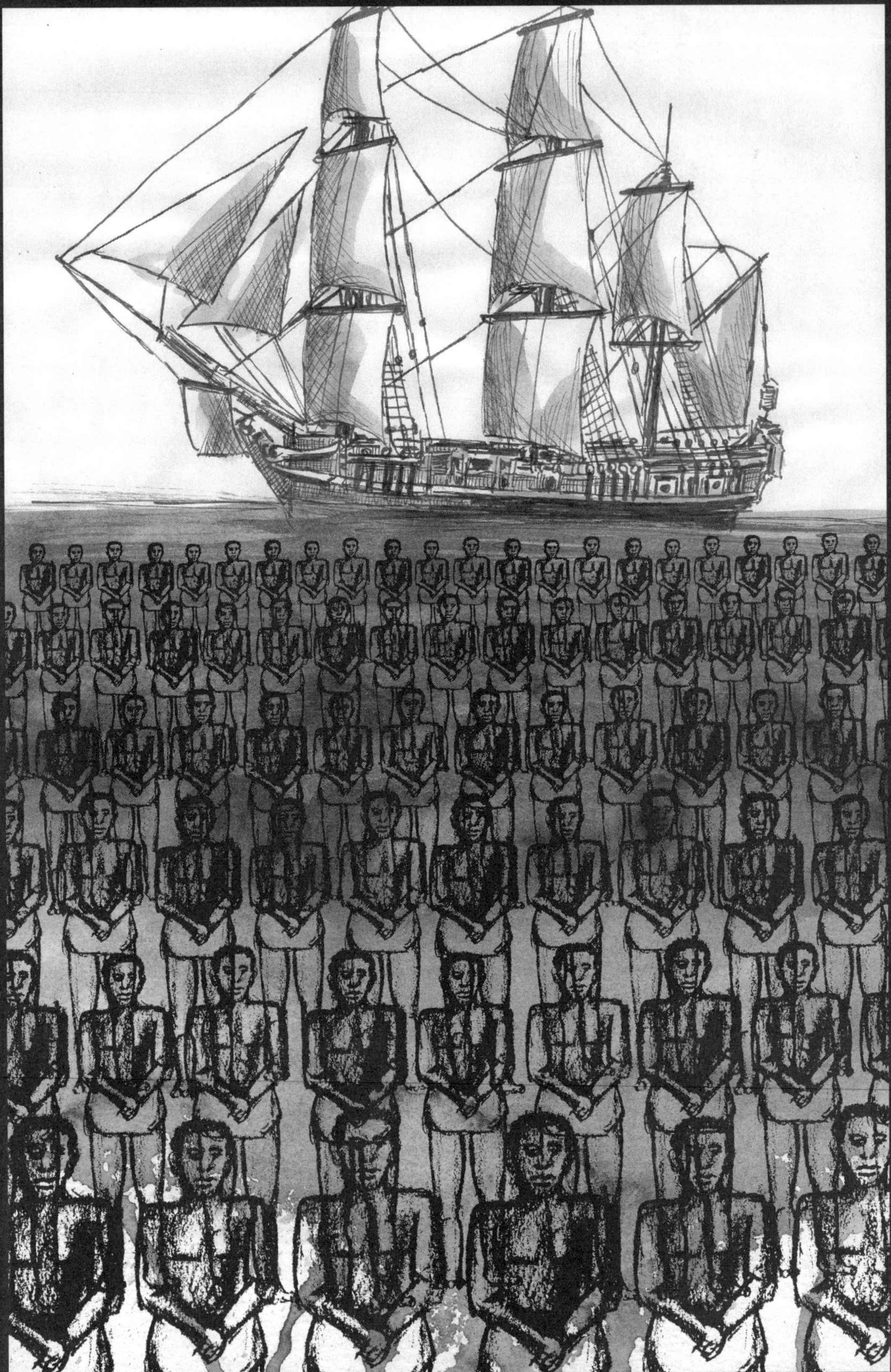

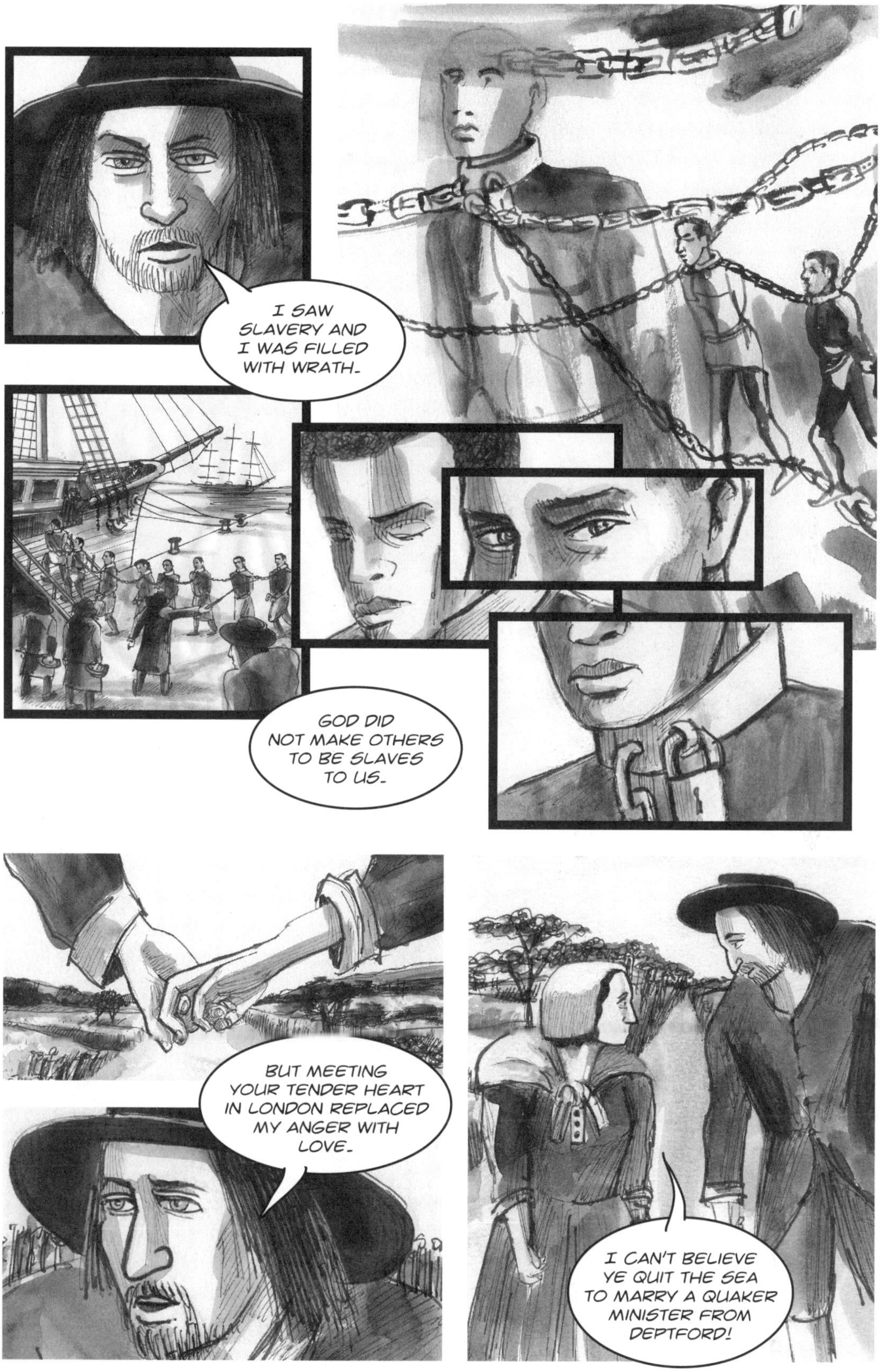
I SAW SLAVERY AND I WAS FILLED WITH WRATH.
GOD DID NOT MAKE OTHERS TO BE SLAVES TO US.
BUT MEETING YOUR TENDER HEART IN LONDON REPLACED MY ANGER WITH LOVE.
I CAN'T BELIEVE YE QUIT THE SEA TO MARRY A QUAKER MINISTER FROM DEPTFORD!

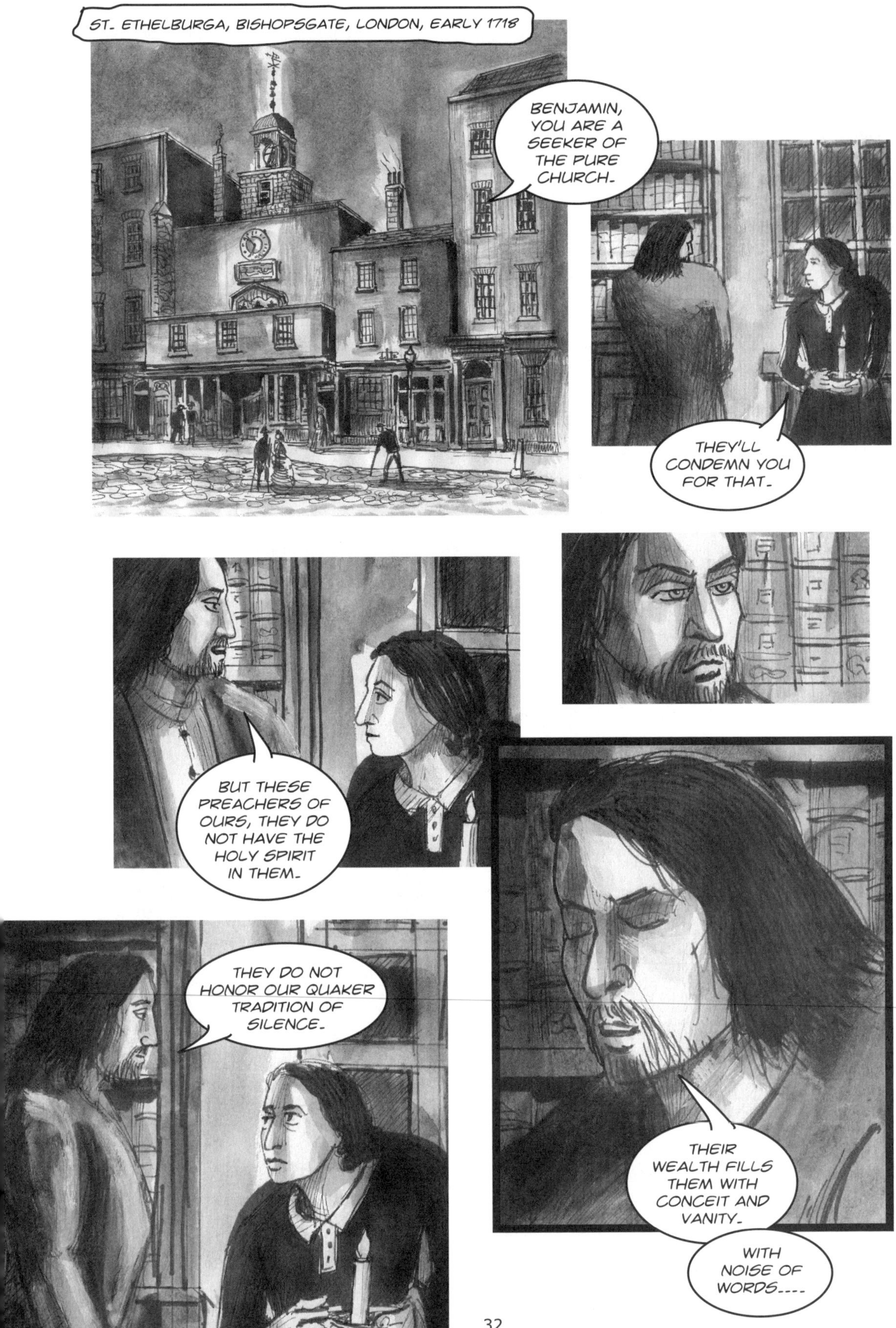
ST. ETHELBURGA, BISHOPSGATE, LONDON, EARLY 1718
BENJAMIN, YOU ARE A SEEKER OF THE PURE CHURCH.
THEY'LL CONDEMN YOU FOR THAT.
BUT THESE PREACHERS OF OURS, THEY DO NOT HAVE THE HOLY SPIRIT IN THEM.
THEY DO NOT HONOR OUR QUAKER TRADITION OF SILENCE.
THEIR WEALTH FILLS THEM WITH CONCEIT AND VANITY.
WITH NOISE OF WORDS....

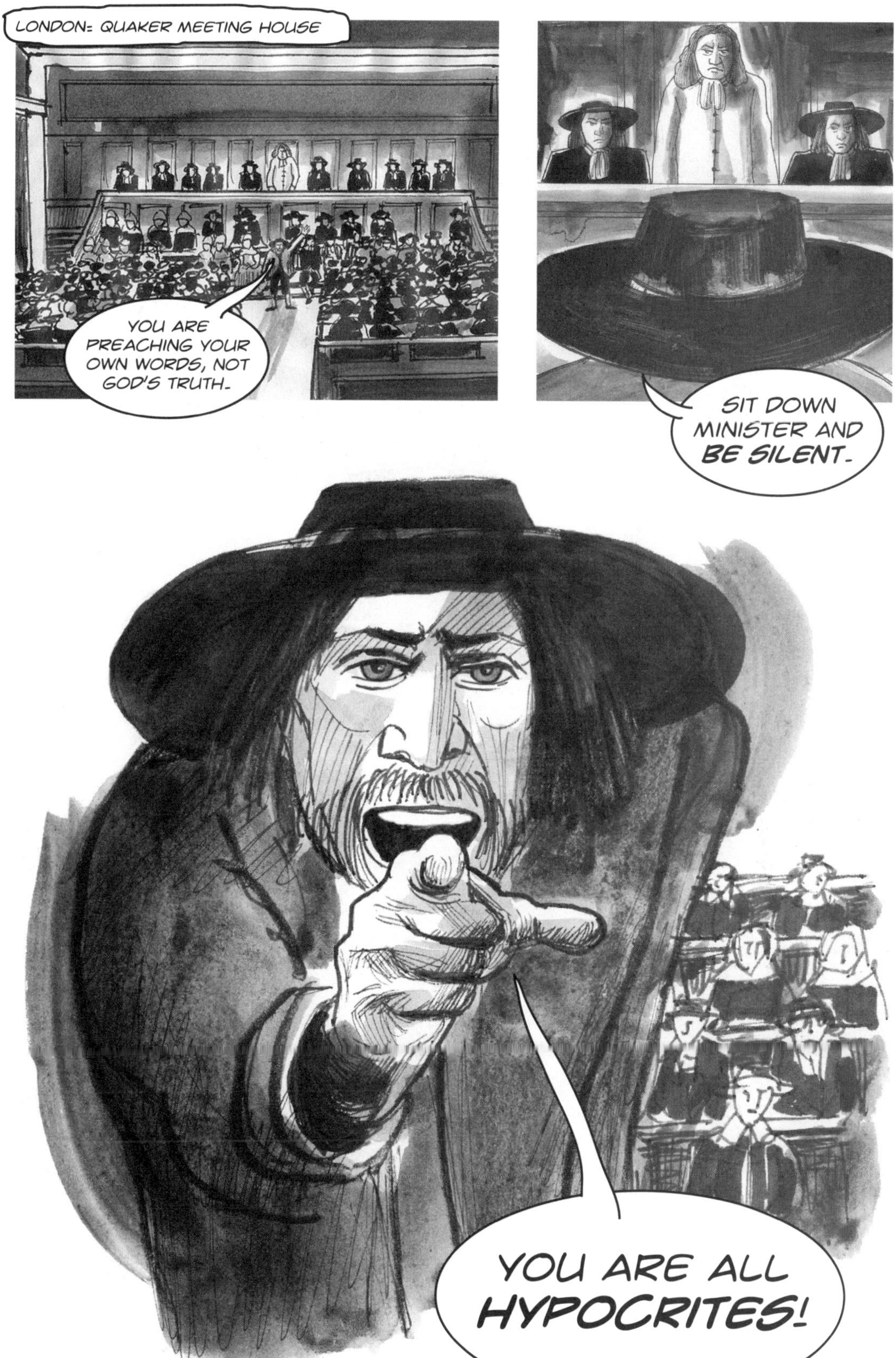
LONDON: QUAKER MEETING HOUSE
YOU ARE PREACHING YOUR OWN WORDS, NOT GOD'S TRUTH.
SIT DOWN MINISTER AND BE SILENT.
YOU ARE ALL HYPOCRITES!

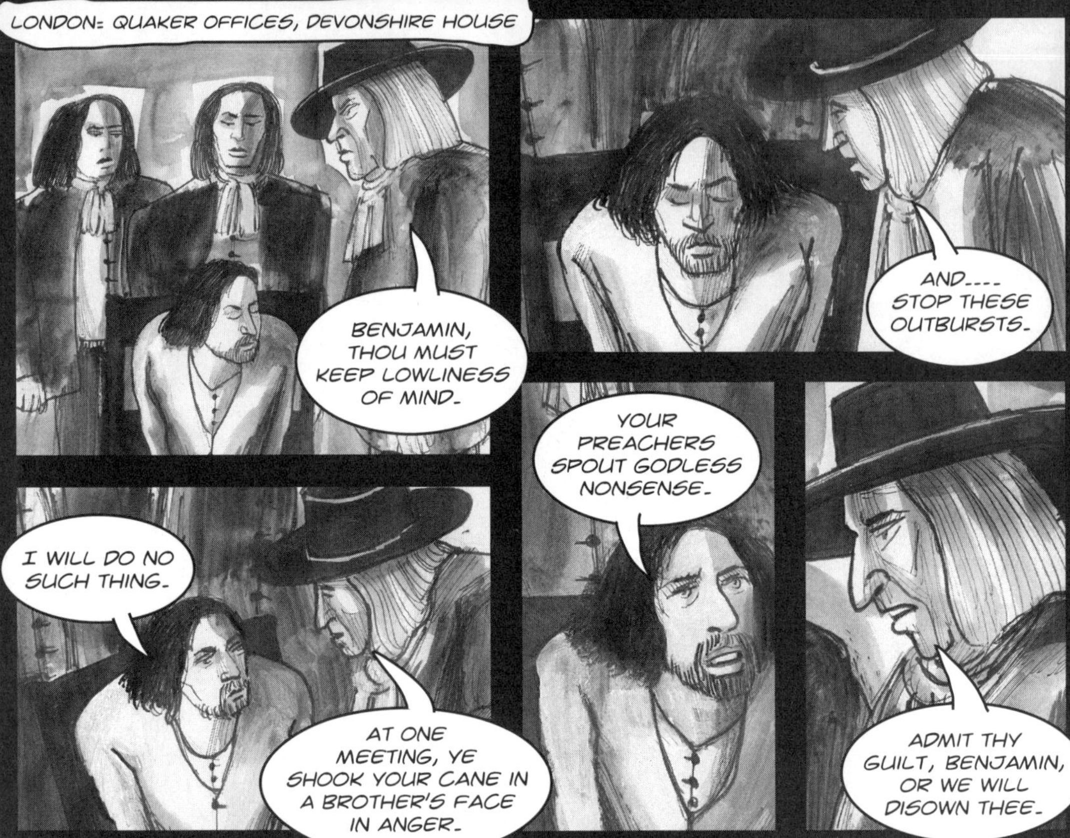
LONDON: QUAKER OFFICES, DEVONSHIRE HOUSE
BENJAMIN, THOU MUST KEEP LOWLINESS OF MIND.
AND.... STOP THESE OUTBURSTS.
I WILL DO NO SUCH THING.
AT ONE MEETING, YE SHOOK YOUR CANE IN A BROTHER'S FACE IN ANGER.
YOUR PREACHERS SPOUT GODLESS NONSENSE.
ADMIT THY GUILT, BENJAMIN, OR WE WILL DISOWN THEE.

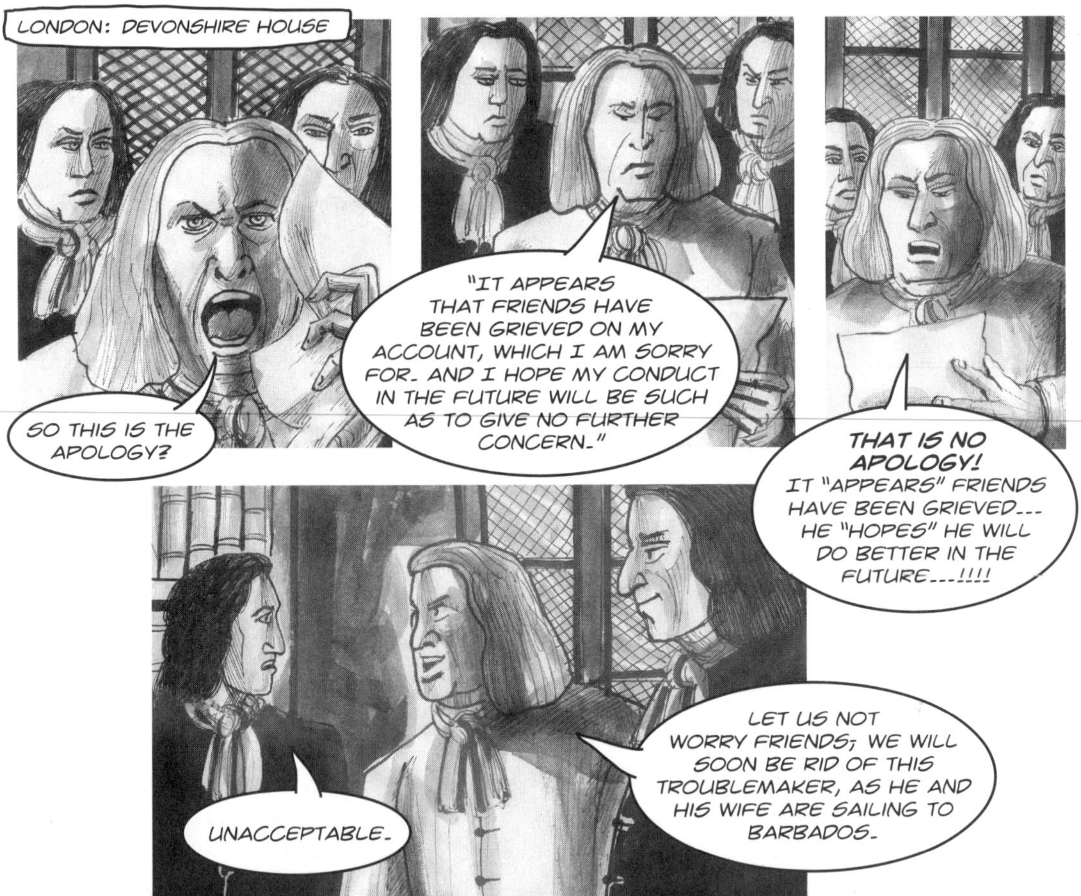
LONDON: DEVONSHIRE HOUSE
SO THIS IS THE APOLOGY?
"IT APPEARS THAT FRIENDS HAVE BEEN GRIEVED ON MY ACCOUNT, WHICH I AM SORRY FOR. AND I HOPE MY CONDUCT IN THE FUTURE WILL BE SUCH AS TO GIVE NO FURTHER CONCERN."
THAT IS NO APOLOGY! IT "APPEARS" FRIENDS HAVE BEEN GRIEVED... HE "HOPES" HE WILL DO BETTER IN THE FUTURE...!!!!
UNACCEPTABLE.
LET US NOT WORRY FRIENDS; WE WILL SOON BE RID OF THIS TROUBLEMAKER, AS HE AND HIS WIFE ARE SAILING TO BARBADOS.

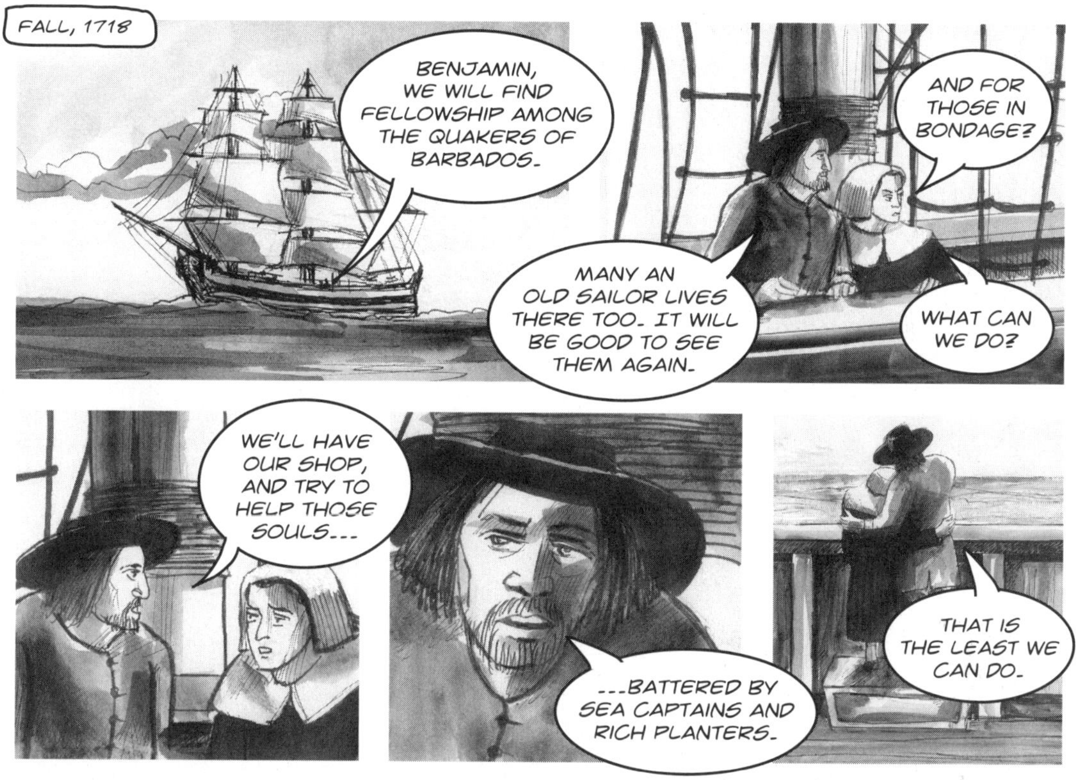
FALL, 1718
BENJAMIN, WE WILL FIND FELLOWSHIP AMONG THE QUAKERS OF BARBADOS.
MANY AN OLD SAILOR LIVES THERE TOO. IT WILL BE GOOD TO SEE THEM AGAIN.
AND FOR THOSE IN BONDAGE?
WHAT CAN WE DO?
WE'LL HAVE OUR SHOP, AND TRY TO HELP THOSE SOULS...
...BATTERED BY SEA CAPTAINS AND RICH PLANTERS.
THAT IS THE LEAST WE CAN DO.

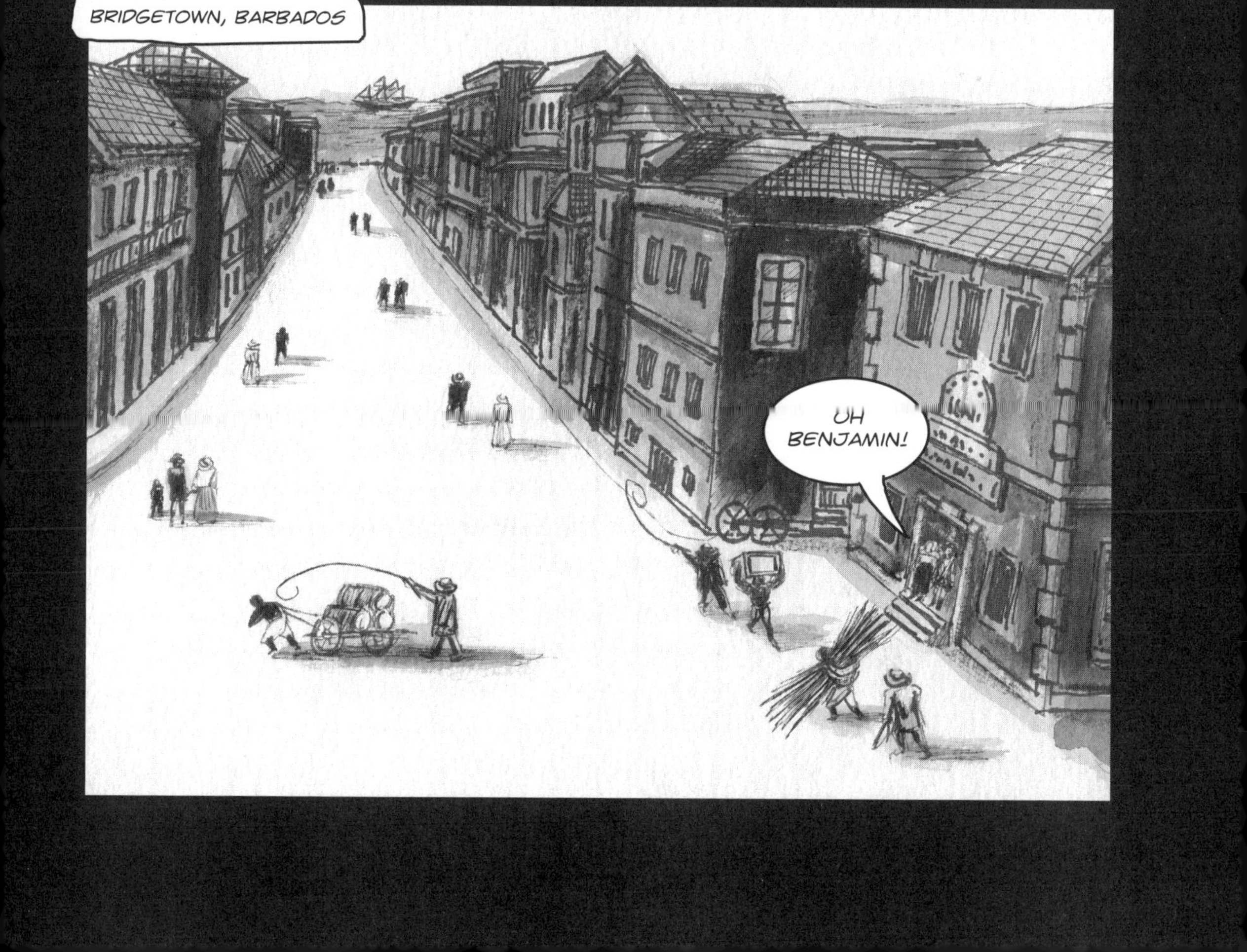
BRIDGETOWN, BARBADOS
UH BENJAMIN!

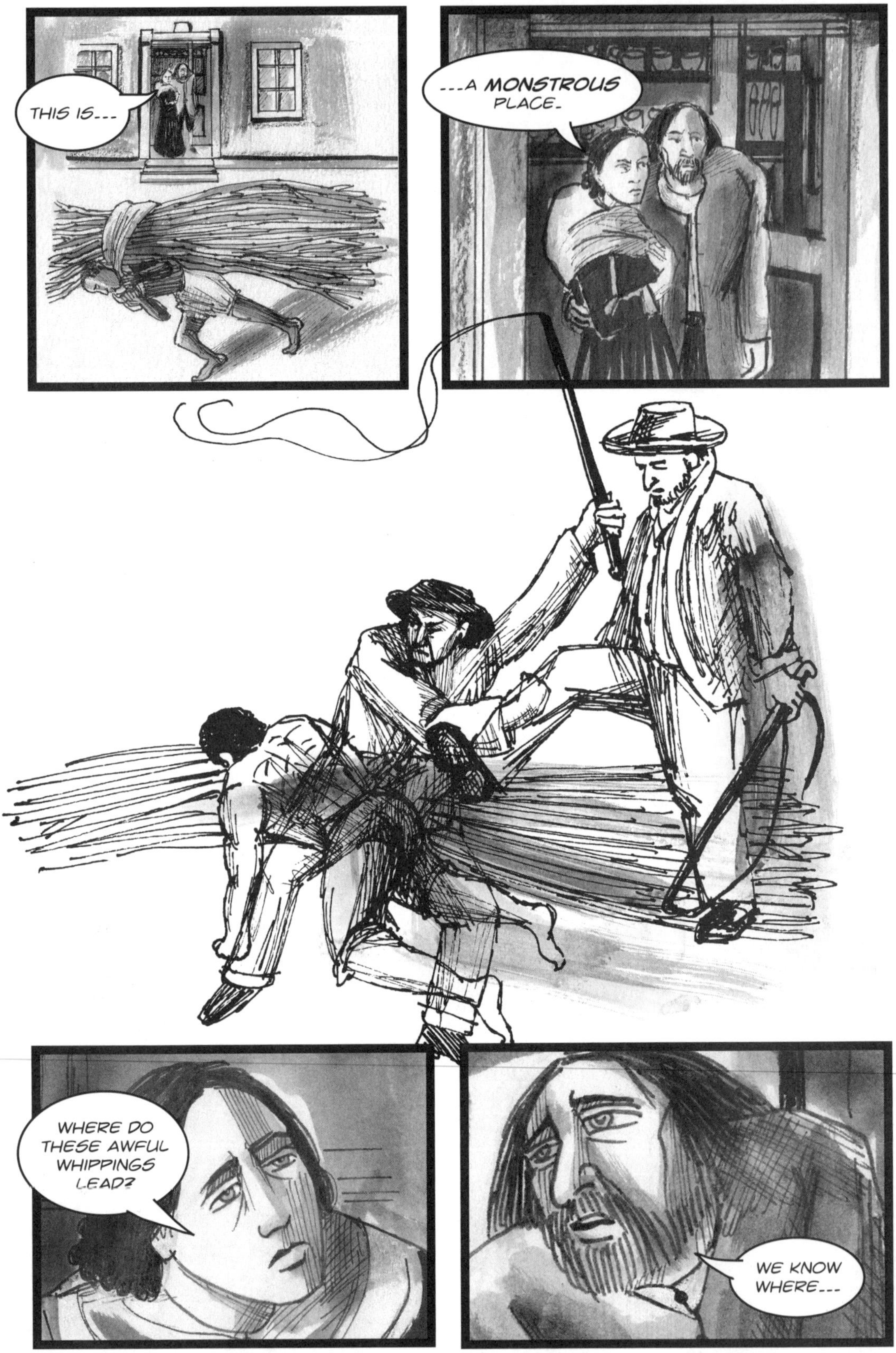
THIS IS...
...A MONSTROUS PLACE.
WHERE DO THESE AWFUL WHIPPINGS LEAD?
WE KNOW WHERE...

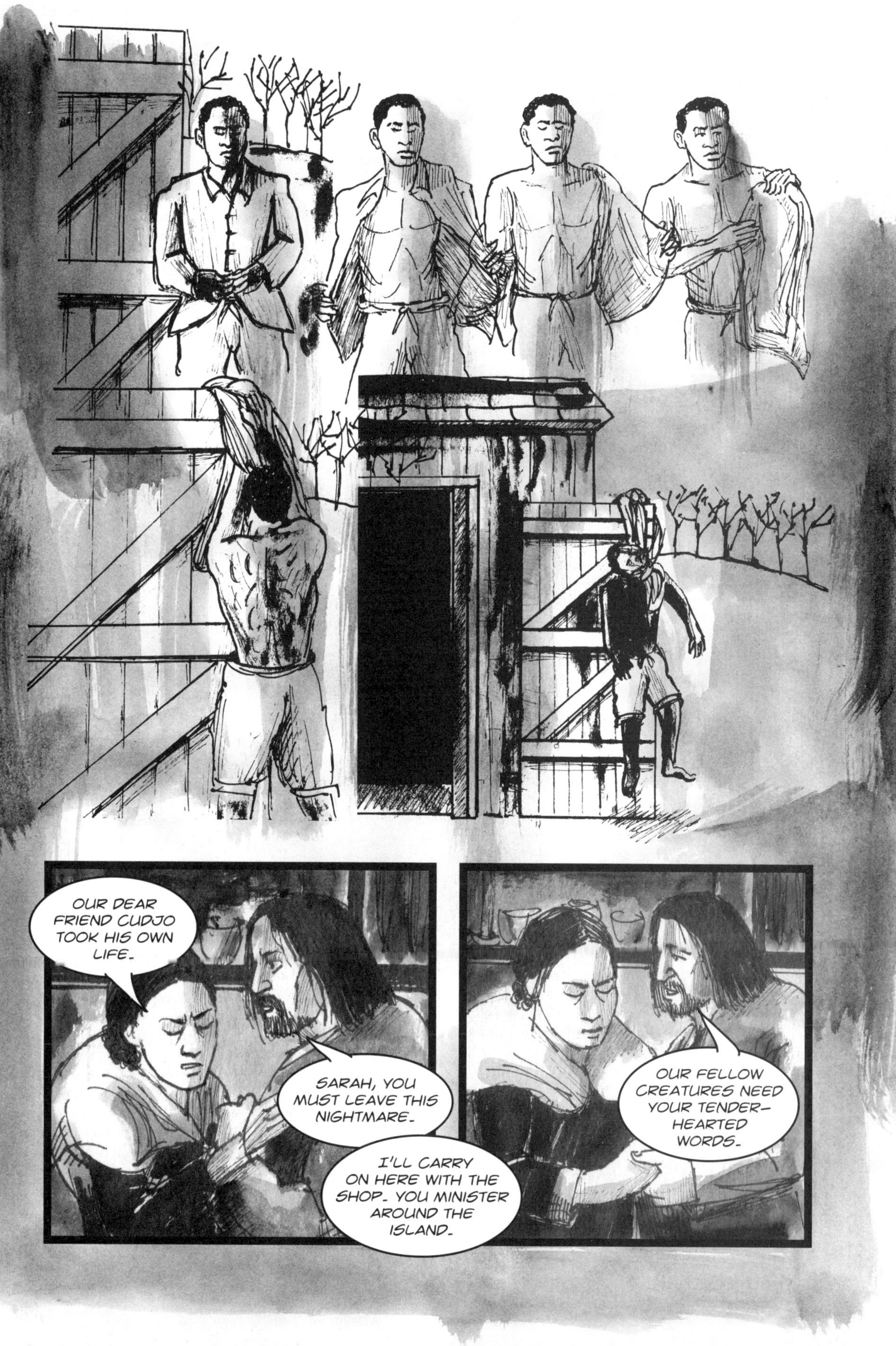
OUR DEAR FRIEND CUDJO TOOK HIS OWN LIFE.
SARAH, YOU MUST LEAVE THIS NIGHTMARE.
I'LL CARRY ON HERE WITH THE SHOP. YOU MINISTER AROUND THE ISLAND.
OUR FELLOW CREATURES NEED YOUR TENDER-HEARTED WORDS.

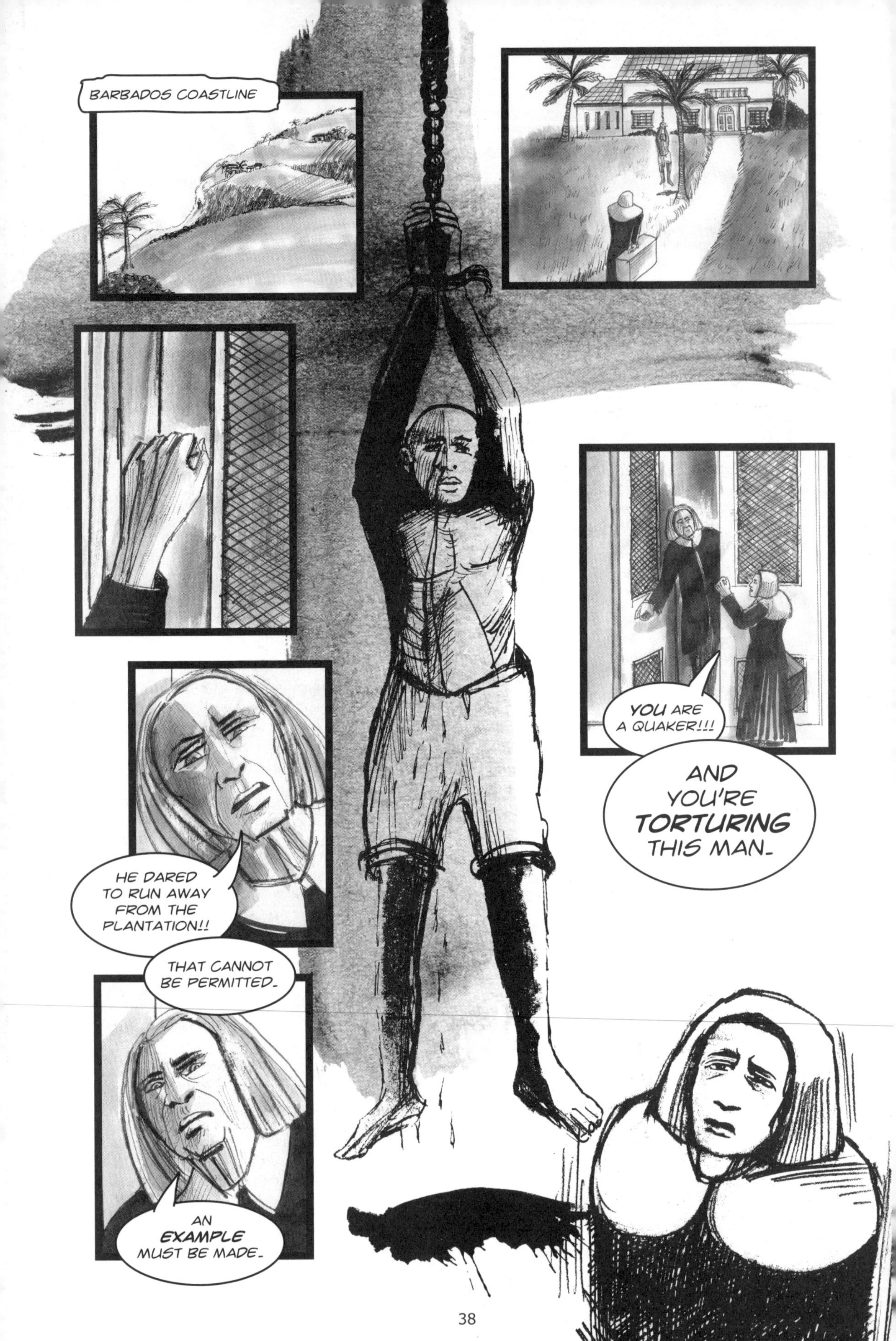
BARBADOS COASTLINE
YOU ARE A QUAKER!!!
AND YOU'RE TORTURING THIS MAN.
HE DARED TO RUN AWAY FROM THE PLANTATION!!
THAT CANNOT BE PERMITTED.
AN EXAMPLE MUST BE MADE.

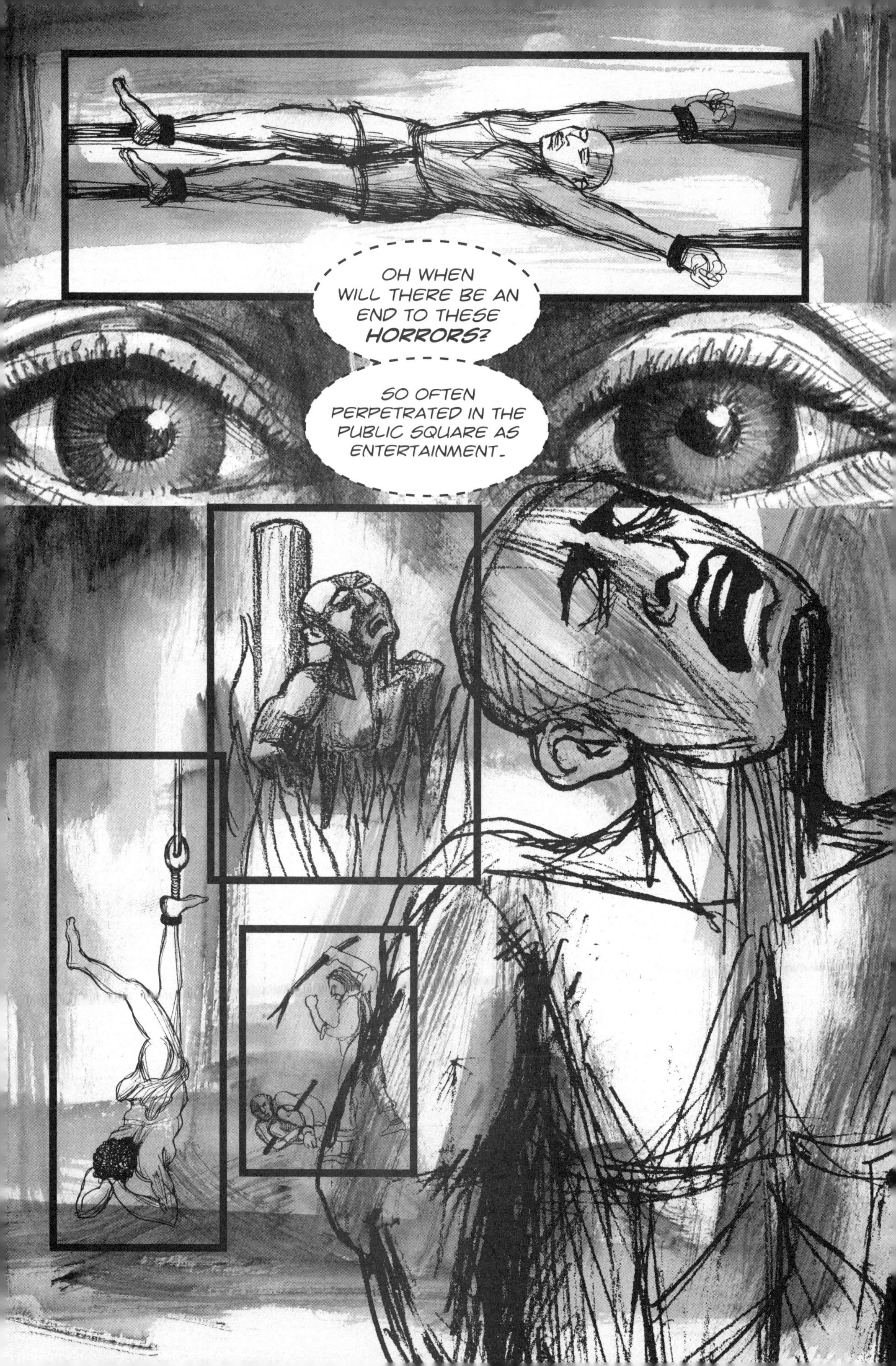
OH WHEN WILL THERE BE AN END TO THESE HORRORS?
SO OFTEN PERPETRATED IN THE PUBLIC SQUARE AS ENTERTAINMENT.

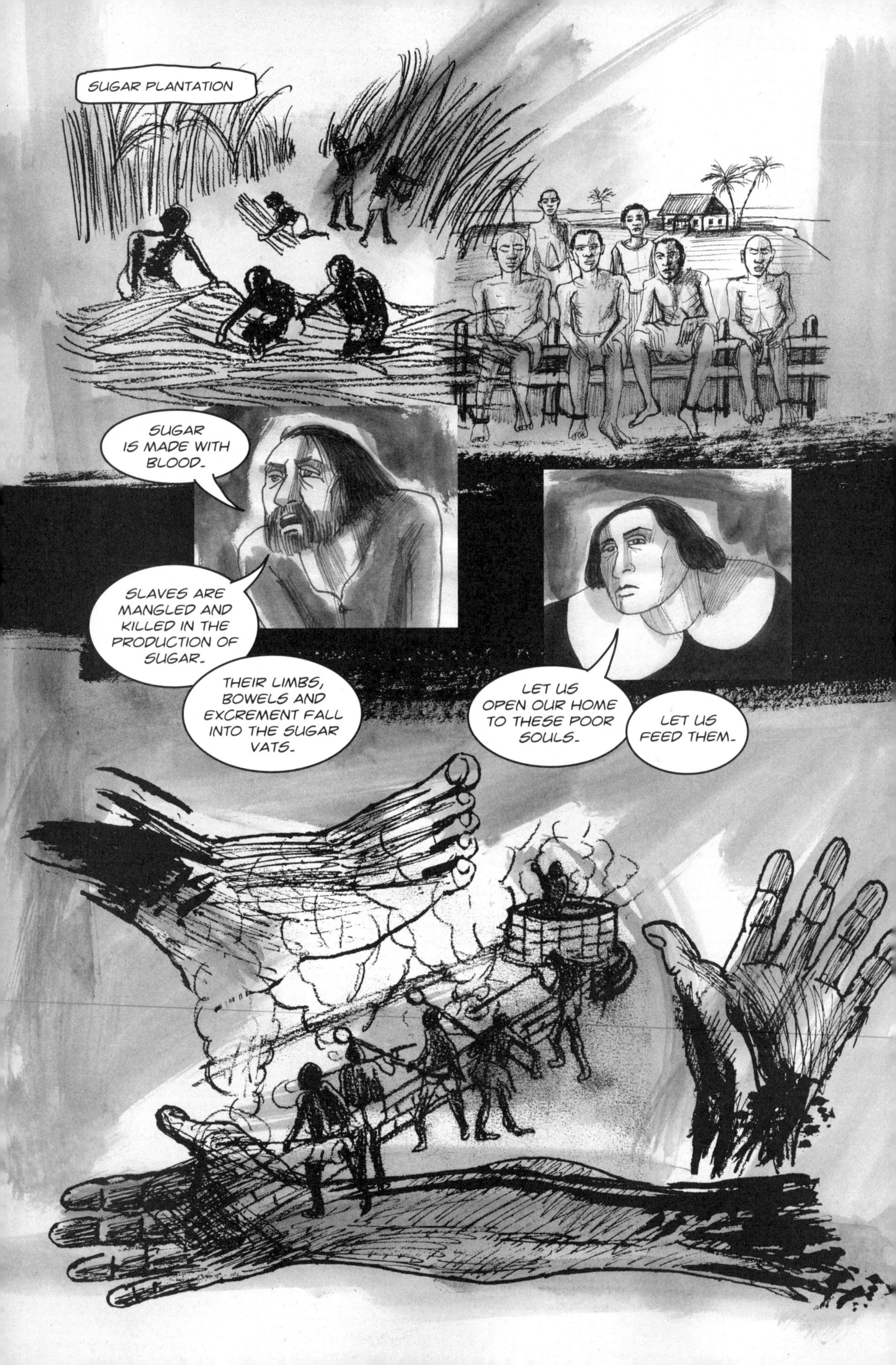
SUGAR PLANTATION
SUGAR IS MADE WITH BLOOD.
SLAVES ARE MANGLED AND KILLED IN THE PRODUCTION OF SUGAR.
THEIR LIMBS, BOWELS AND EXCREMENT FALL INTO THE SUGAR VATS.
LET US OPEN OUR HOME TO THESE POOR SOULS.
LET US FEED THEM.

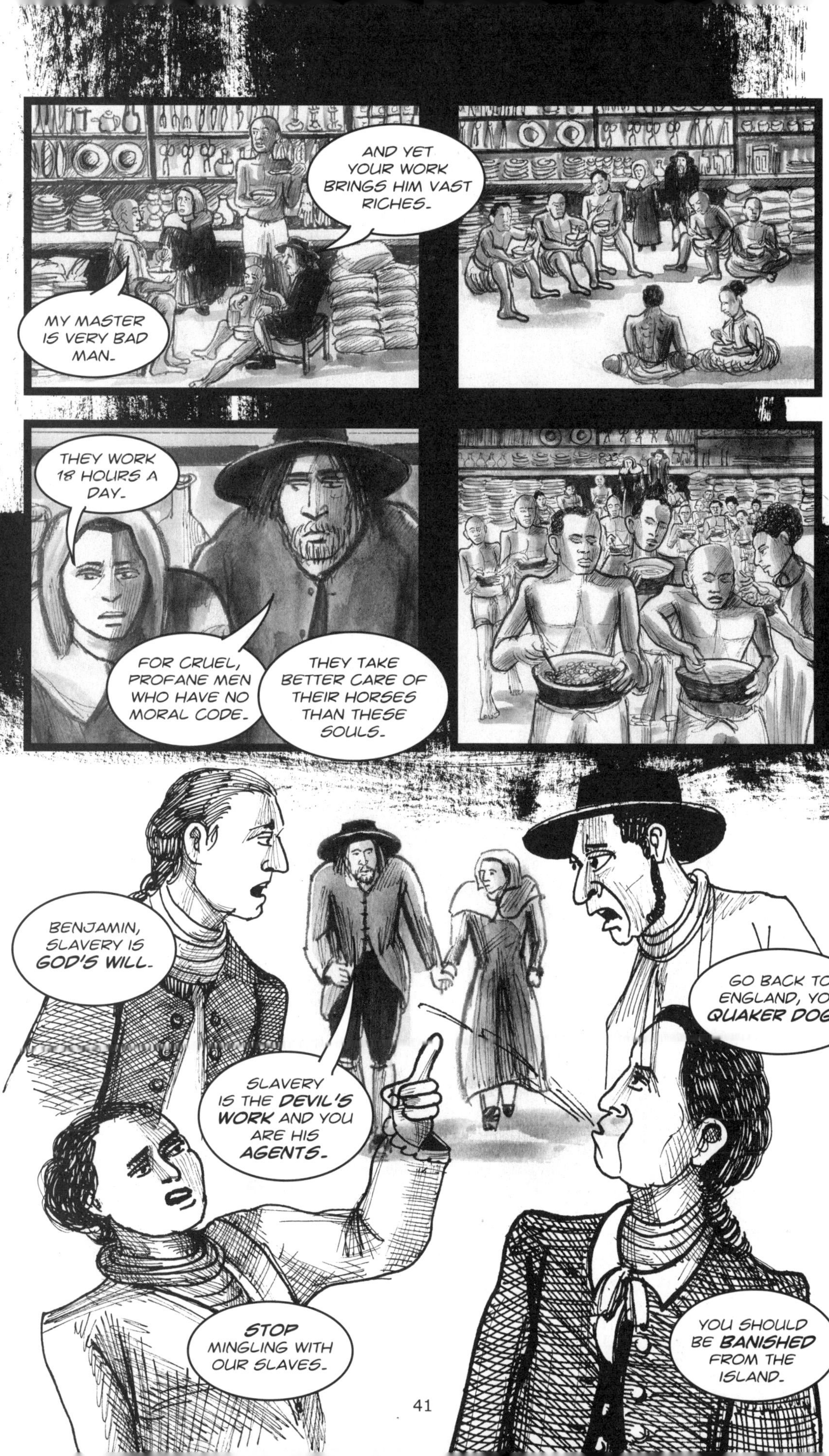
MY MASTER IS VERY BAD MAN.
AND YET YOUR WORK BRINGS HIM VAST RICHES.
THEY WORK 18 HOURS A DAY.
FOR CRUEL, PROFANE MEN WHO HAVE NO MORAL CODE.
THEY TAKE BETTER CARE OF THEIR HORSES THAN THESE SOULS.
BENJAMIN, SLAVERY IS GOD'S WILL.
GO BACK TO ENGLAND, YOU QUAKER DOGS!
SLAVERY IS THE DEVIL'S WORK AND YOU ARE HIS AGENTS.
STOP MINGLING WITH OUR SLAVES.
YOU SHOULD BE BANISHED FROM THE ISLAND.

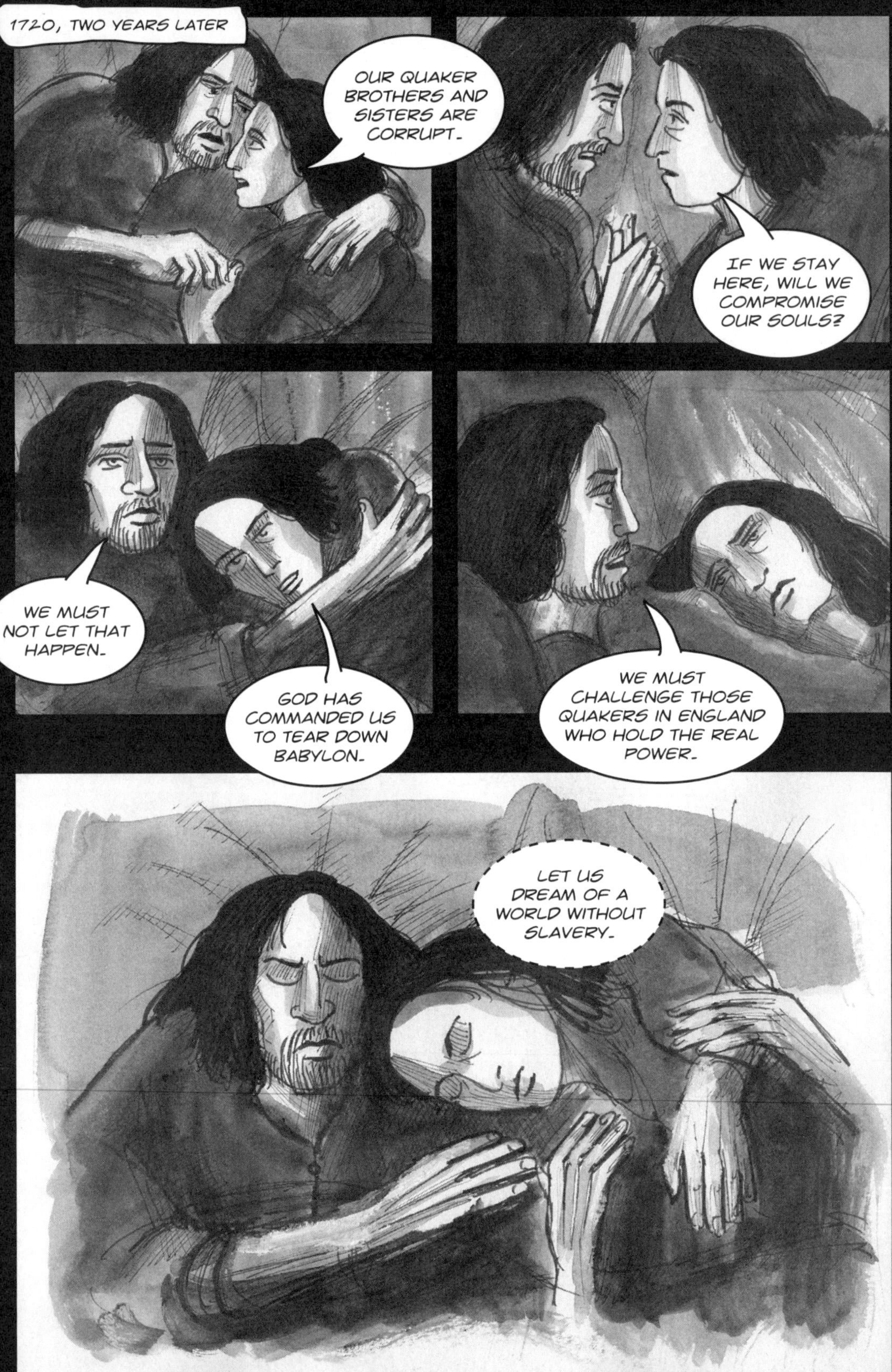
1720, TWO YEARS LATER
OUR QUAKER BROTHERS AND SISTERS ARE CORRUPT.
IF WE STAY HERE, WILL WE COMPROMISE OUR SOULS?
WE MUST NOT LET THAT HAPPEN.
GOD HAS COMMANDED US TO TEAR DOWN BABYLON.
WE MUST CHALLENGE THOSE QUAKERS IN ENGLAND WHO HOLD THE REAL POWER.
LET US DREAM OF A WORLD WITHOUT SLAVERY.

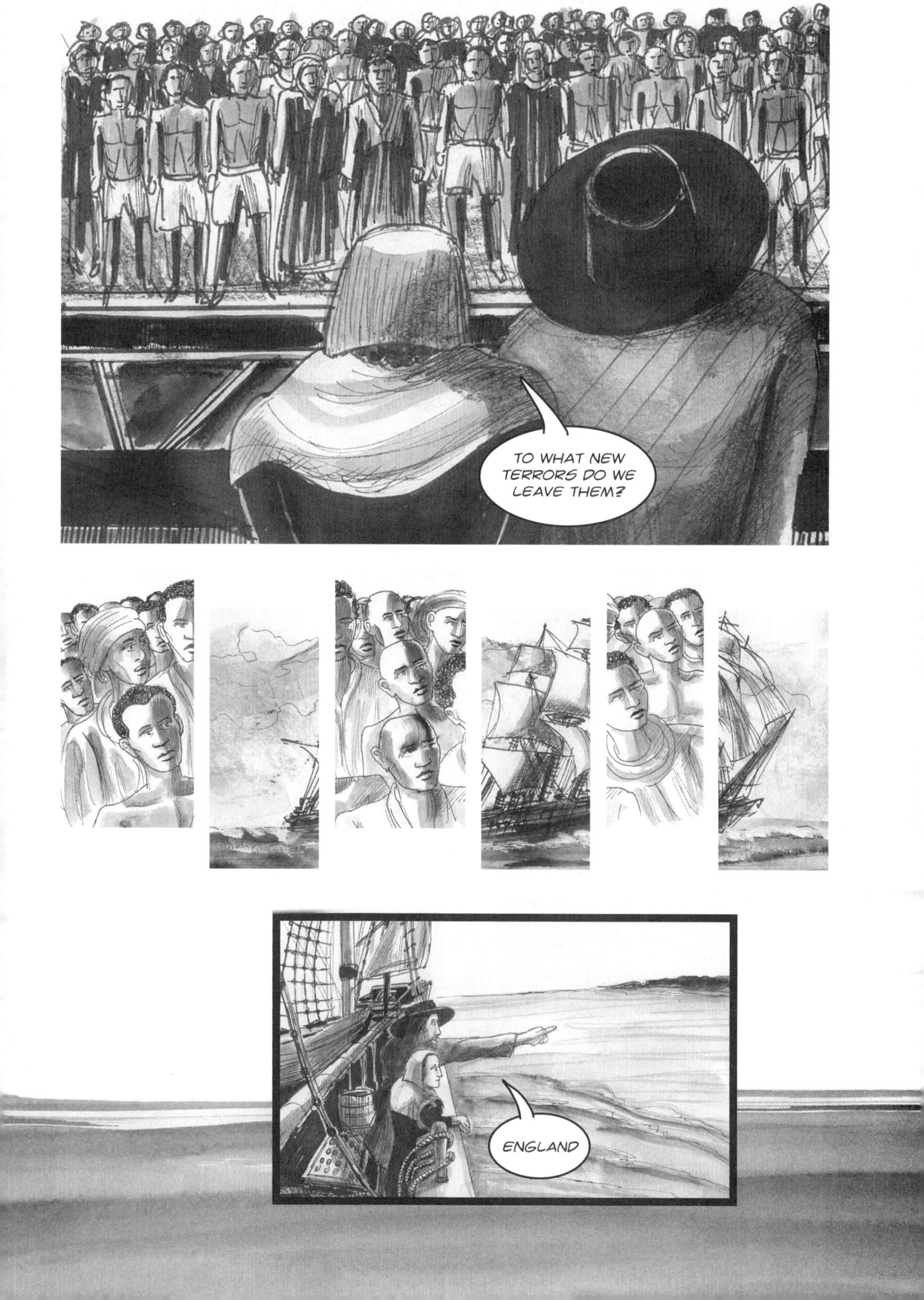
TO WHAT NEW TERRORS DO WE LEAVE THEM?
ENGLAND

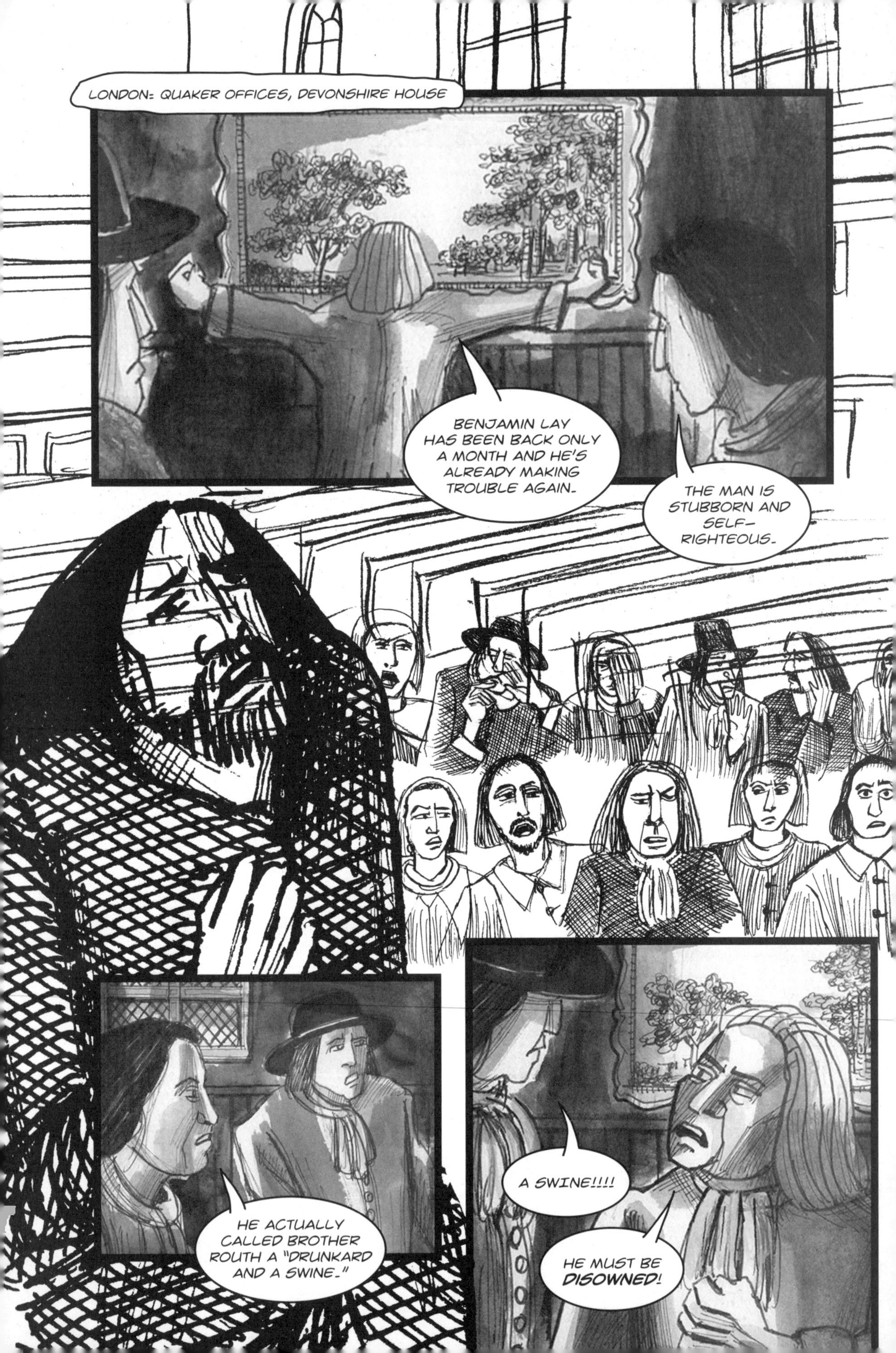
LONDON: QUAKER OFFICES, DEVONSHIRE HOUSE
BENJAMIN LAY HAS BEEN BACK ONLY A MONTH AND HE'S ALREADY MAKING TROUBLE AGAIN.
THE MAN IS STUBBORN AND SELF-RIGHTEOUS.
HE ACTUALLY CALLED BROTHER ROUTH A "DRUNKARD AND A SWINE."
A SWINE!!!!
HE MUST BE DISOWNED!

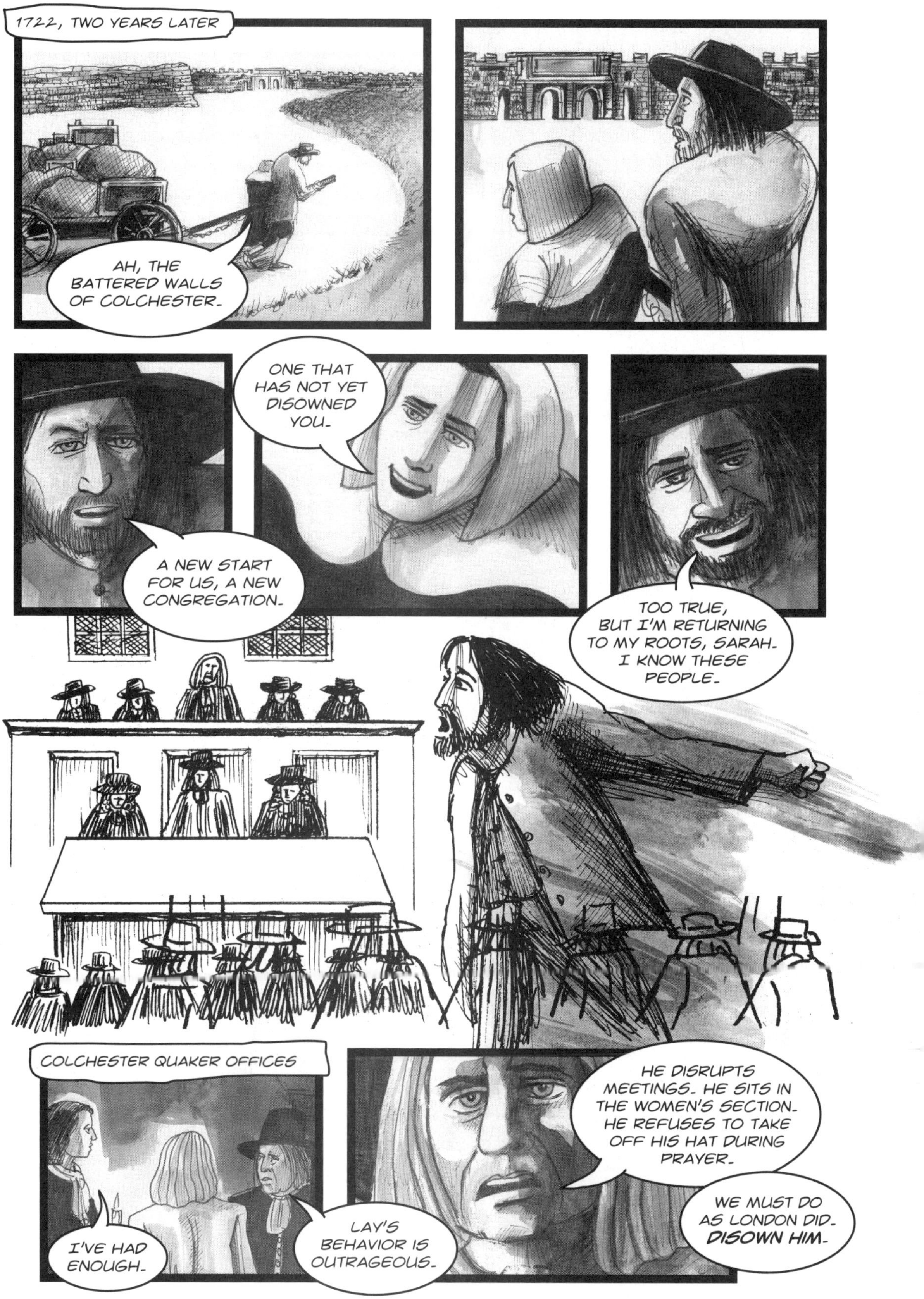

1722, TWO YEARS LATER
AH, THE BATTERED WALLS OF COLCHESTER.
A NEW START FOR US, A NEW CONGREGATION.
ONE THAT HAS NOT YET DISOWNED YOU.
TOO TRUE, BUT I'M RETURNING TO MY ROOTS, SARAH. I KNOW THESE PEOPLE.
COLCHESTER QUAKER OFFICES
I'VE HAD ENOUGH.
LAY'S BEHAVIOR IS OUTRAGEOUS.
HE DISRUPTS MEETINGS. HE SITS IN THE WOMEN'S SECTION. HE REFUSES TO TAKE OFF HIS HAT DURING PRAYER.
WE MUST DO AS LONDON DID. DISOWN HIM.

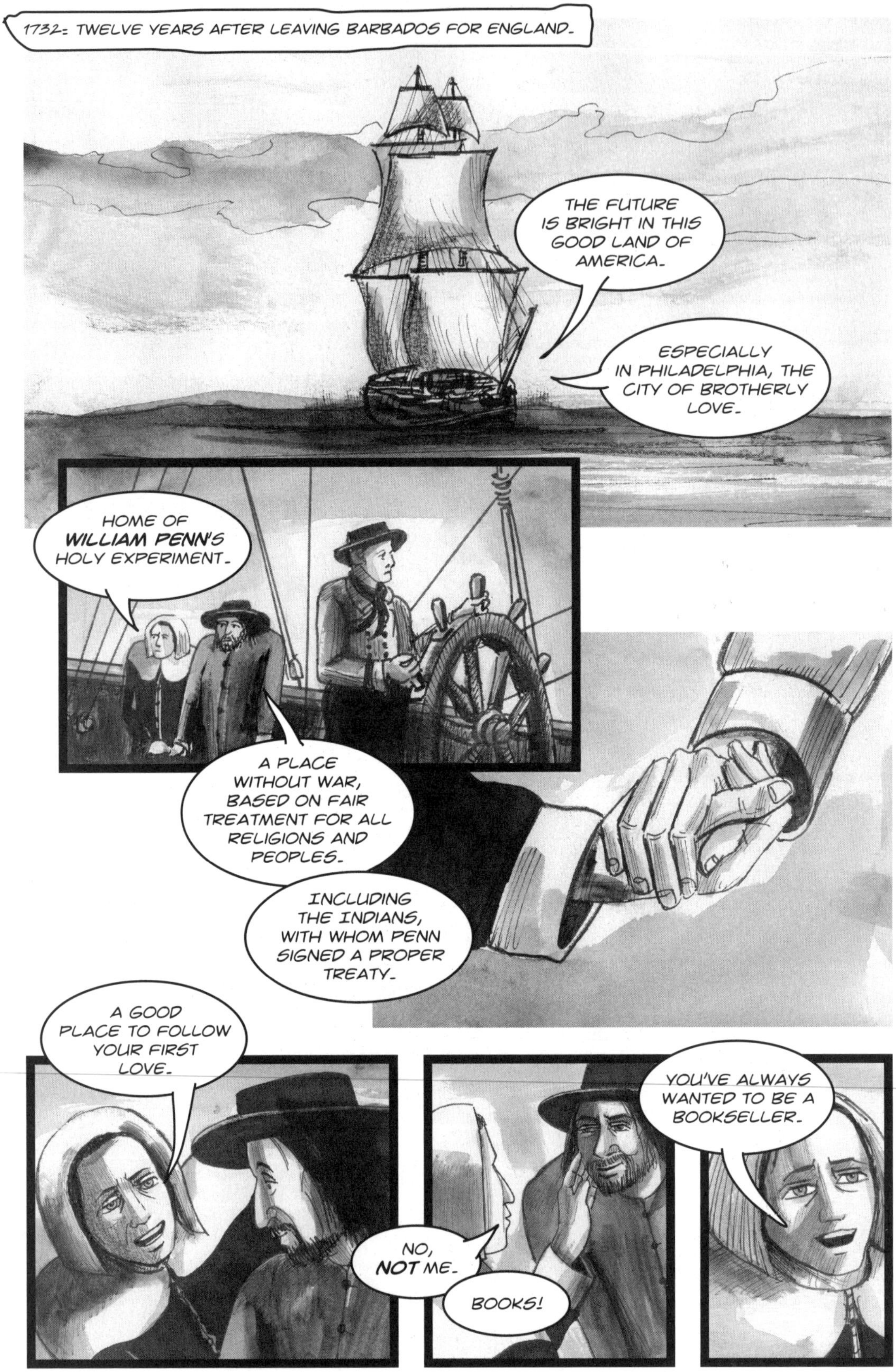
1732: TWELVE YEARS AFTER LEAVING BARBADOS FOR ENGLAND.
THE FUTURE IS BRIGHT IN THIS GOOD LAND OF AMERICA.
ESPECIALLY IN PHILADELPHIA, THE CITY OF BROTHERLY LOVE.
HOME OF **WILLIAM PENN**'S HOLY EXPERIMENT.
A PLACE WITHOUT WAR, BASED ON FAIR TREATMENT FOR ALL RELIGIONS AND PEOPLES.
INCLUDING THE INDIANS, WITH WHOM PENN SIGNED A PROPER TREATY.
A GOOD PLACE TO FOLLOW YOUR FIRST LOVE.
YOU'VE ALWAYS WANTED TO BE A BOOKSELLER.
NO, **NOT** ME.
BOOKS!

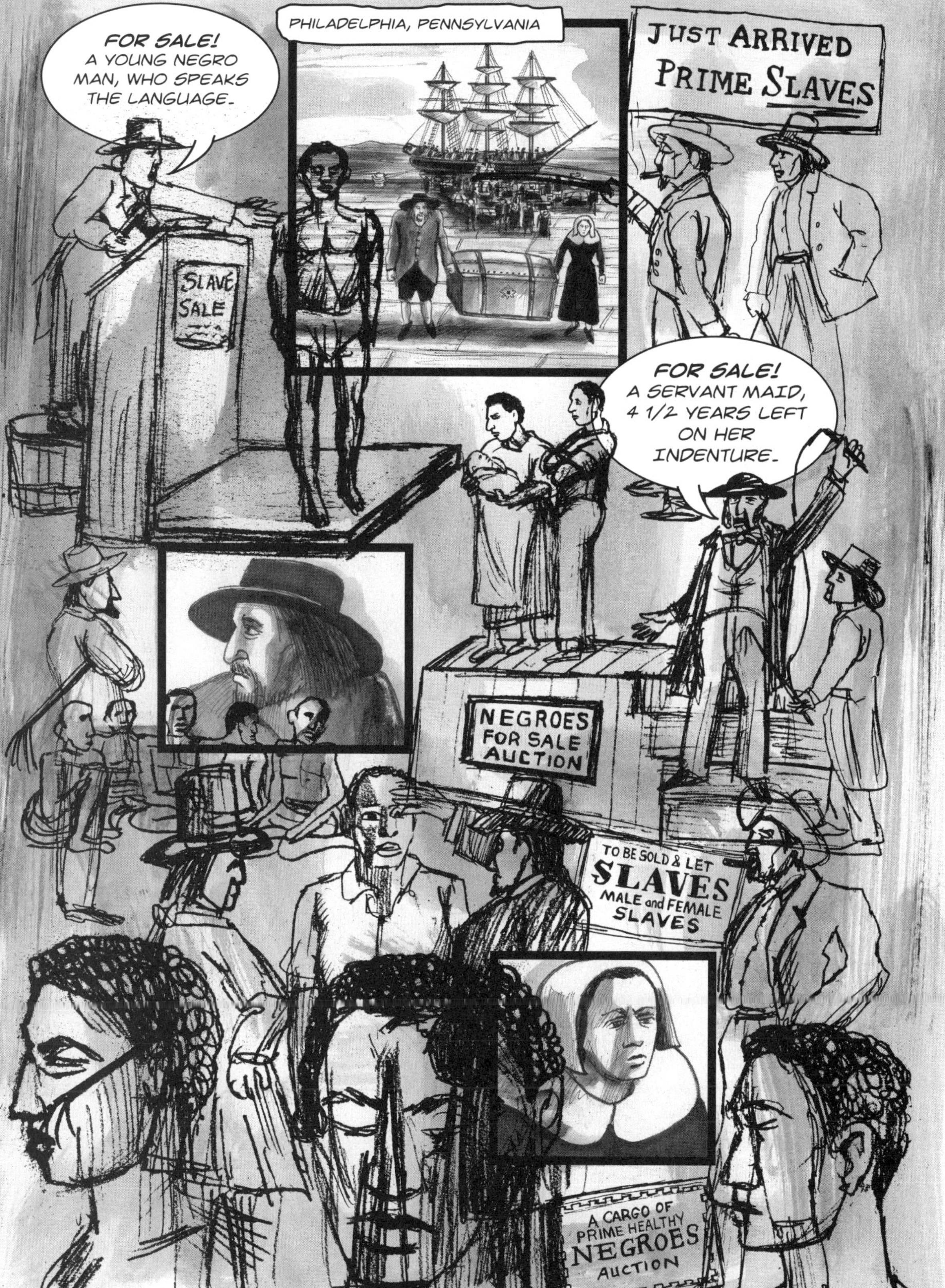

FOR SALE! A YOUNG NEGRO MAN, WHO SPEAKS THE LANGUAGE.
SLAVE SALE
PHILADELPHIA, PENNSYLVANIA
JUST ARRIVED PRIME SLAVES
FOR SALE! A SERVANT MAID, 4 1/2 YEARS LEFT ON HER INDENTURE.
NEGROES FOR SALE AUCTION
TO BE SOLD & LET SLAVES MALE and FEMALE SLAVES
A CARGO OF PRIME HEALTHY NEGROES AUCTION

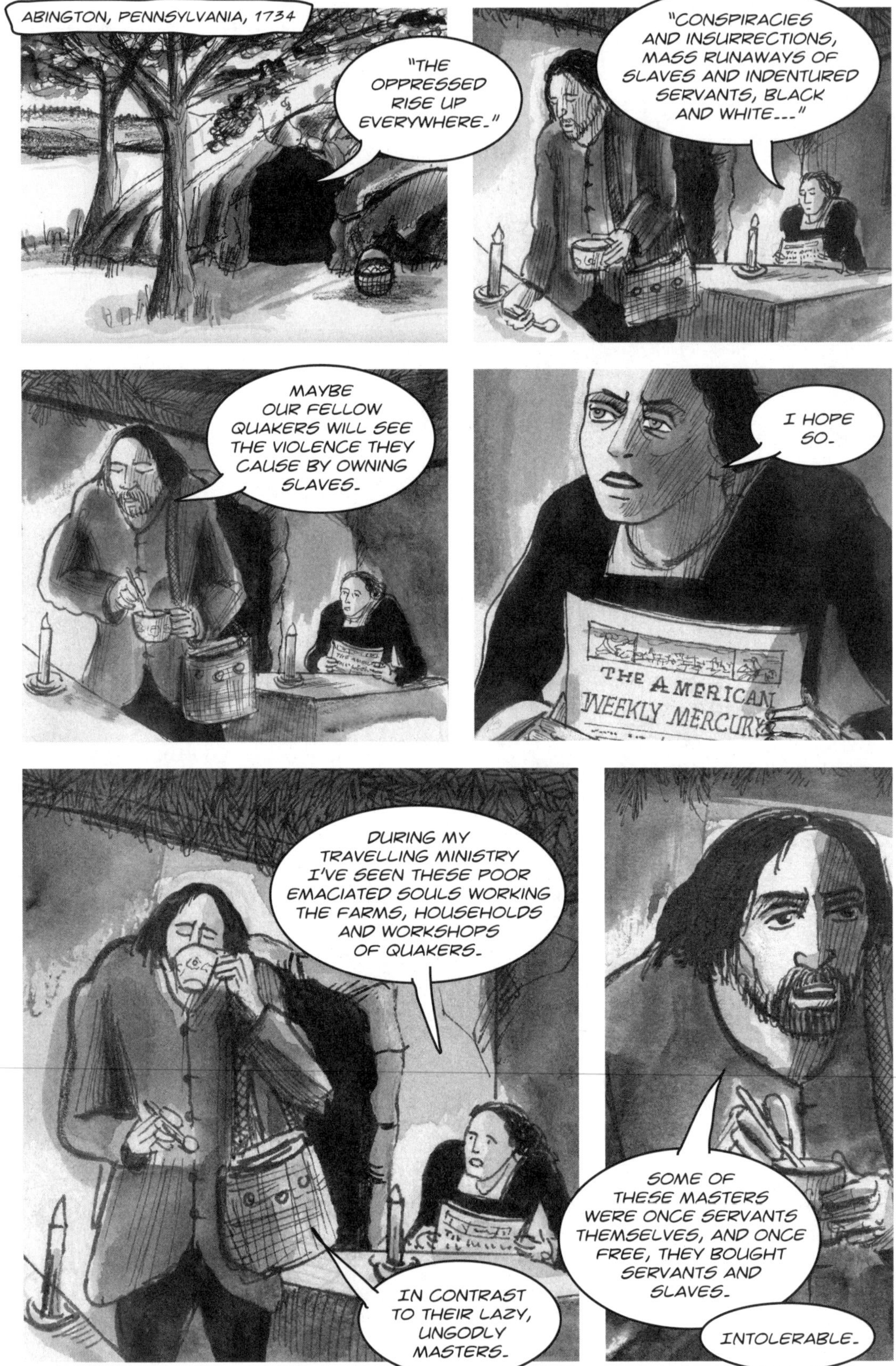
ABINGTON, PENNSYLVANIA, 1734
"THE OPPRESSED RISE UP EVERYWHERE."
"CONSPIRACIES AND INSURRECTIONS, MASS RUNAWAYS OF SLAVES AND INDENTURED SERVANTS, BLACK AND WHITE..."
MAYBE OUR FELLOW QUAKERS WILL SEE THE VIOLENCE THEY CAUSE BY OWNING SLAVES.
I HOPE SO.
THE AMERICAN WEEKLY MERCURY
DURING MY TRAVELLING MINISTRY I'VE SEEN THESE POOR EMACIATED SOULS WORKING THE FARMS, HOUSEHOLDS AND WORKSHOPS OF QUAKERS.
IN CONTRAST TO THEIR LAZY, UNGODLY MASTERS.
SOME OF THESE MASTERS WERE ONCE SERVANTS THEMSELVES, AND ONCE FREE, THEY BOUGHT SERVANTS AND SLAVES.
INTOLERABLE.

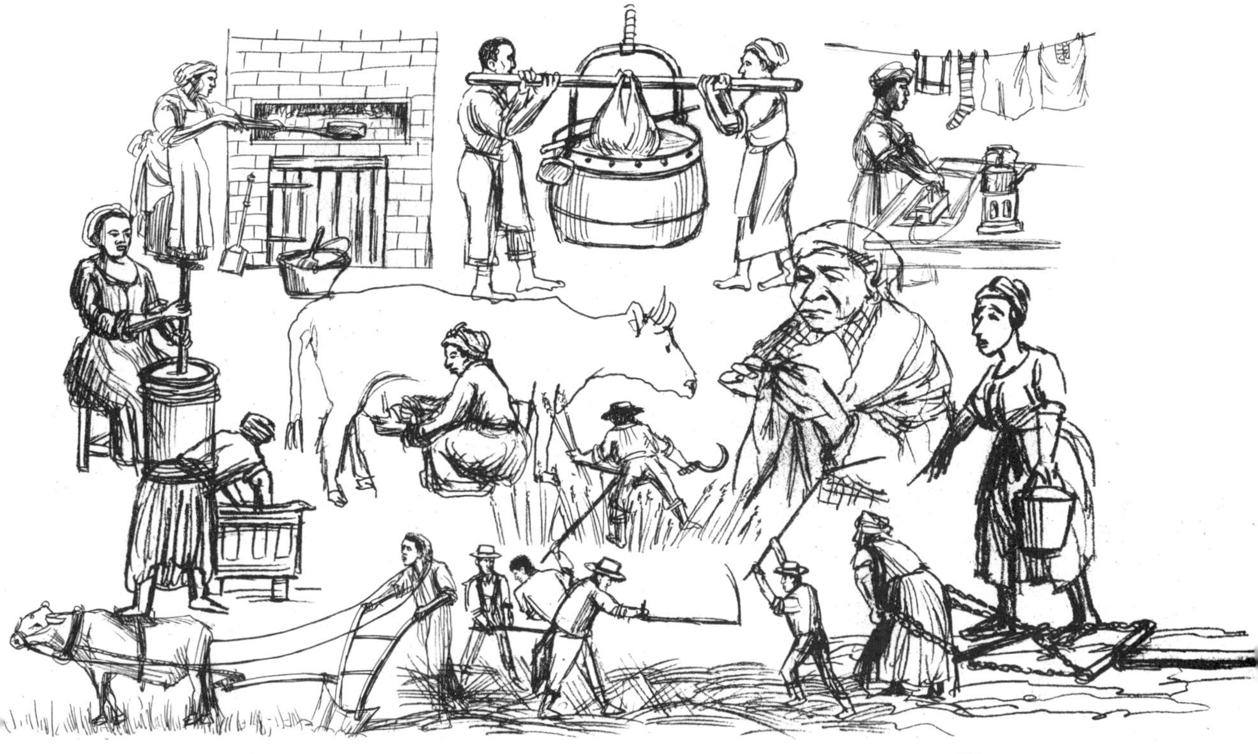

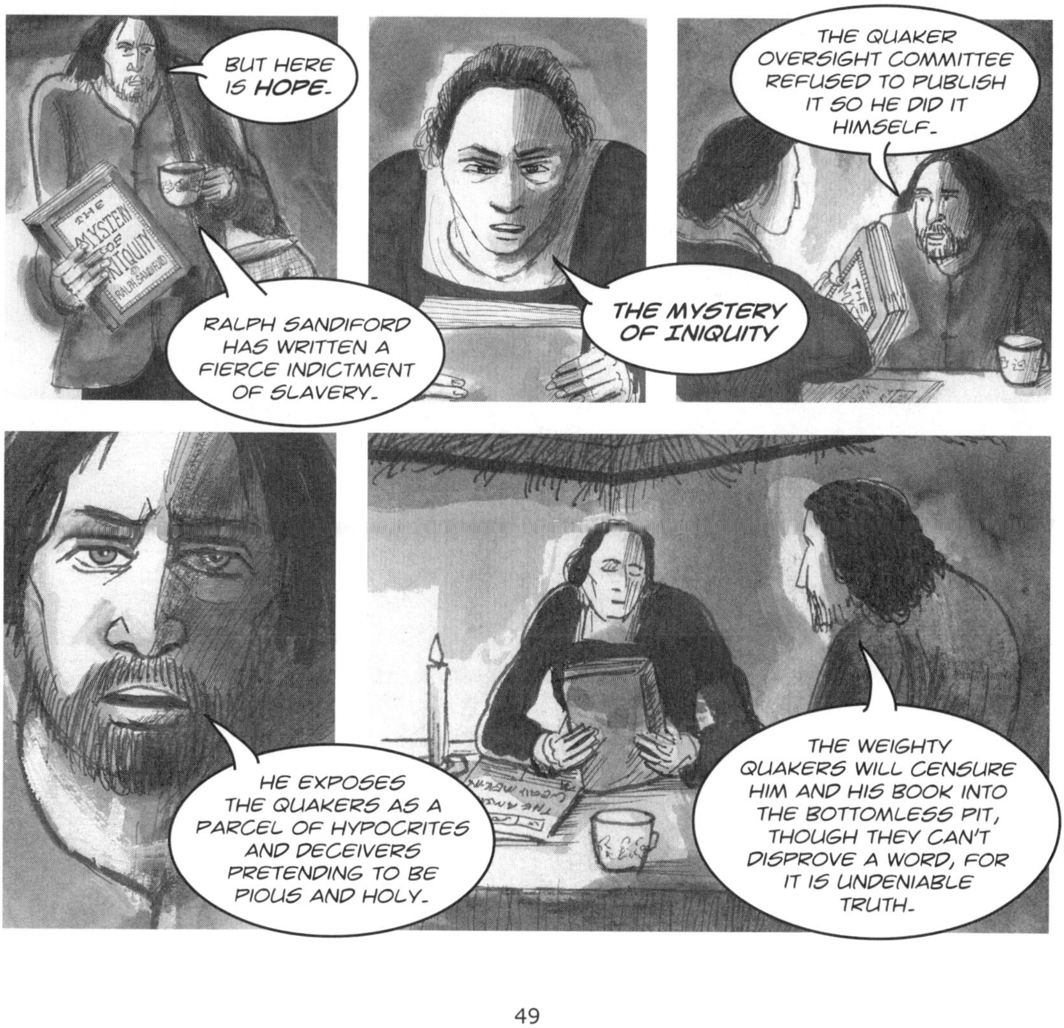

BUT HERE IS HOPE.
RALPH SANDIFORD HAS WRITTEN A FIERCE INDICTMENT OF SLAVERY.
THE MYSTERY OF INIQUITY
THE QUAKER OVERSIGHT COMMITTEE REFUSED TO PUBLISH IT SO HE DID IT HIMSELF.
HE EXPOSES THE QUAKERS AS A PARCEL OF HYPOCRITES AND DECEIVERS PRETENDING TO BE PIOUS AND HOLY.
THE WEIGHTY QUAKERS WILL CENSURE HIM AND HIS BOOK INTO THE BOTTOMLESS PIT, THOUGH THEY CAN'T DISPROVE A WORD, FOR IT IS UNDENIABLE TRUTH.

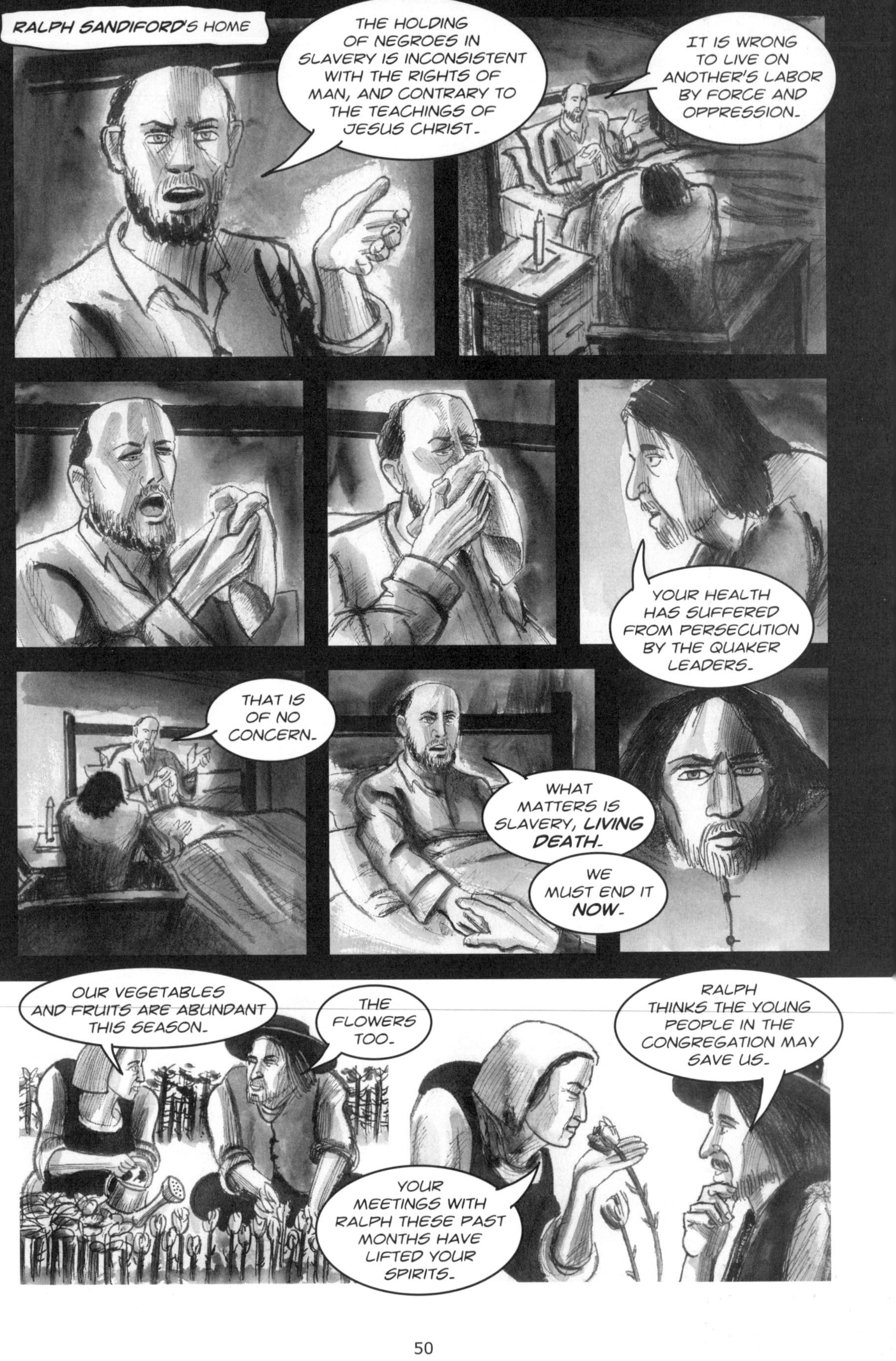
RALPH SANDIFORD'S HOME
THE HOLDING OF NEGROES IN SLAVERY IS INCONSISTENT WITH THE RIGHTS OF MAN, AND CONTRARY TO THE TEACHINGS OF JESUS CHRIST.
IT IS WRONG TO LIVE ON ANOTHER'S LABOR BY FORCE AND OPPRESSION.
YOUR HEALTH HAS SUFFERED FROM PERSECUTION BY THE QUAKER LEADERS.
THAT IS OF NO CONCERN.
WHAT MATTERS IS SLAVERY, LIVING DEATH.
WE MUST END IT NOW.
OUR VEGETABLES AND FRUITS ARE ABUNDANT THIS SEASON.
THE FLOWERS TOO.
YOUR MEETINGS WITH RALPH THESE PAST MONTHS HAVE LIFTED YOUR SPIRITS.
RALPH THINKS THE YOUNG PEOPLE IN THE CONGREGATION MAY SAVE US.

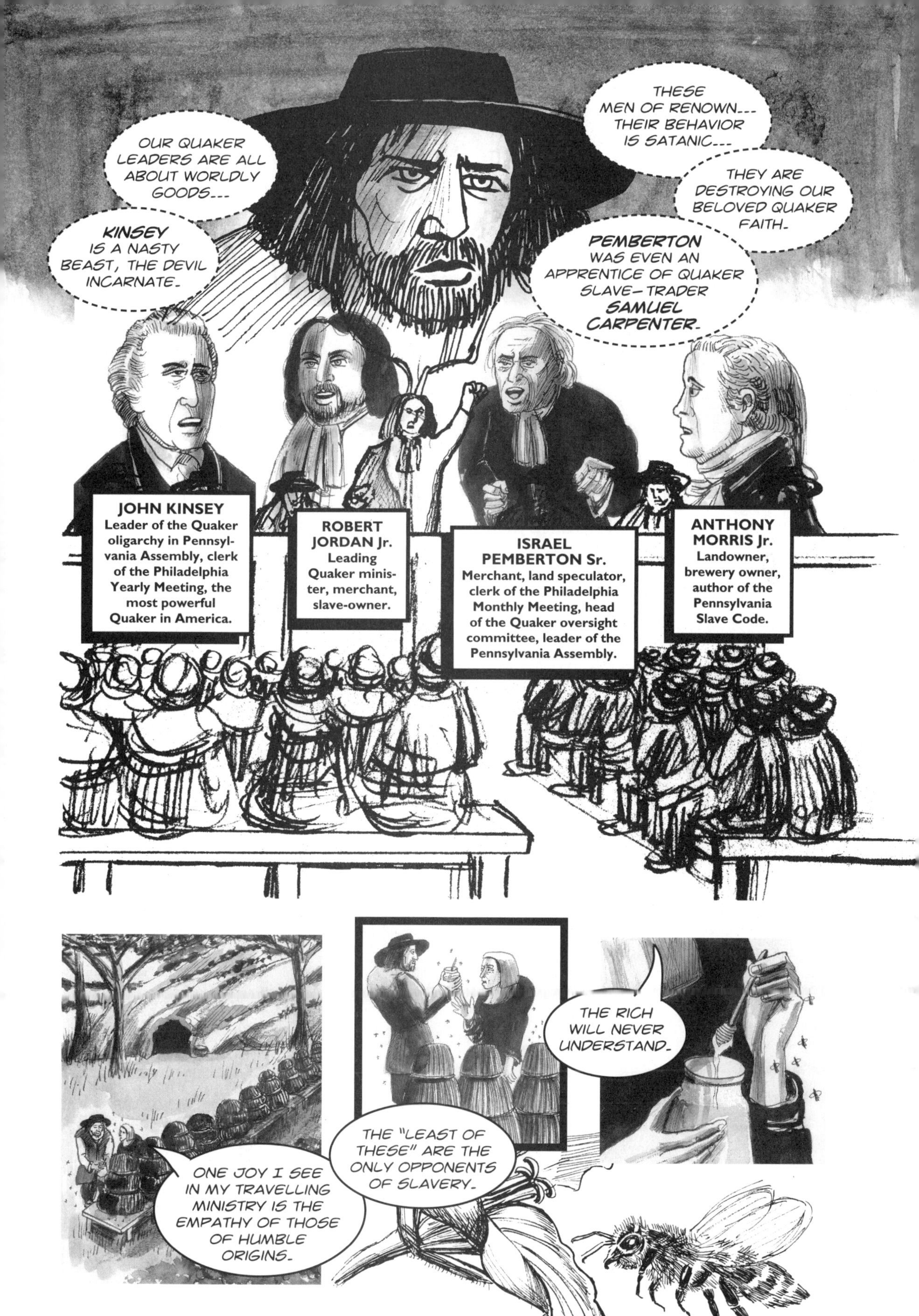
OUR QUAKER LEADERS ARE ALL ABOUT WORLDLY GOODS...
KINSEY IS A NASTY BEAST, THE DEVIL INCARNATE.
THESE MEN OF RENOWN... THEIR BEHAVIOR IS SATANIC...
THEY ARE DESTROYING OUR BELOVED QUAKER FAITH.
PEMBERTON WAS EVEN AN APPRENTICE OF QUAKER SLAVE-TRADER SAMUEL CARPENTER.
JOHN KINSEY
Leader of the Quaker oligarchy in Pennsylvania Assembly, clerk of the Philadelphia Yearly Meeting, the most powerful Quaker in America.
ROBERT JORDAN Jr.
Leading Quaker minister, merchant, slave-owner.
ISRAEL PEMBERTON Sr.
Merchant, land speculator, clerk of the Philadelphia Monthly Meeting, head of the Quaker oversight committee, leader of the Pennsylvania Assembly.
ANTHONY MORRIS Jr.
Landowner, brewery owner, author of the Pennsylvania Slave Code.
ONE JOY I SEE IN MY TRAVELLING MINISTRY IS THE EMPATHY OF THOSE OF HUMBLE ORIGINS.
THE "LEAST OF THESE" ARE THE ONLY OPPONENTS OF SLAVERY.
THE RICH WILL NEVER UNDERSTAND.

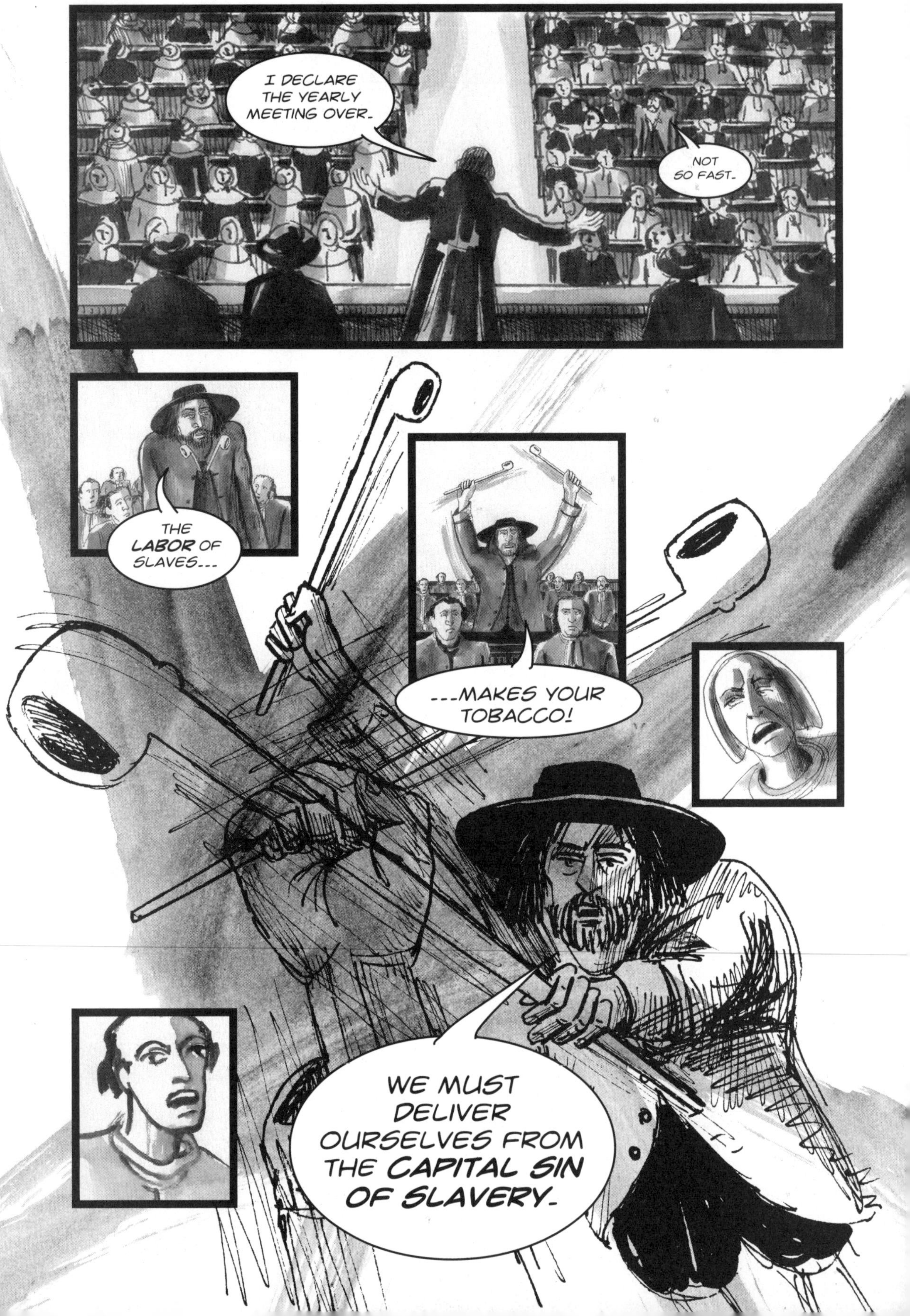
I DECLARE THE YEARLY MEETING OVER.
NOT SO FAST.
THE LABOR OF SLAVES...
...MAKES YOUR TOBACCO!
WE MUST DELIVER OURSELVES FROM THE CAPITAL SIN OF SLAVERY.

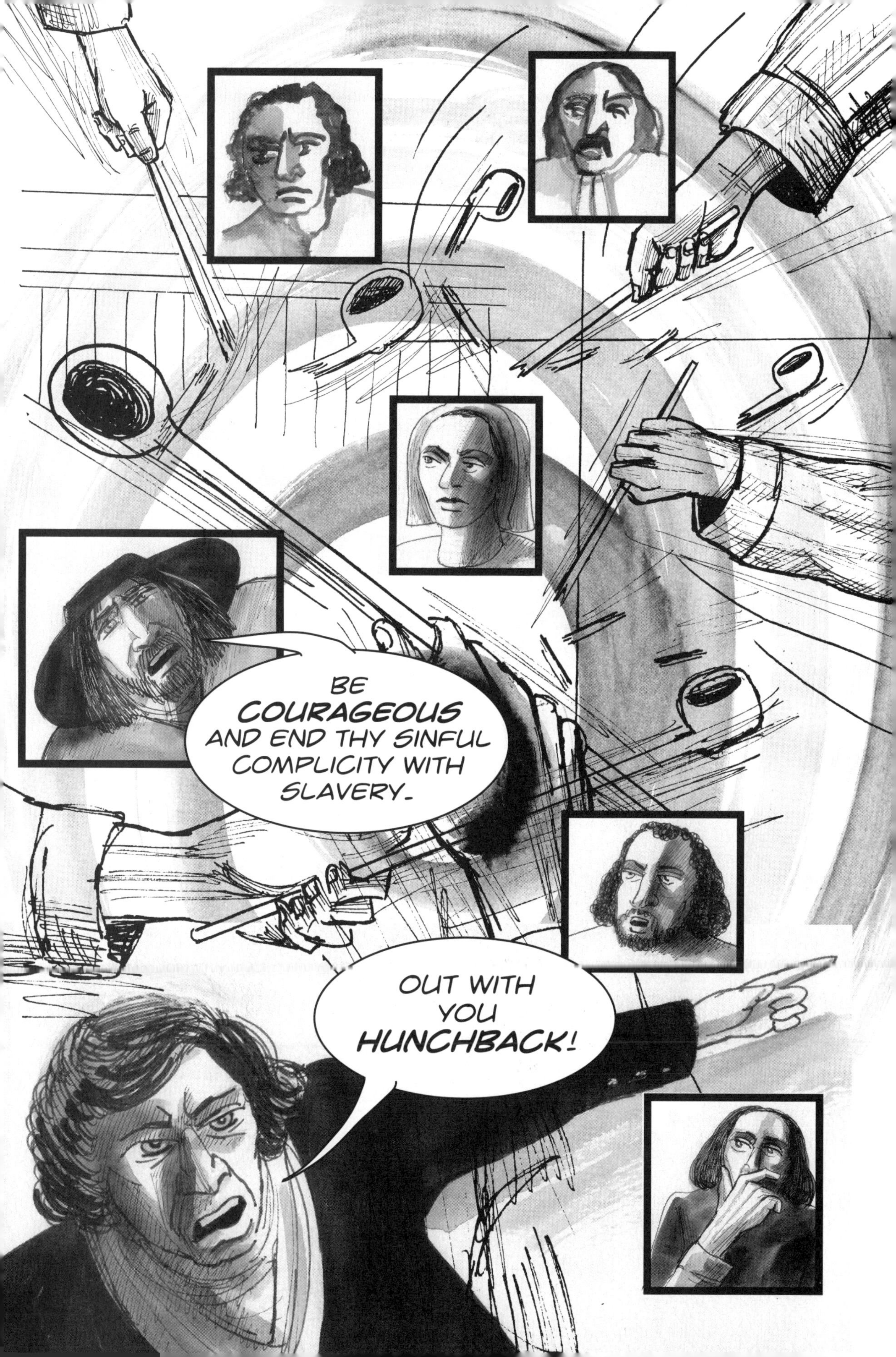
BE COURAGEOUS AND END THY SINFUL COMPLICITY WITH SLAVERY.
OUT WITH YOU HUNCHBACK!

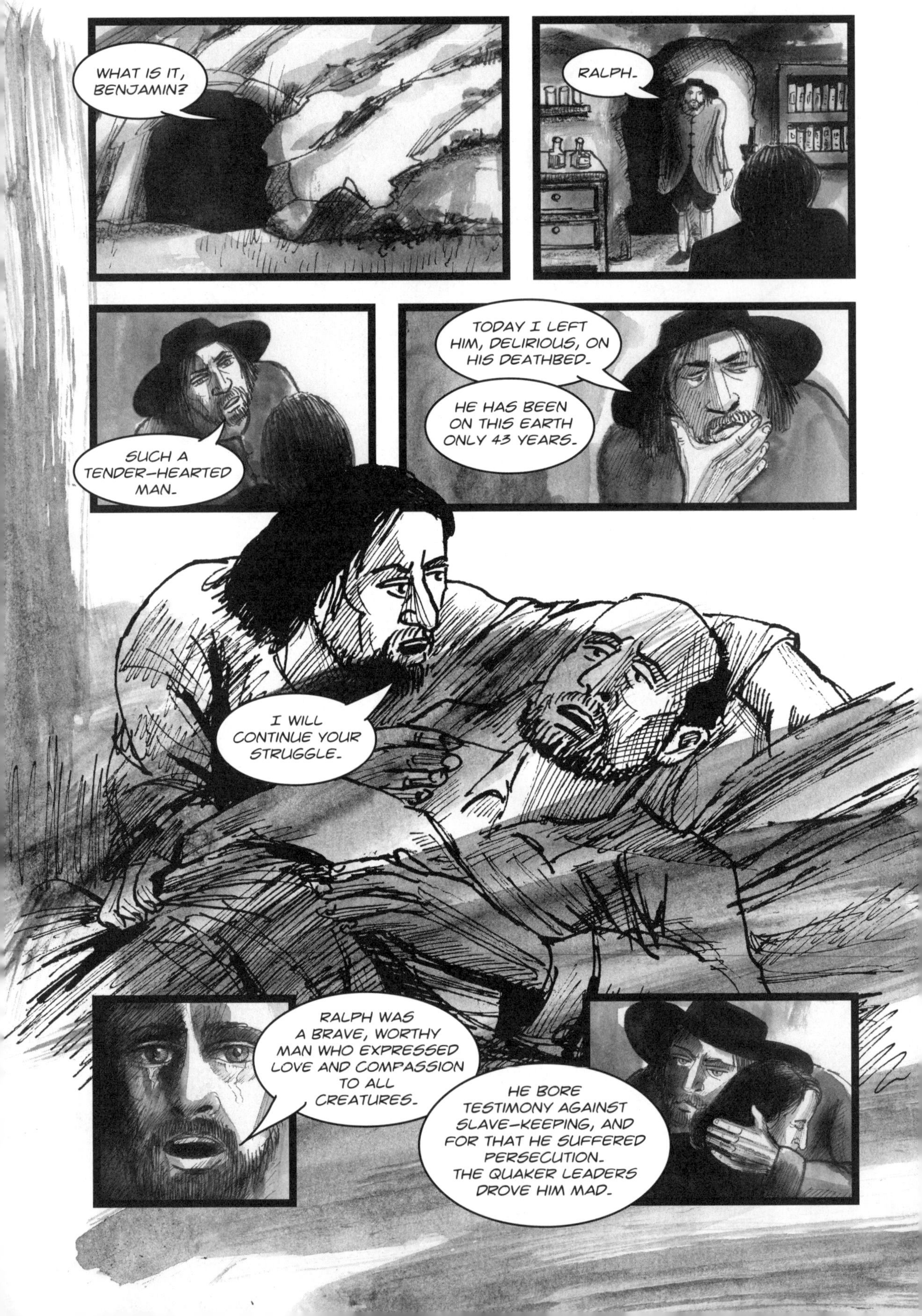
WHAT IS IT, BENJAMIN?
RALPH.
SUCH A TENDER-HEARTED MAN.
TODAY I LEFT HIM, DELIRIOUS, ON HIS DEATHBED.
HE HAS BEEN ON THIS EARTH ONLY 43 YEARS.
I WILL CONTINUE YOUR STRUGGLE.
RALPH WAS A BRAVE, WORTHY MAN WHO EXPRESSED LOVE AND COMPASSION TO ALL CREATURES.
HE BORE TESTIMONY AGAINST SLAVE-KEEPING, AND FOR THAT HE SUFFERED PERSECUTION.
THE QUAKER LEADERS DROVE HIM MAD.

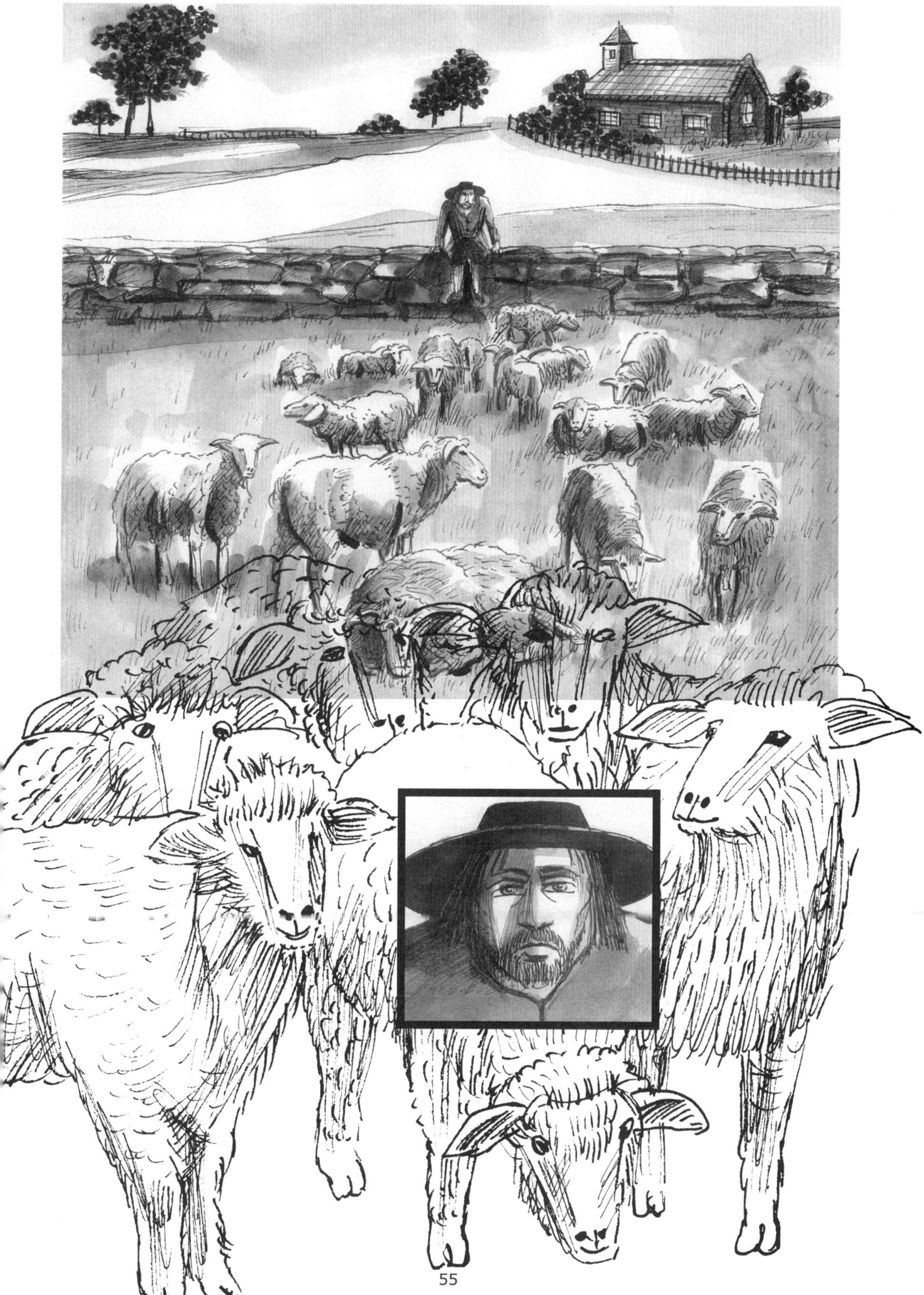

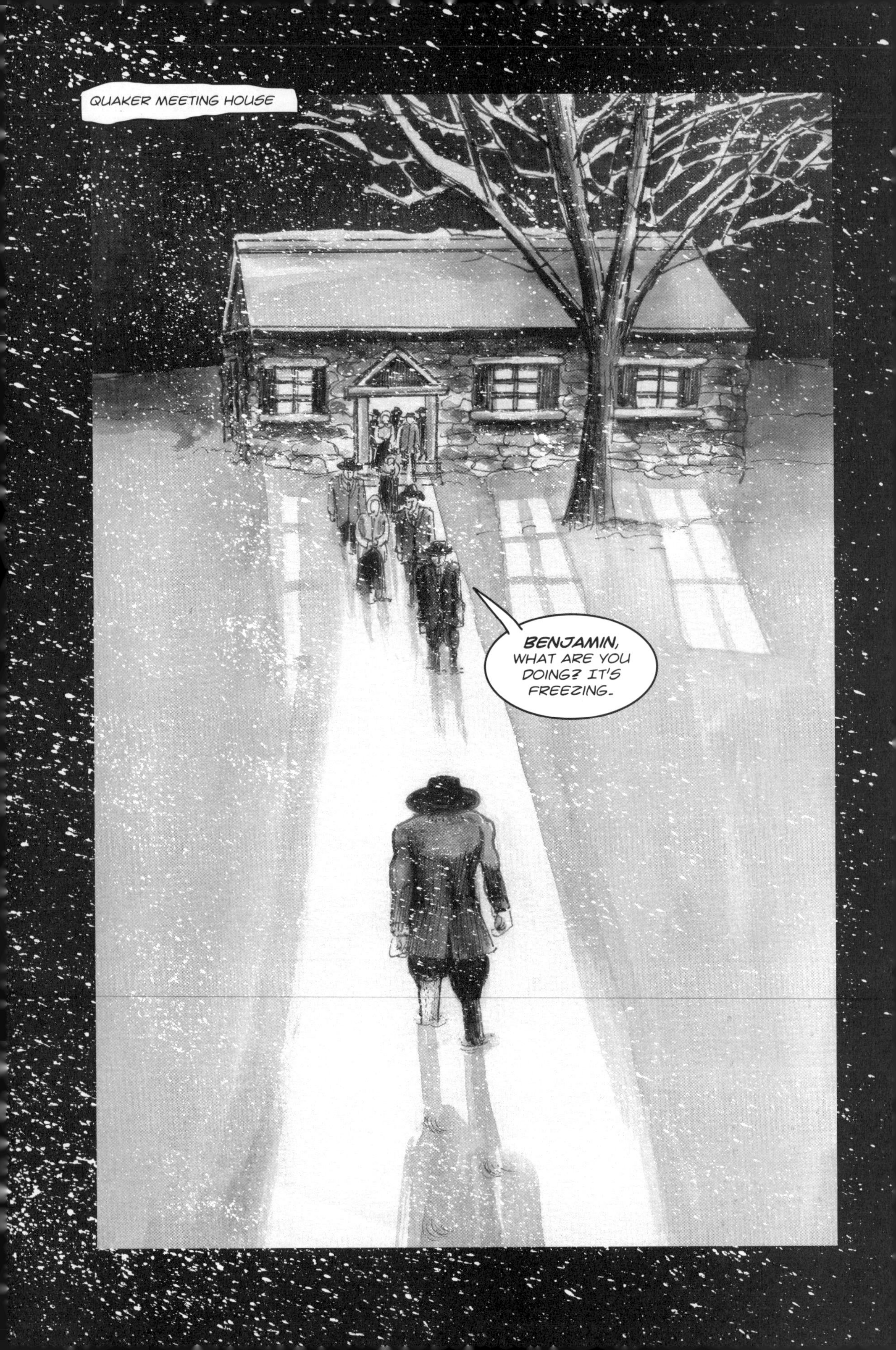
QUAKER MEETING HOUSE
BENJAMIN, WHAT ARE YOU DOING? IT'S FREEZING.

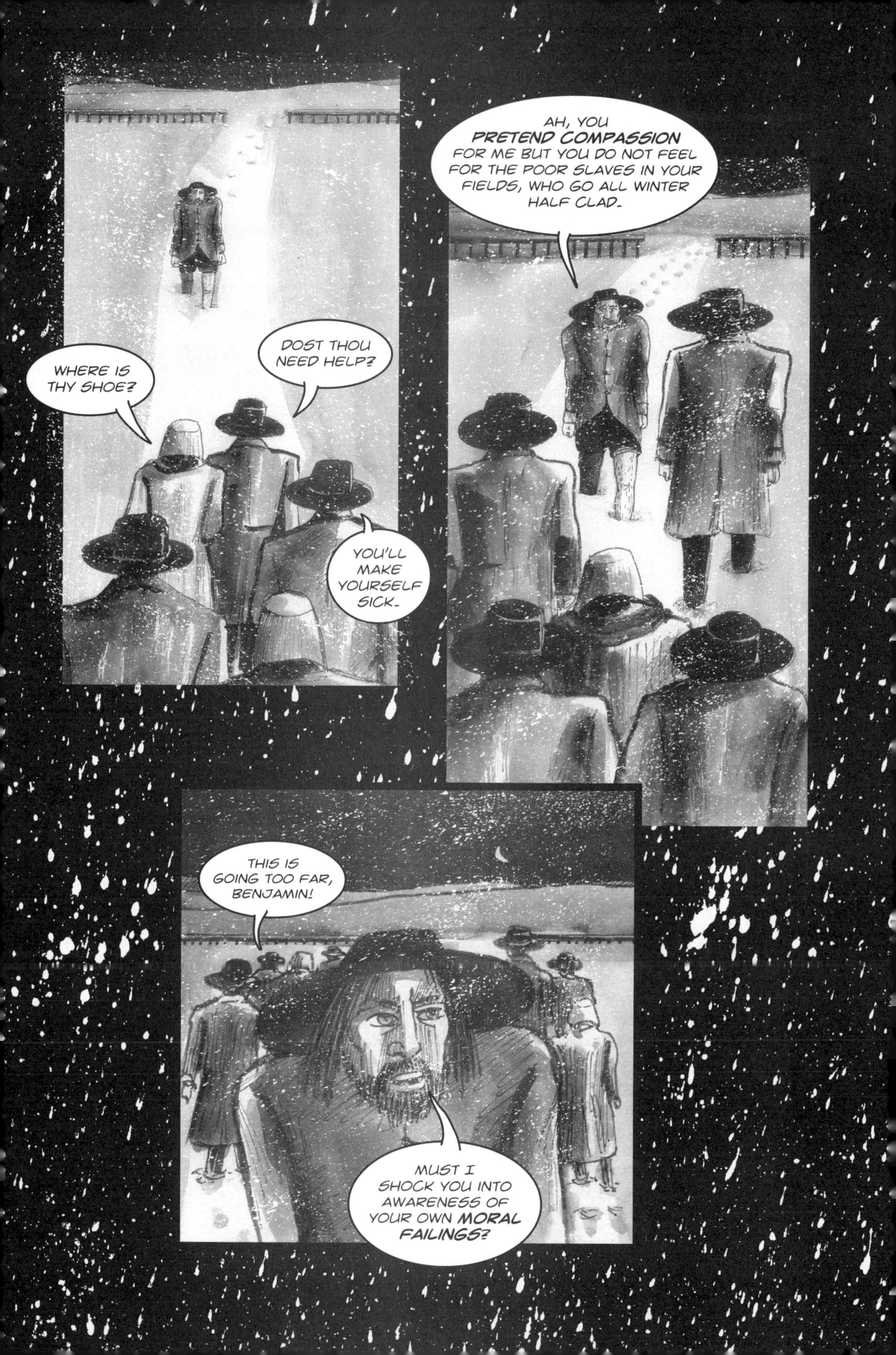
WHERE IS THY SHOE?
DOST THOU NEED HELP?
YOU'LL MAKE YOURSELF SICK.
AH, YOU **PRETEND COMPASSION** FOR ME BUT YOU DO NOT FEEL FOR THE POOR SLAVES IN YOUR FIELDS, WHO GO ALL WINTER HALF CLAD.
THIS IS GOING TOO FAR, BENJAMIN!
MUST I SHOCK YOU INTO AWARENESS OF YOUR OWN **MORAL FAILINGS**?

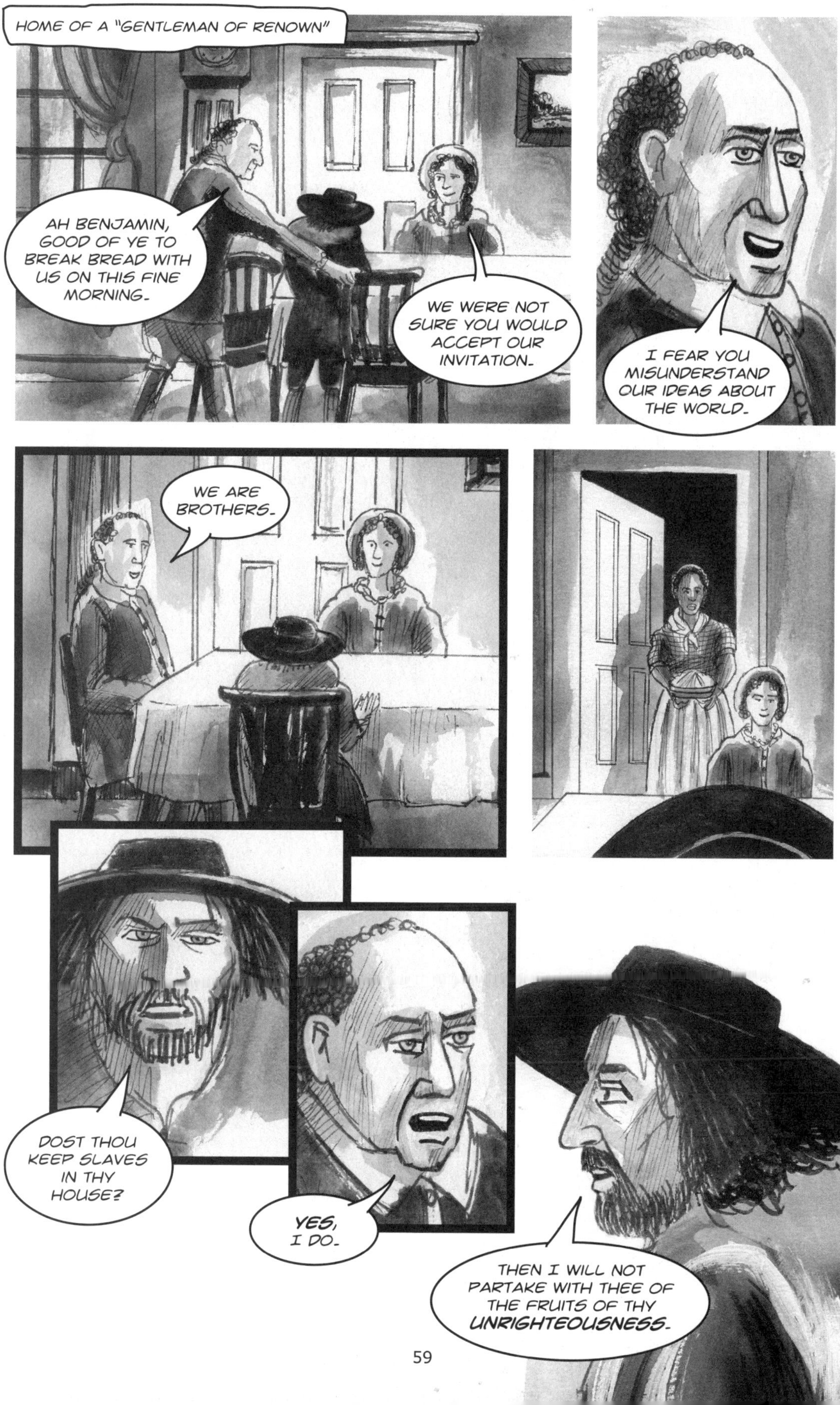

HOME OF A "GENTLEMAN OF RENOWN"
AH BENJAMIN, GOOD OF YE TO BREAK BREAD WITH US ON THIS FINE MORNING.
WE WERE NOT SURE YOU WOULD ACCEPT OUR INVITATION.
I FEAR YOU MISUNDERSTAND OUR IDEAS ABOUT THE WORLD.
WE ARE BROTHERS.
DOST THOU KEEP SLAVES IN THY HOUSE?
YES, I DO.
THEN I WILL NOT PARTAKE WITH THEE OF THE FRUITS OF THY UNRIGHTEOUSNESS.

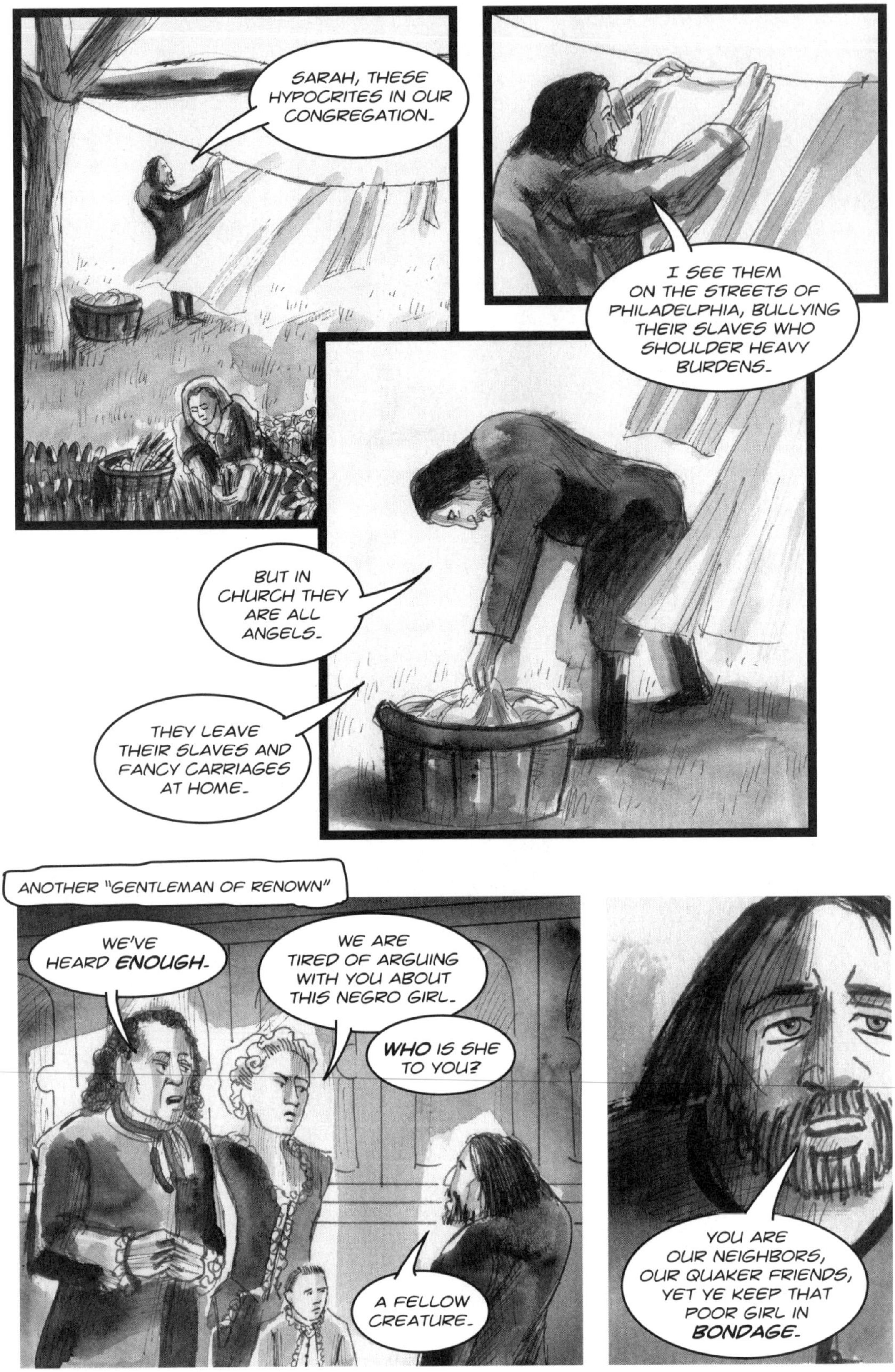
SARAH, THESE HYPOCRITES IN OUR CONGREGATION.
I SEE THEM ON THE STREETS OF PHILADELPHIA, BULLYING THEIR SLAVES WHO SHOULDER HEAVY BURDENS.
BUT IN CHURCH THEY ARE ALL ANGELS.
THEY LEAVE THEIR SLAVES AND FANCY CARRIAGES AT HOME.
ANOTHER "GENTLEMAN OF RENOWN"
WE'VE HEARD **ENOUGH**.
WE ARE TIRED OF ARGUING WITH YOU ABOUT THIS NEGRO GIRL.
WHO IS SHE TO YOU?
A FELLOW CREATURE.
YOU ARE OUR NEIGHBORS, OUR QUAKER FRIENDS, YET YE KEEP THAT POOR GIRL IN **BONDAGE**.

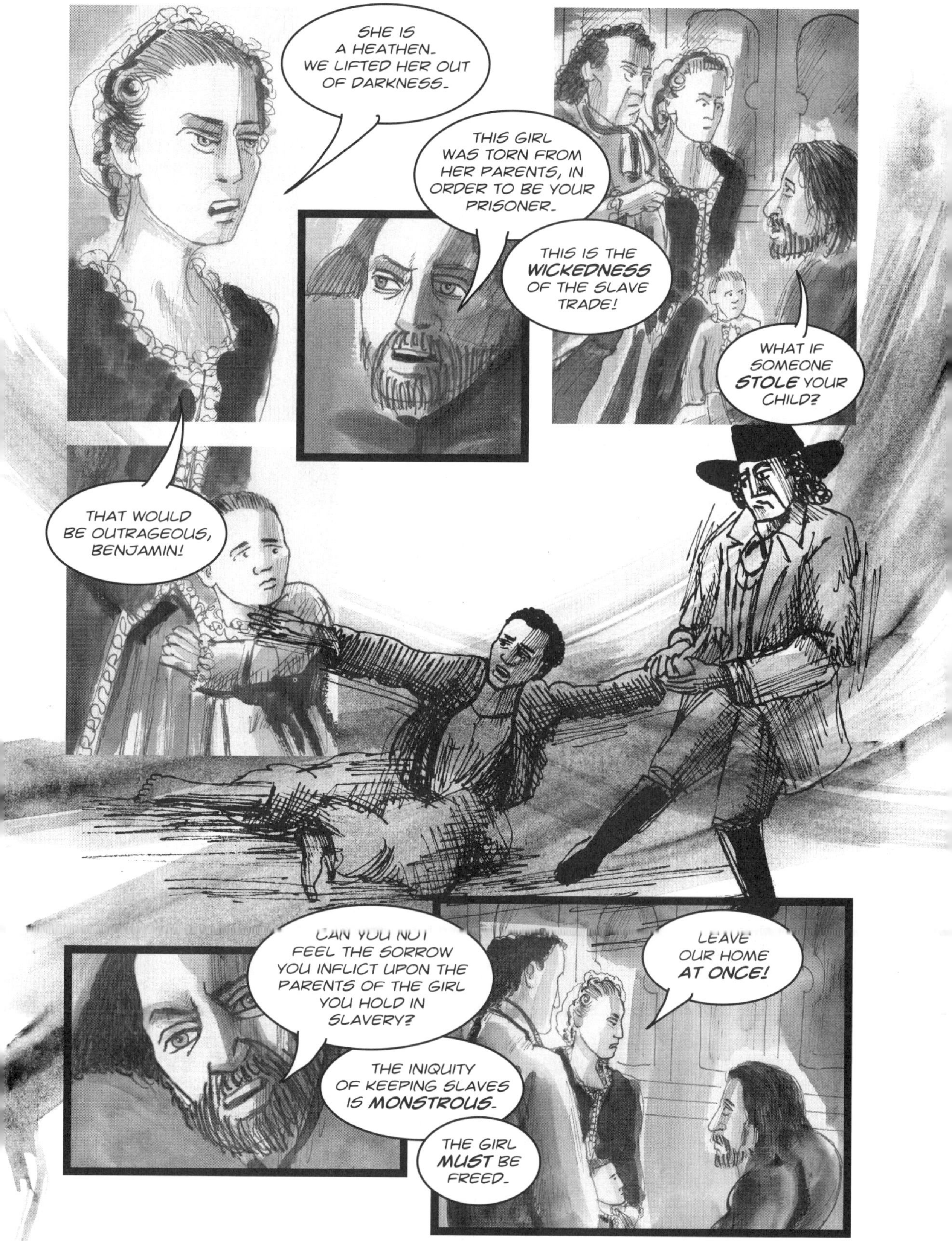
SHE IS A HEATHEN. WE LIFTED HER OUT OF DARKNESS.
THIS GIRL WAS TORN FROM HER PARENTS, IN ORDER TO BE YOUR PRISONER.
THIS IS THE WICKEDNESS OF THE SLAVE TRADE!
WHAT IF SOMEONE STOLE YOUR CHILD?
THAT WOULD BE OUTRAGEOUS, BENJAMIN!
CAN YOU NOT FEEL THE SORROW YOU INFLICT UPON THE PARENTS OF THE GIRL YOU HOLD IN SLAVERY?
THE INIQUITY OF KEEPING SLAVES IS MONSTROUS.
THE GIRL MUST BE FREED.
LEAVE OUR HOME AT ONCE!

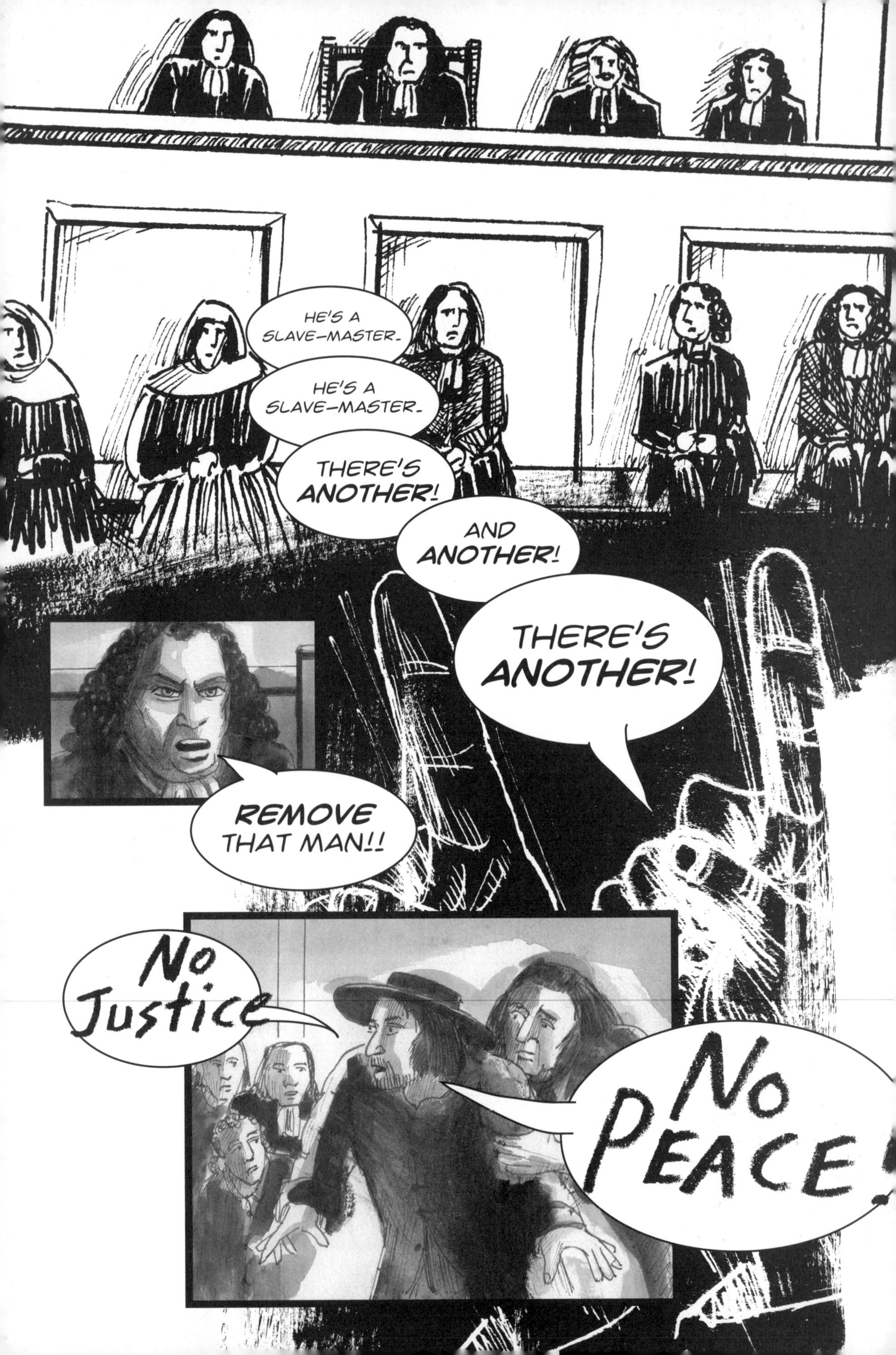
HE'S A SLAVE-MASTER.
HE'S A SLAVE-MASTER.
THERE'S ANOTHER!
AND ANOTHER!
THERE'S ANOTHER!
REMOVE THAT MAN!!
No Justice
No PEACE!

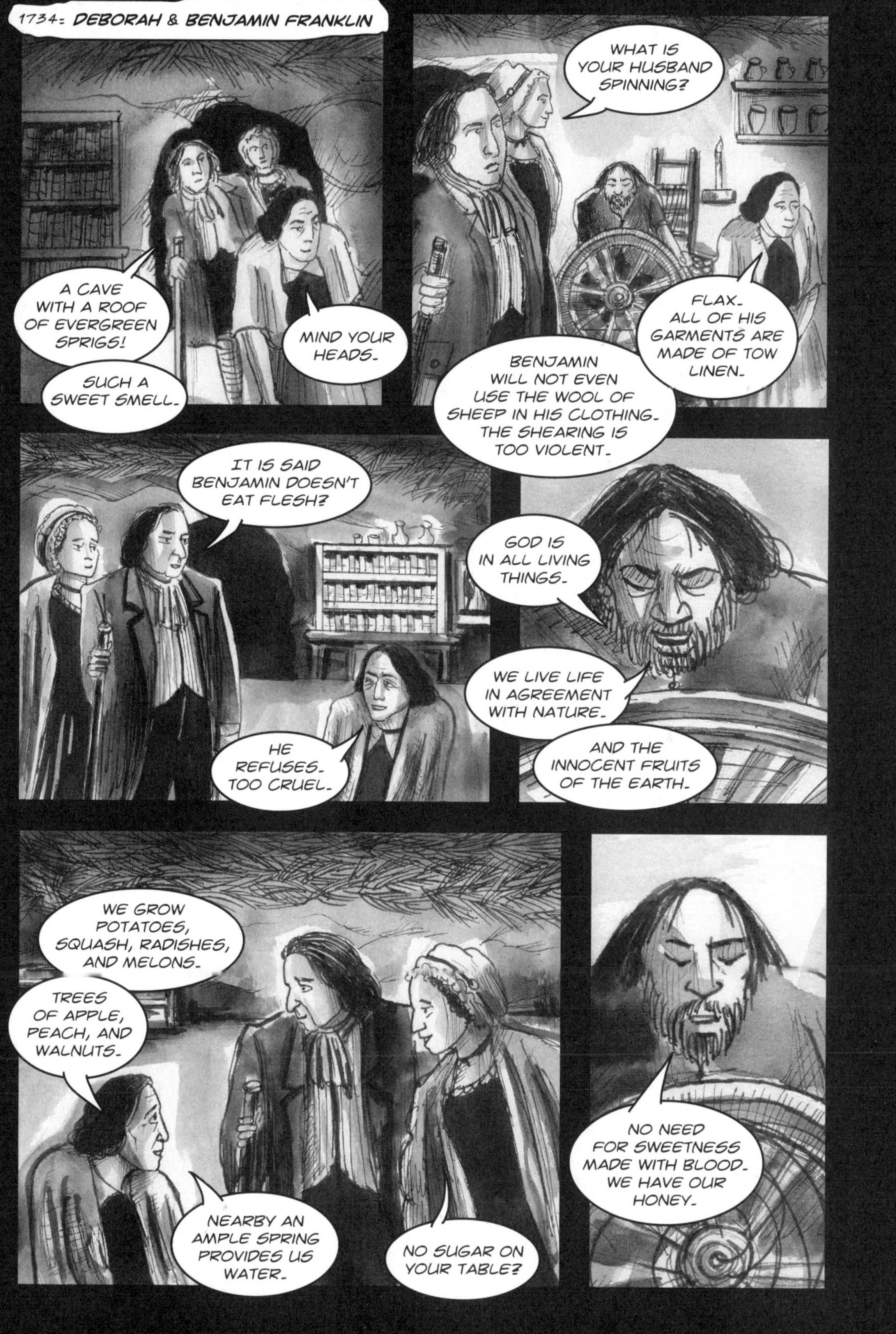
1734: DEBORAH & BENJAMIN FRANKLIN
A CAVE WITH A ROOF OF EVERGREEN SPRIGS!
SUCH A SWEET SMELL.
MIND YOUR HEADS.
WHAT IS YOUR HUSBAND SPINNING?
FLAX. ALL OF HIS GARMENTS ARE MADE OF TOW LINEN.
BENJAMIN WILL NOT EVEN USE THE WOOL OF SHEEP IN HIS CLOTHING. THE SHEARING IS TOO VIOLENT.
IT IS SAID BENJAMIN DOESN'T EAT FLESH?
HE REFUSES. TOO CRUEL.
GOD IS IN ALL LIVING THINGS.
WE LIVE LIFE IN AGREEMENT WITH NATURE.
AND THE INNOCENT FRUITS OF THE EARTH.
WE GROW POTATOES, SQUASH, RADISHES, AND MELONS.
TREES OF APPLE, PEACH, AND WALNUTS.
NEARBY AN AMPLE SPRING PROVIDES US WATER.
NO SUGAR ON YOUR TABLE?
NO NEED FOR SWEETNESS MADE WITH BLOOD. WE HAVE OUR HONEY.

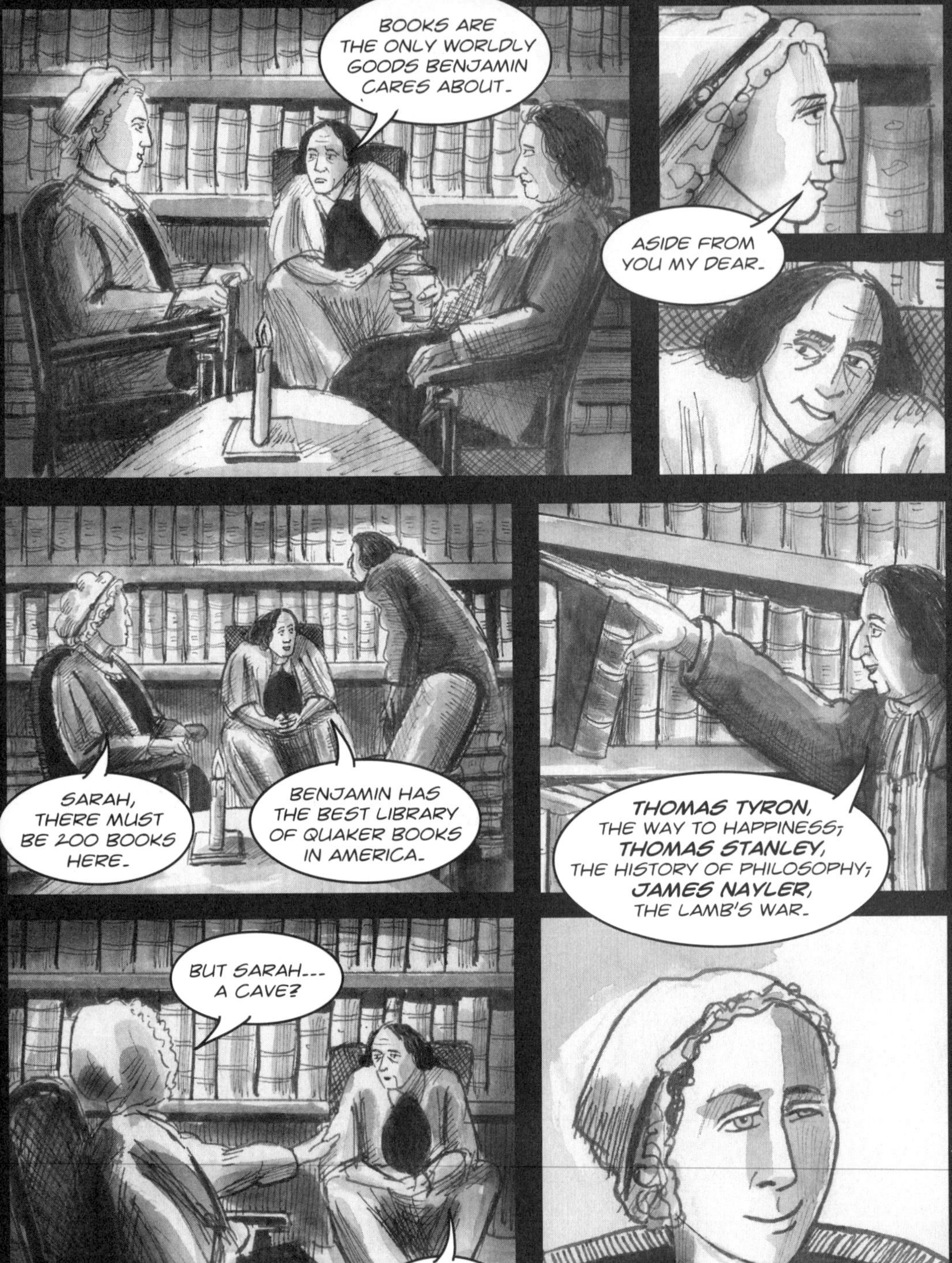
BOOKS ARE THE ONLY WORLDLY GOODS BENJAMIN CARES ABOUT.
ASIDE FROM YOU MY DEAR.
SARAH, THERE MUST BE 200 BOOKS HERE.
BENJAMIN HAS THE BEST LIBRARY OF QUAKER BOOKS IN AMERICA.
THOMAS TYRON, THE WAY TO HAPPINESS; THOMAS STANLEY, THE HISTORY OF PHILOSOPHY; JAMES NAYLER, THE LAMB'S WAR.
BUT SARAH... A CAVE?
SPIRITUAL STRENGTH THROUGH A HUMBLE LIFE.
INDEED, AND WITH LOVE I'M SURE.

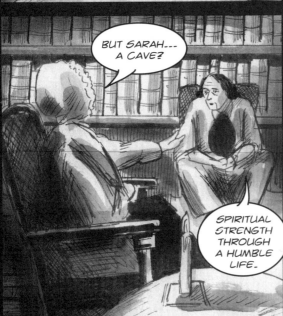

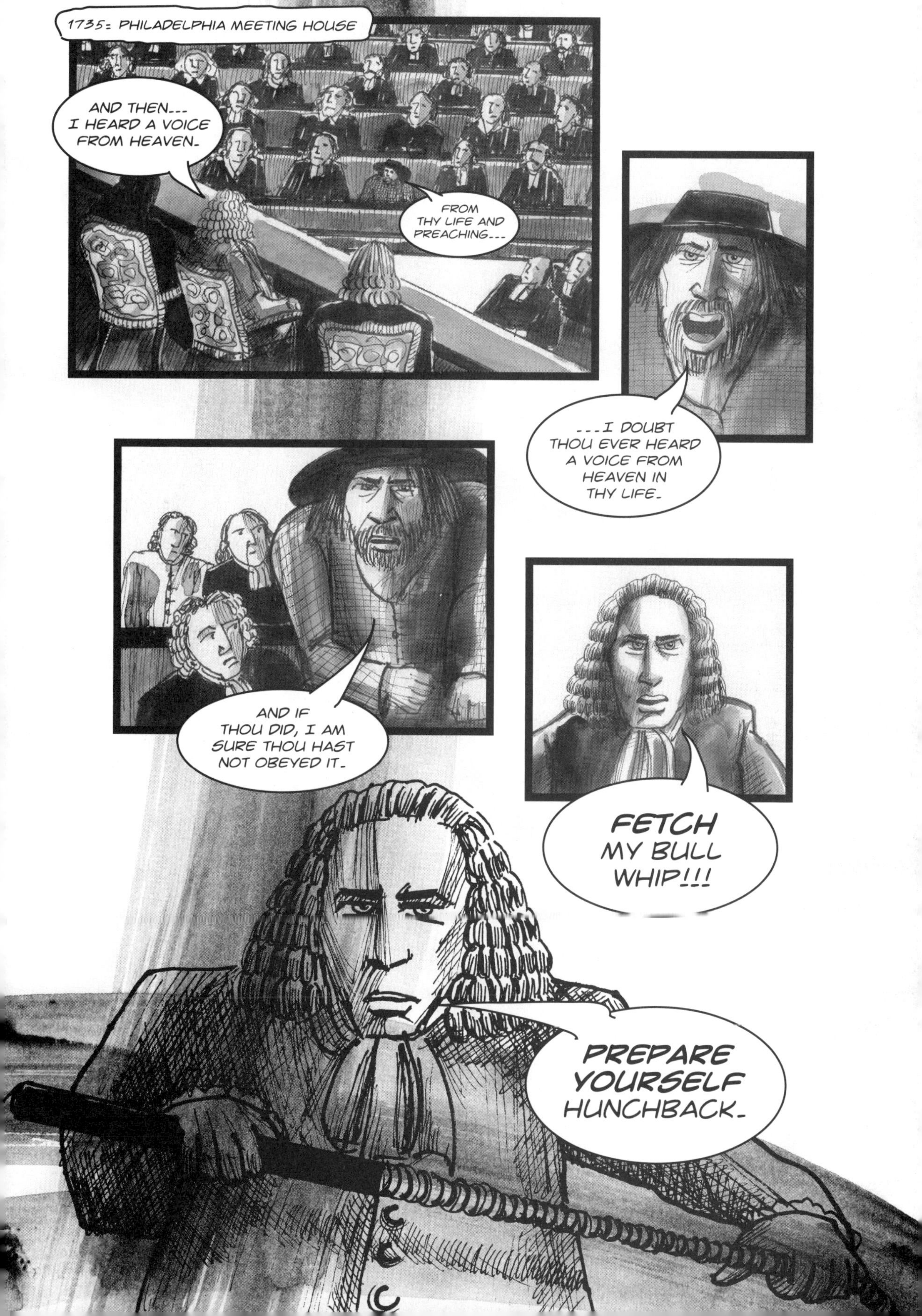

1735: PHILADELPHIA MEETING HOUSE
AND THEN... I HEARD A VOICE FROM HEAVEN.
FROM THY LIFE AND PREACHING...
...I DOUBT THOU EVER HEARD A VOICE FROM HEAVEN IN THY LIFE.
AND IF THOU DID, I AM SURE THOU HAST NOT OBEYED IT.
FETCH MY BULL WHIP!!!
PREPARE YOURSELF HUNCHBACK.

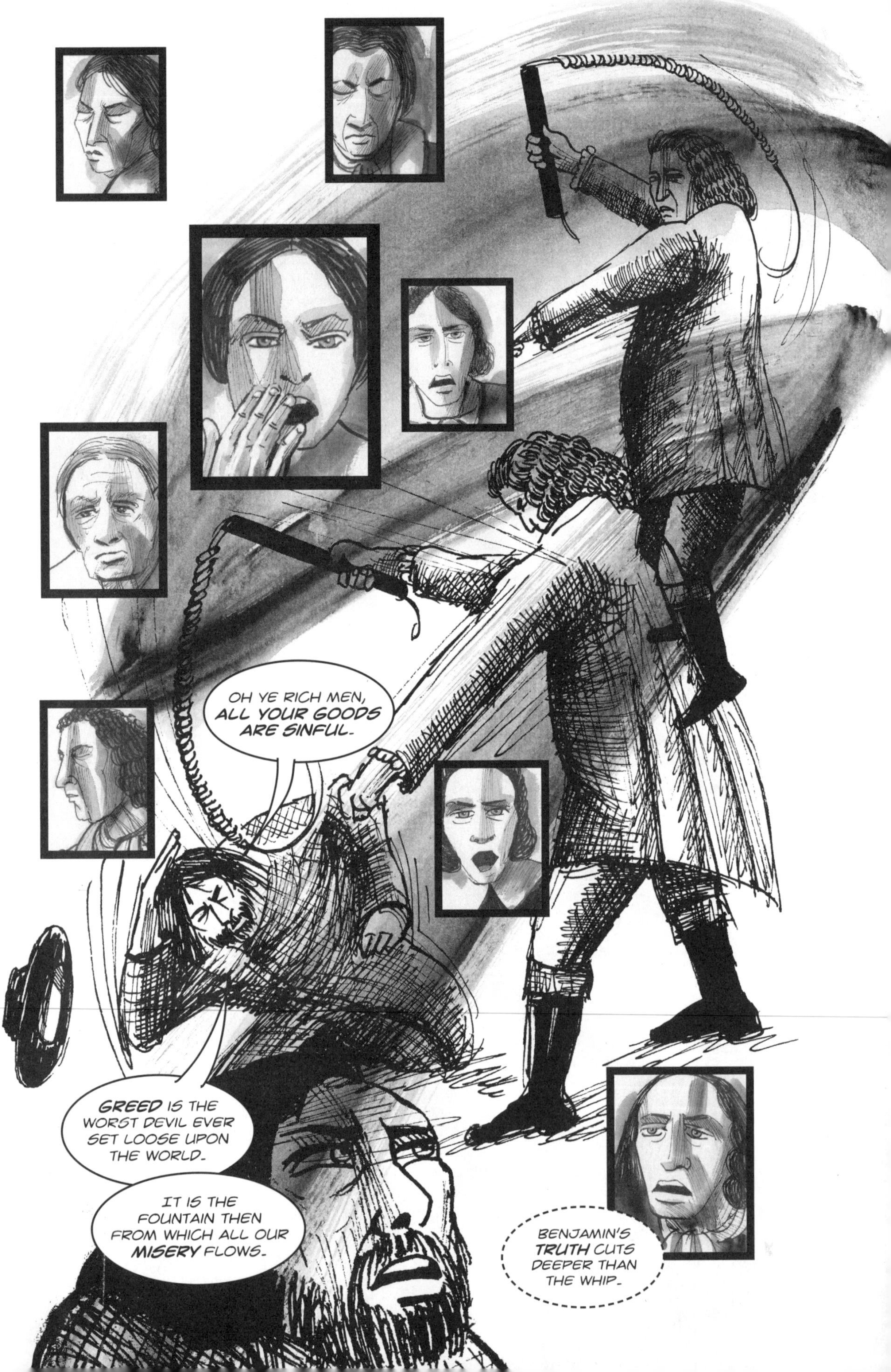
OH YE RICH MEN, ALL YOUR GOODS ARE SINFUL.
GREED IS THE WORST DEVIL EVER SET LOOSE UPON THE WORLD.
IT IS THE FOUNTAIN THEN FROM WHICH ALL OUR MISERY FLOWS.
BENJAMIN'S TRUTH CUTS DEEPER THAN THE WHIP.

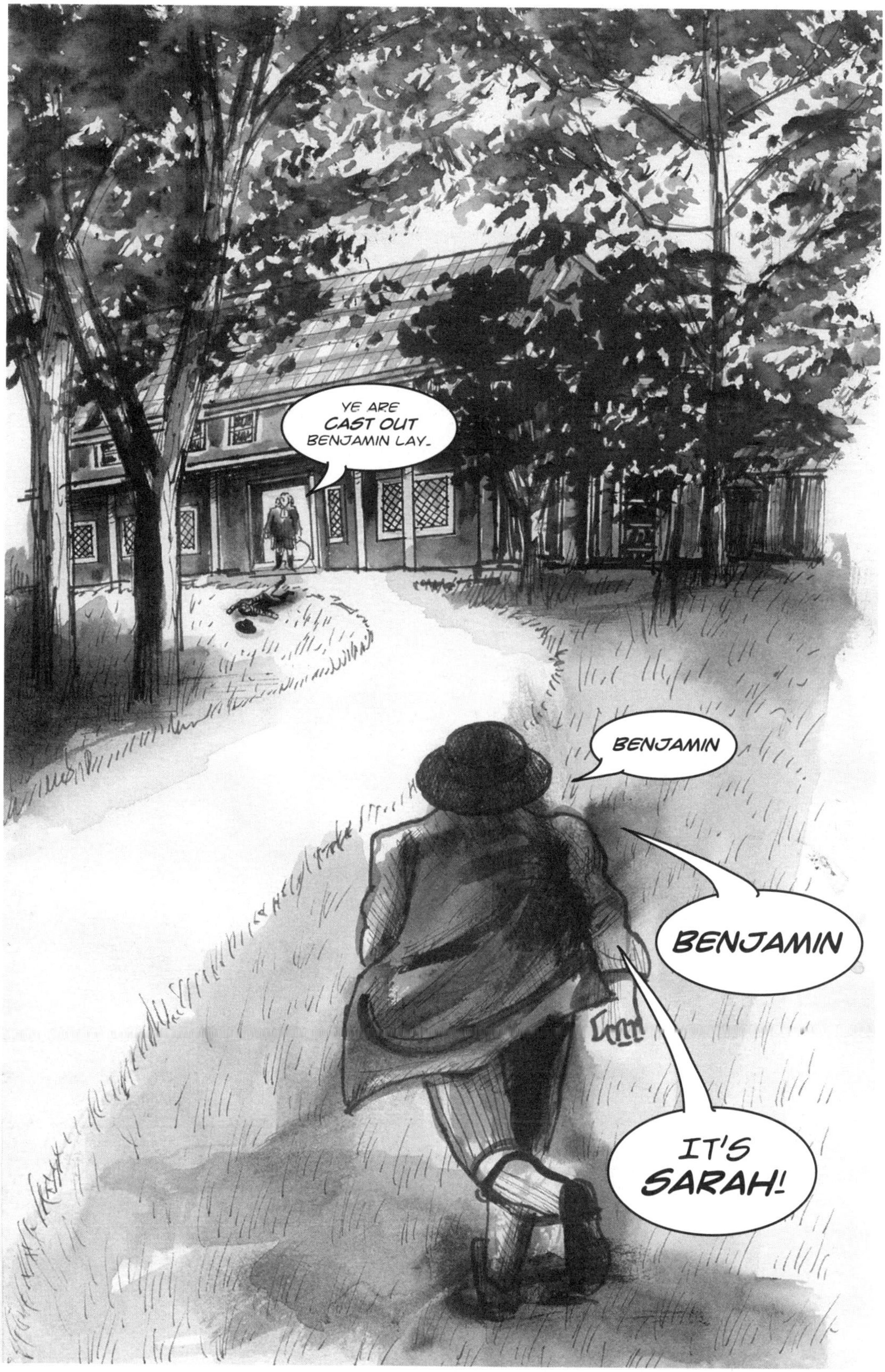
YE ARE CAST OUT BENJAMIN LAY.
BENJAMIN
BENJAMIN
IT'S SARAH!

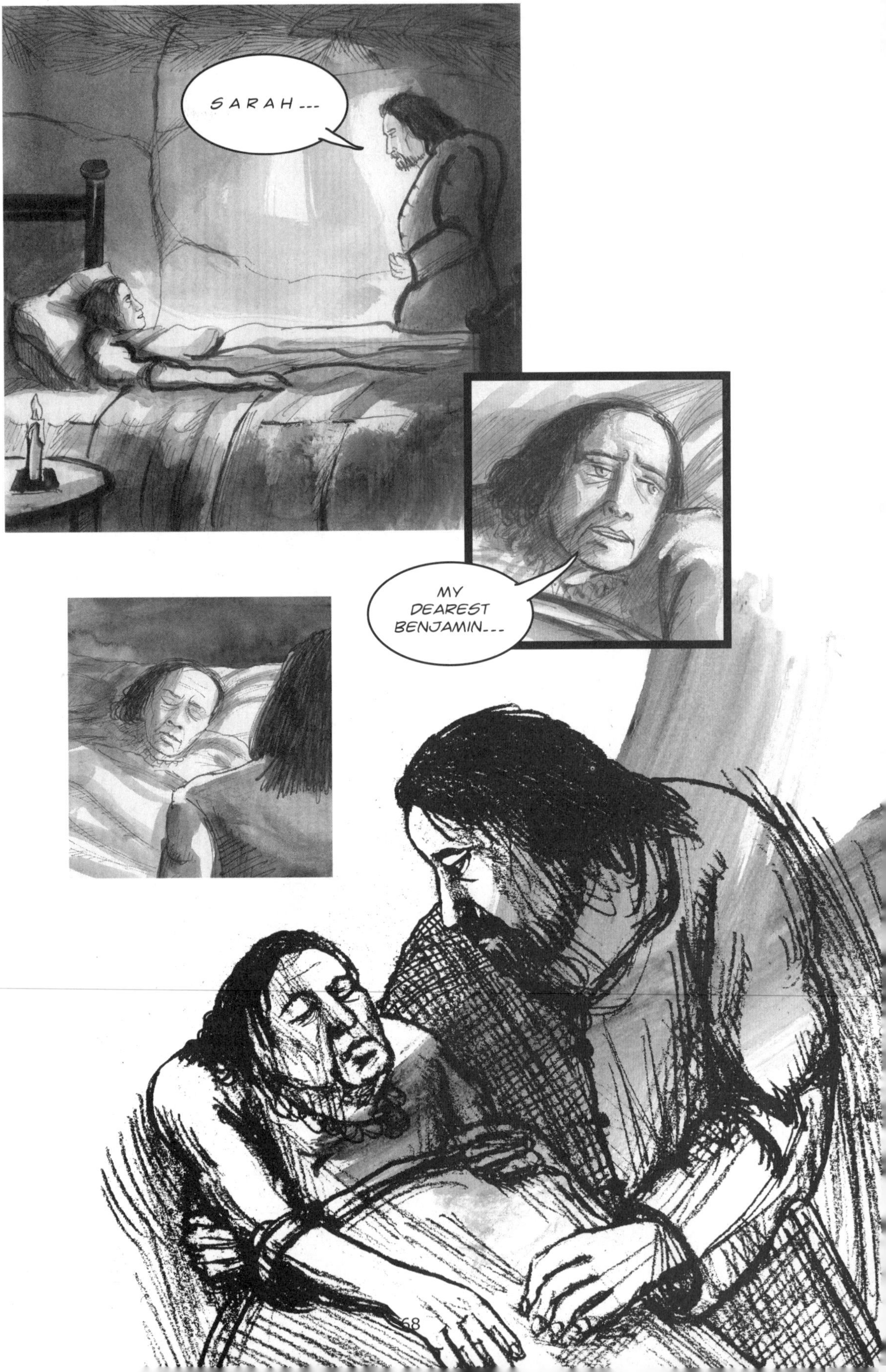
SARAH...
MY DEAREST BENJAMIN...

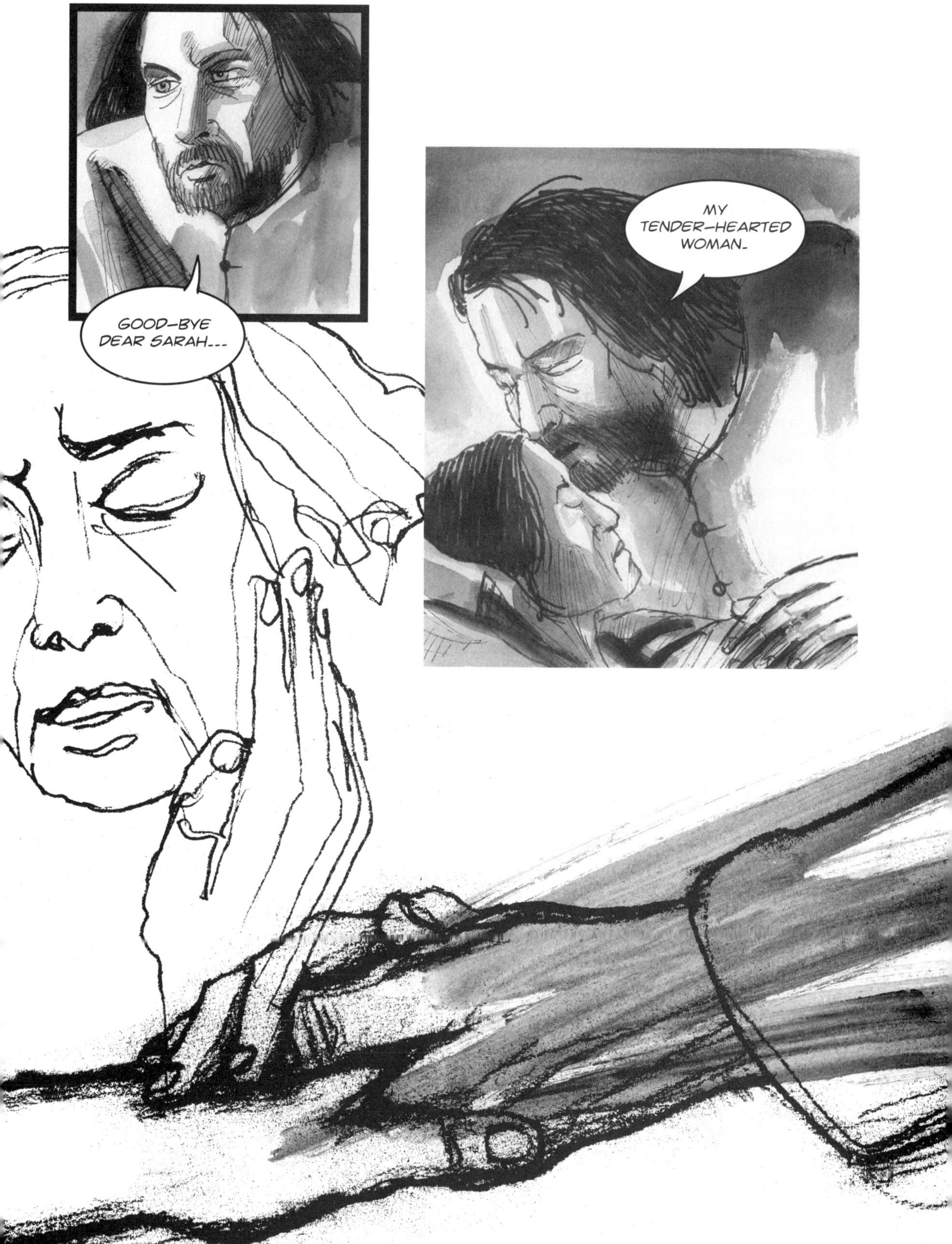
GOOD-BYE DEAR SARAH...
MY TENDER-HEARTED WOMAN.

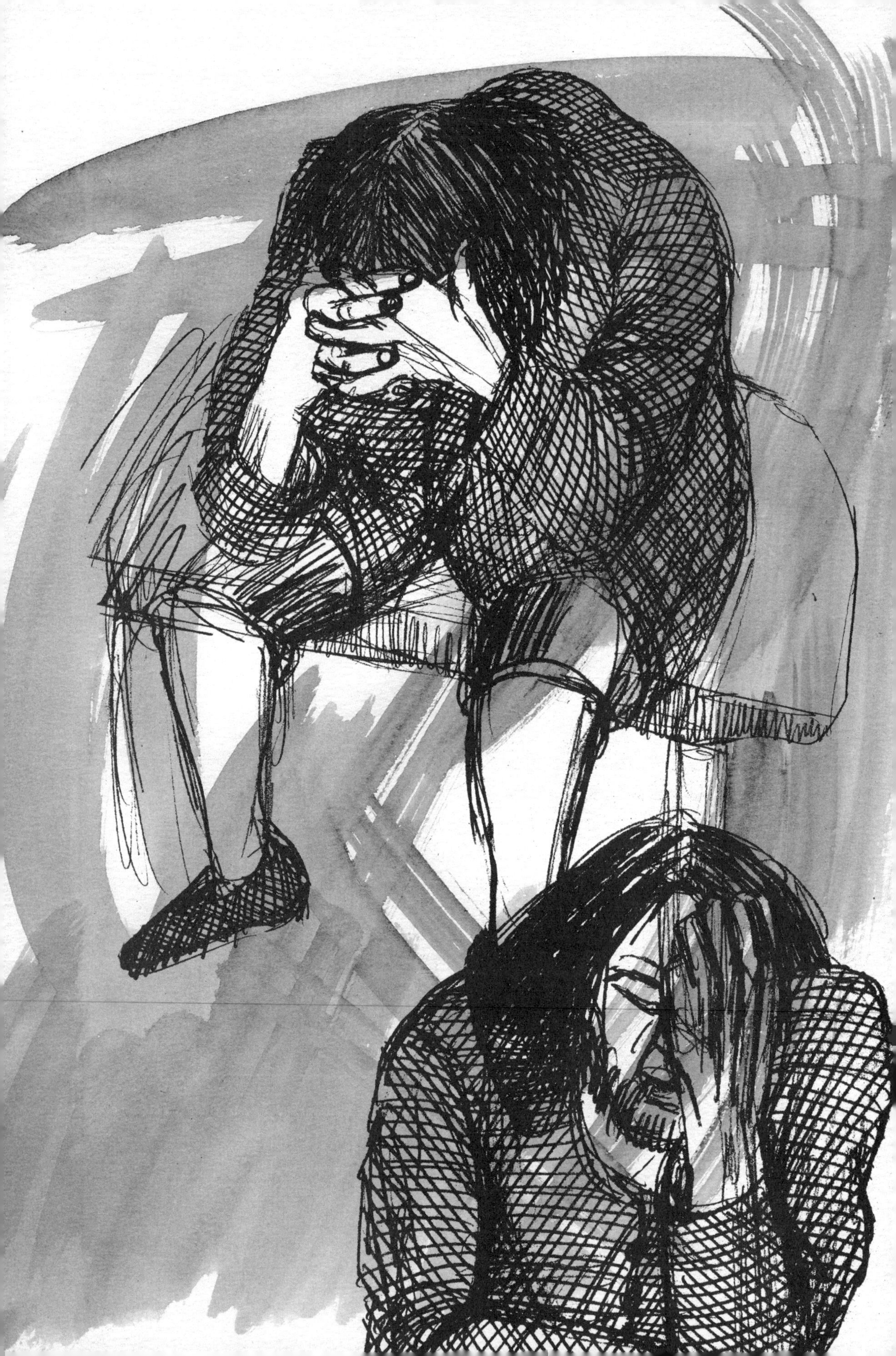

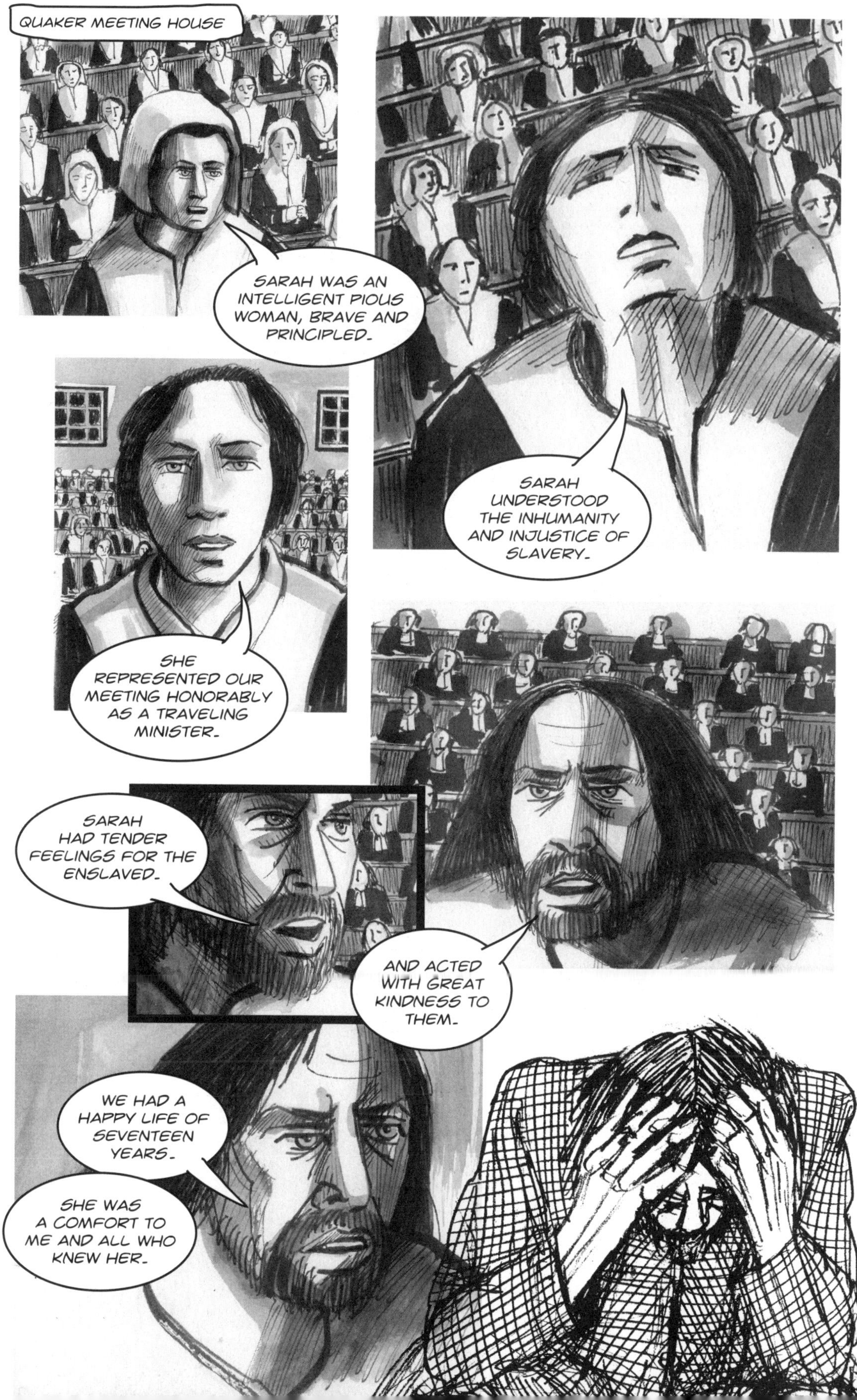
QUAKER MEETING HOUSE
SARAH WAS AN INTELLIGENT PIOUS WOMAN, BRAVE AND PRINCIPLED.
SARAH UNDERSTOOD THE INHUMANITY AND INJUSTICE OF SLAVERY.
SHE REPRESENTED OUR MEETING HONORABLY AS A TRAVELING MINISTER.
SARAH HAD TENDER FEELINGS FOR THE ENSLAVED.
AND ACTED WITH GREAT KINDNESS TO THEM.
WE HAD A HAPPY LIFE OF SEVENTEEN YEARS.
SHE WAS A COMFORT TO ME AND ALL WHO KNEW HER.

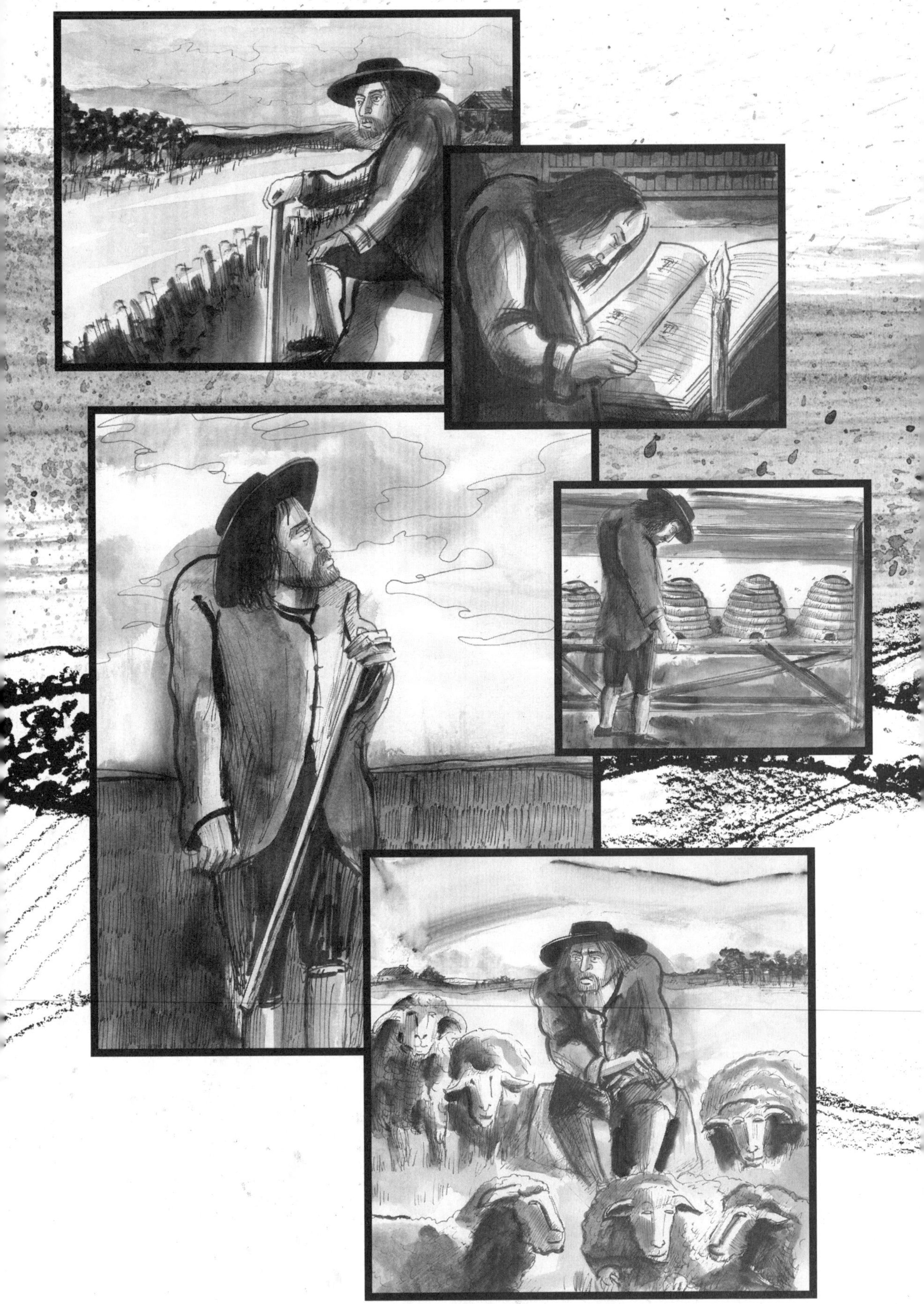

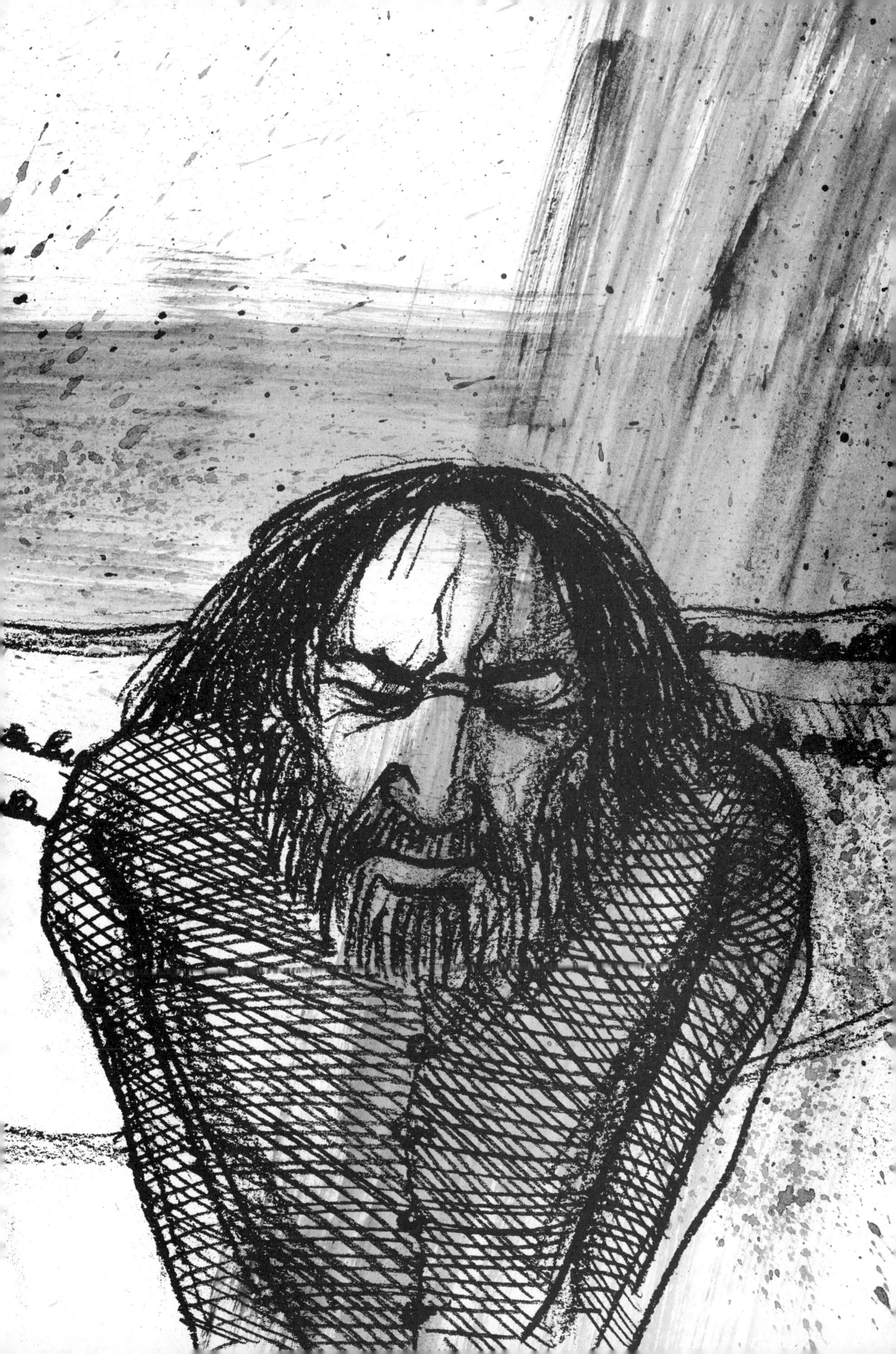

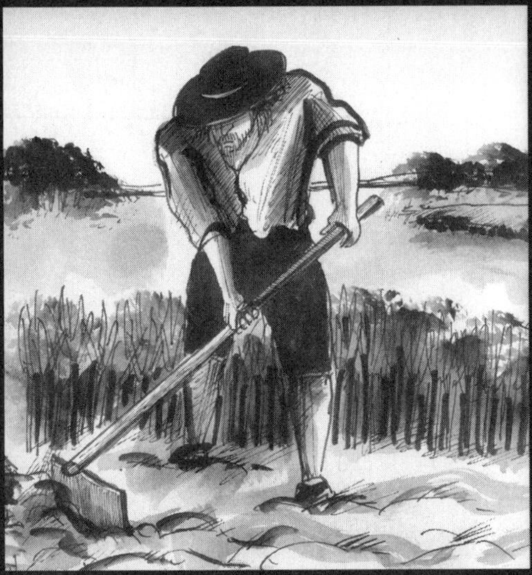

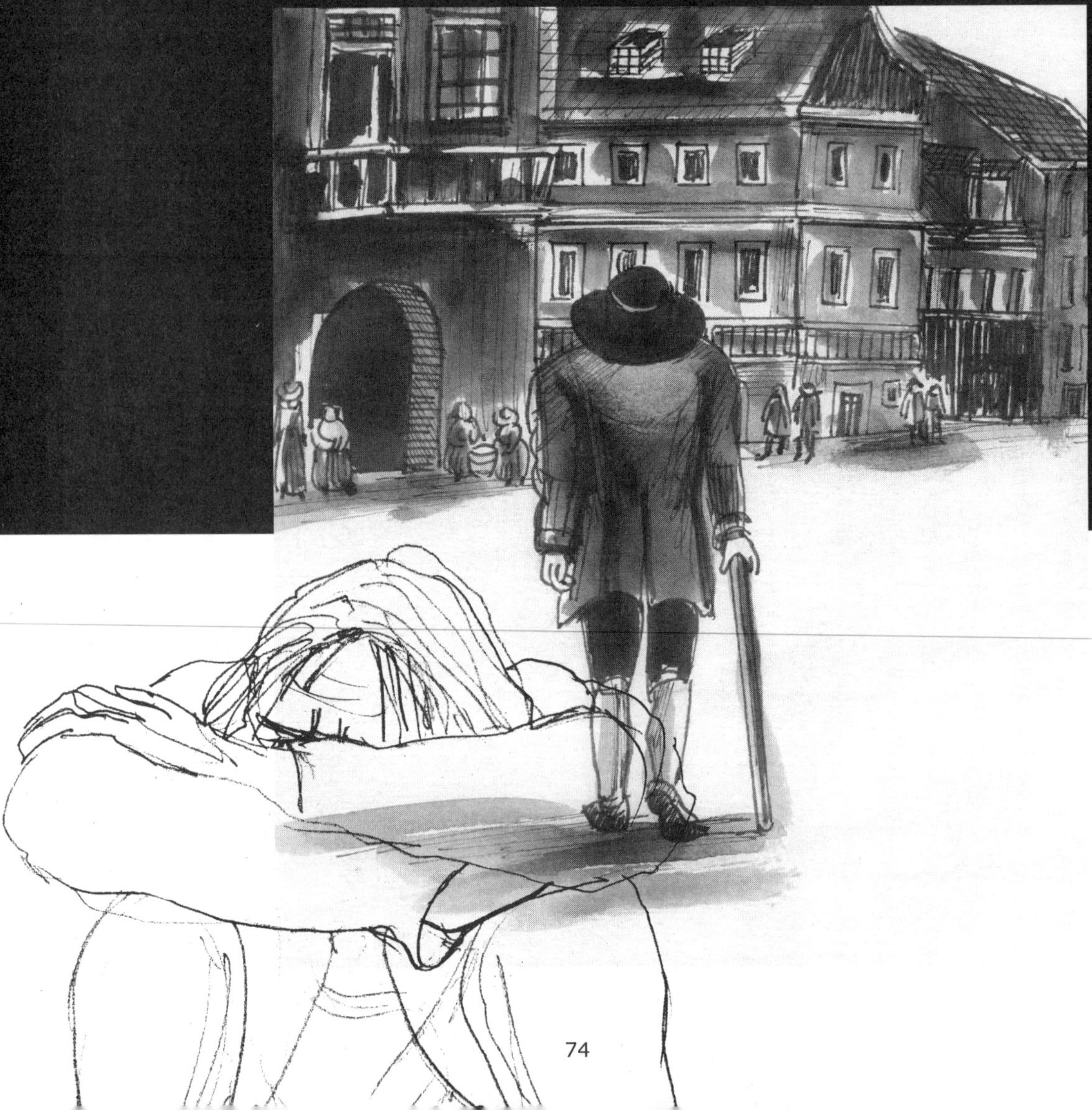

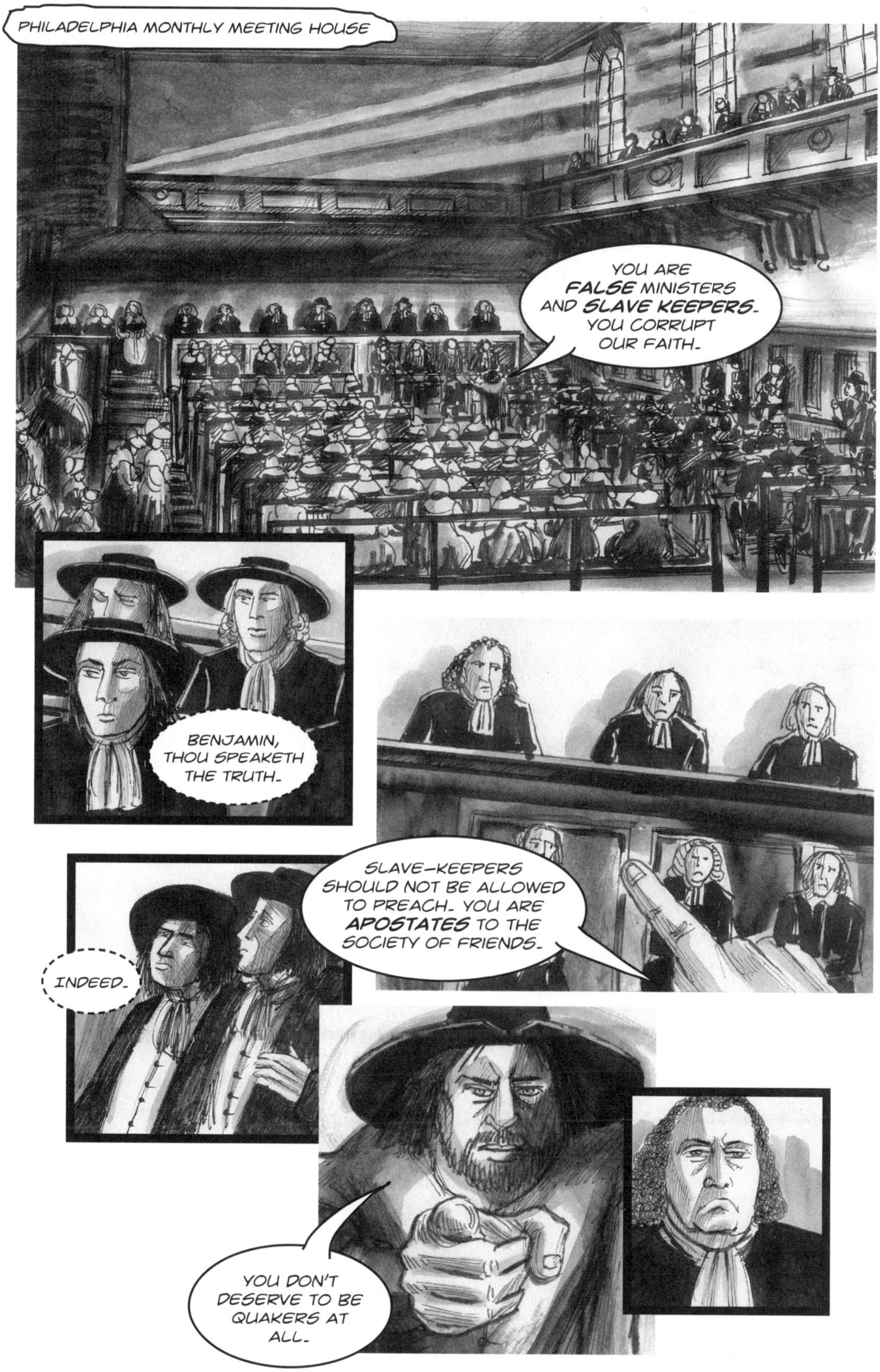
PHILADELPHIA MONTHLY MEETING HOUSE
YOU ARE FALSE MINISTERS AND SLAVE KEEPERS. YOU CORRUPT OUR FAITH.
BENJAMIN, THOU SPEAKETH THE TRUTH.
SLAVE-KEEPERS SHOULD NOT BE ALLOWED TO PREACH. YOU ARE APOSTATES TO THE SOCIETY OF FRIENDS.
INDEED.
YOU DON'T DESERVE TO BE QUAKERS AT ALL.

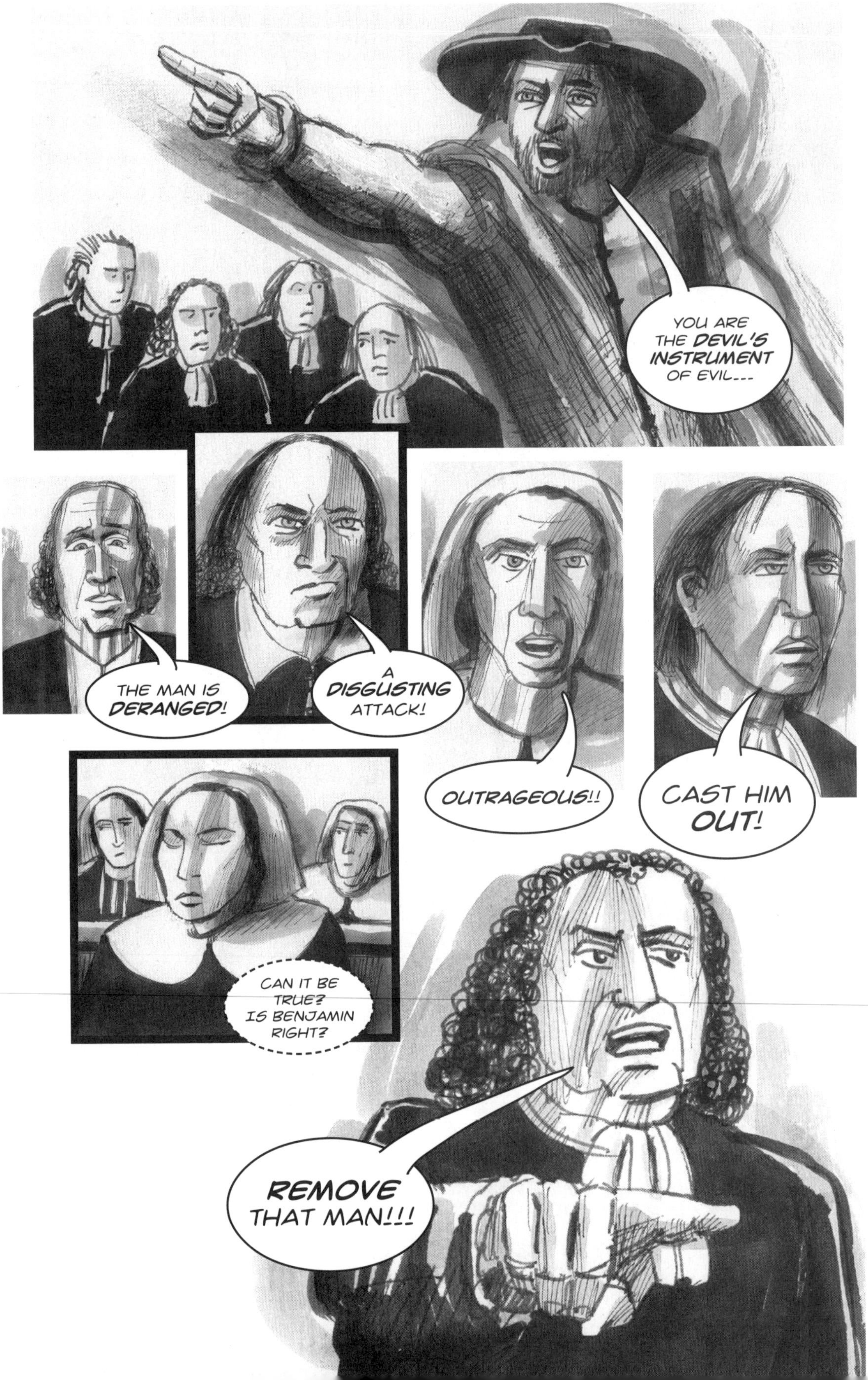
YOU ARE THE DEVIL'S INSTRUMENT OF EVIL...
THE MAN IS DERANGED!
A DISGUSTING ATTACK!
OUTRAGEOUS!!
CAST HIM OUT!
CAN IT BE TRUE? IS BENJAMIN RIGHT?
REMOVE THAT MAN!!!

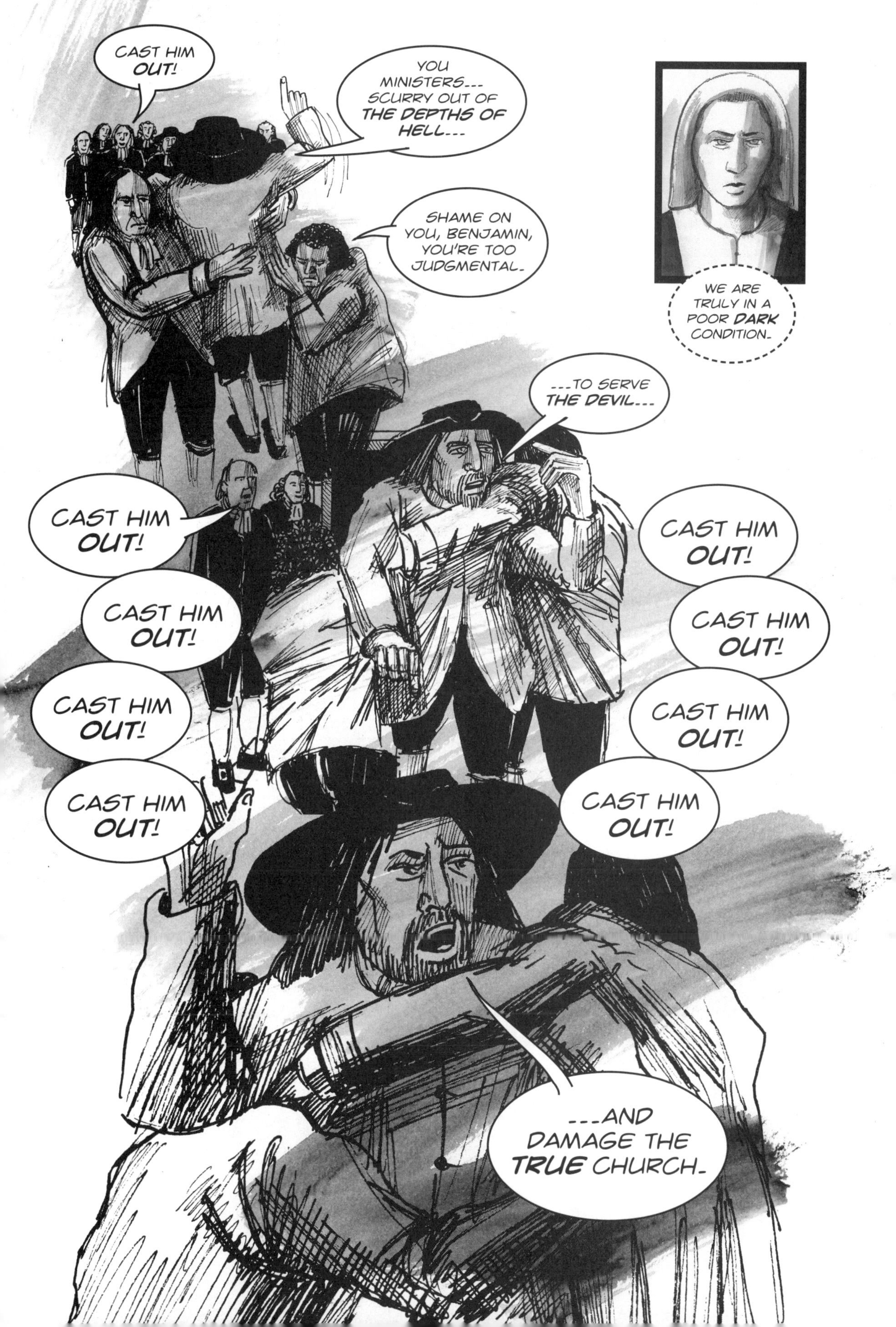
CAST HIM OUT!
YOU MINISTERS--- SCURRY OUT OF THE DEPTHS OF HELL---
SHAME ON YOU, BENJAMIN, YOU'RE TOO JUDGMENTAL.
WE ARE TRULY IN A POOR DARK CONDITION.
---TO SERVE THE DEVIL---
CAST HIM OUT!
CAST HIM OUT!
CAST HIM OUT!
CAST HIM OUT!
CAST HIM OUT!
CAST HIM OUT!
CAST HIM OUT!
CAST HIM OUT!
---AND DAMAGE THE TRUE CHURCH.

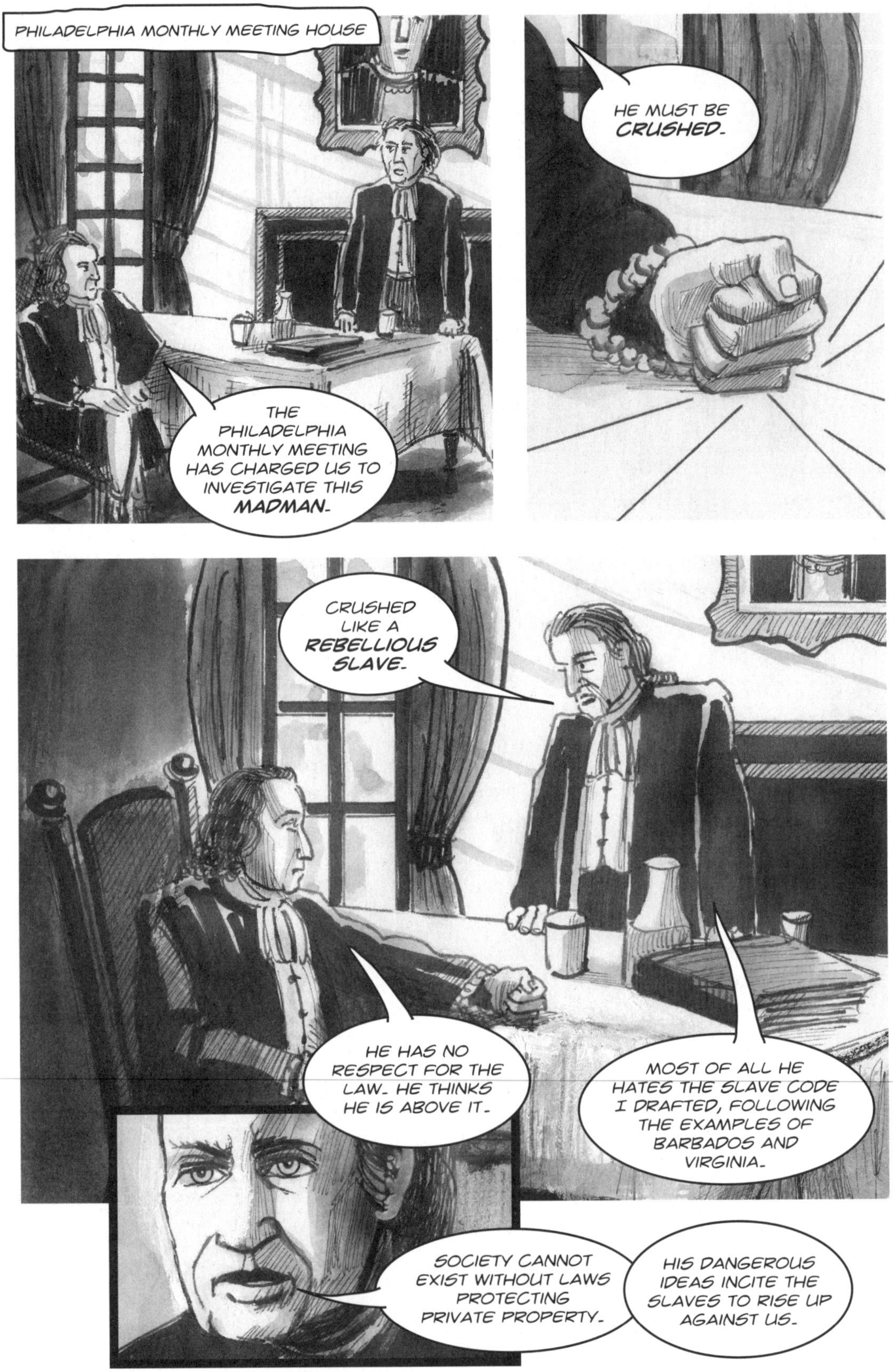
PHILADELPHIA MONTHLY MEETING HOUSE
THE PHILADELPHIA MONTHLY MEETING HAS CHARGED US TO INVESTIGATE THIS MADMAN.
HE MUST BE CRUSHED.
CRUSHED LIKE A REBELLIOUS SLAVE.
HE HAS NO RESPECT FOR THE LAW. HE THINKS HE IS ABOVE IT.
MOST OF ALL HE HATES THE SLAVE CODE I DRAFTED, FOLLOWING THE EXAMPLES OF BARBADOS AND VIRGINIA.
SOCIETY CANNOT EXIST WITHOUT LAWS PROTECTING PRIVATE PROPERTY.
HIS DANGEROUS IDEAS INCITE THE SLAVES TO RISE UP AGAINST US.

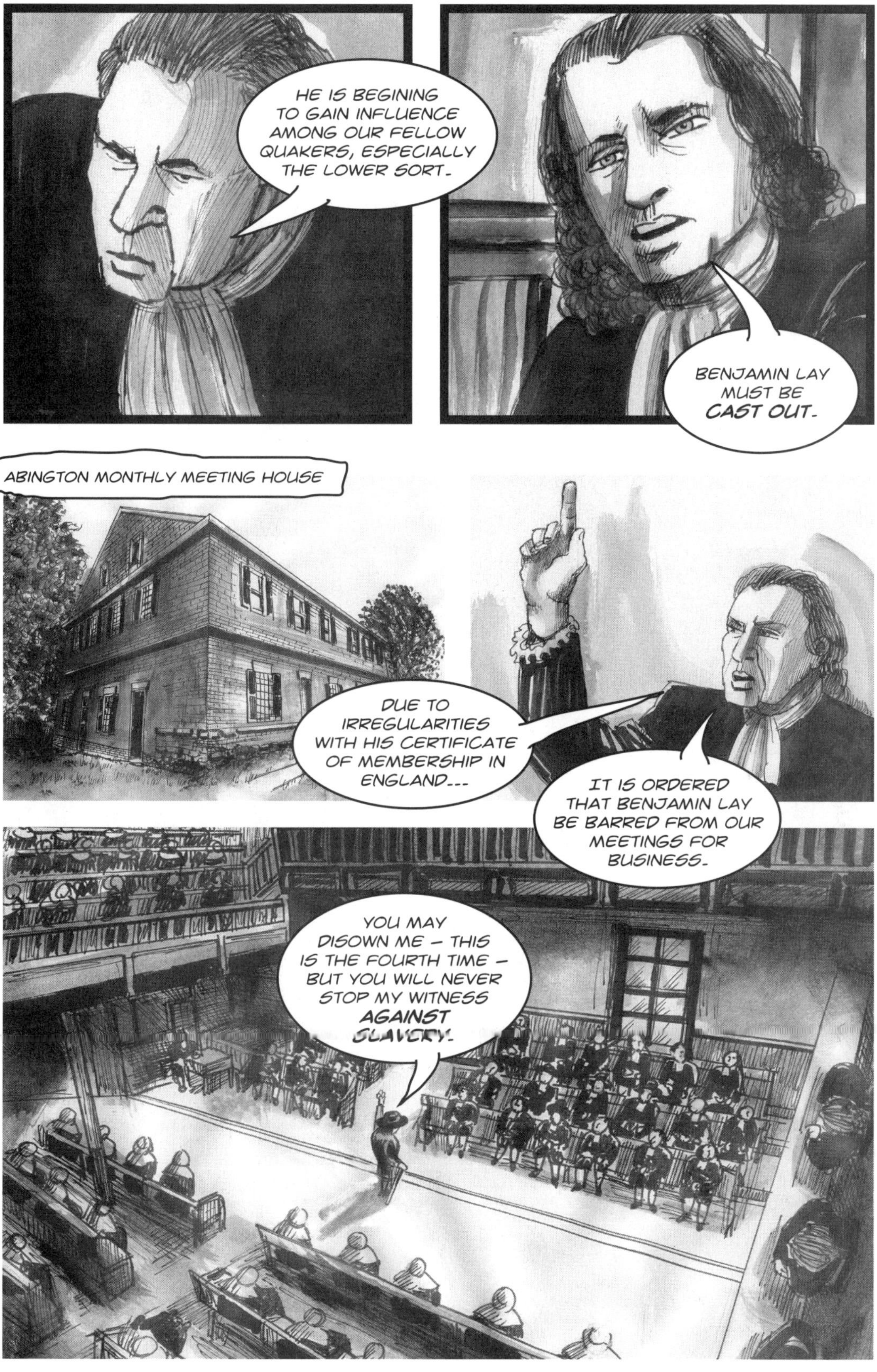
HE IS BEGINING TO GAIN INFLUENCE AMONG OUR FELLOW QUAKERS, ESPECIALLY THE LOWER SORT.
BENJAMIN LAY MUST BE CAST OUT.
ABINGTON MONTHLY MEETING HOUSE
DUE TO IRREGULARITIES WITH HIS CERTIFICATE OF MEMBERSHIP IN ENGLAND...
IT IS ORDERED THAT BENJAMIN LAY BE BARRED FROM OUR MEETINGS FOR BUSINESS.
YOU MAY DISOWN ME – THIS IS THE FOURTH TIME – BUT YOU WILL NEVER STOP MY WITNESS AGAINST SLAVERY.

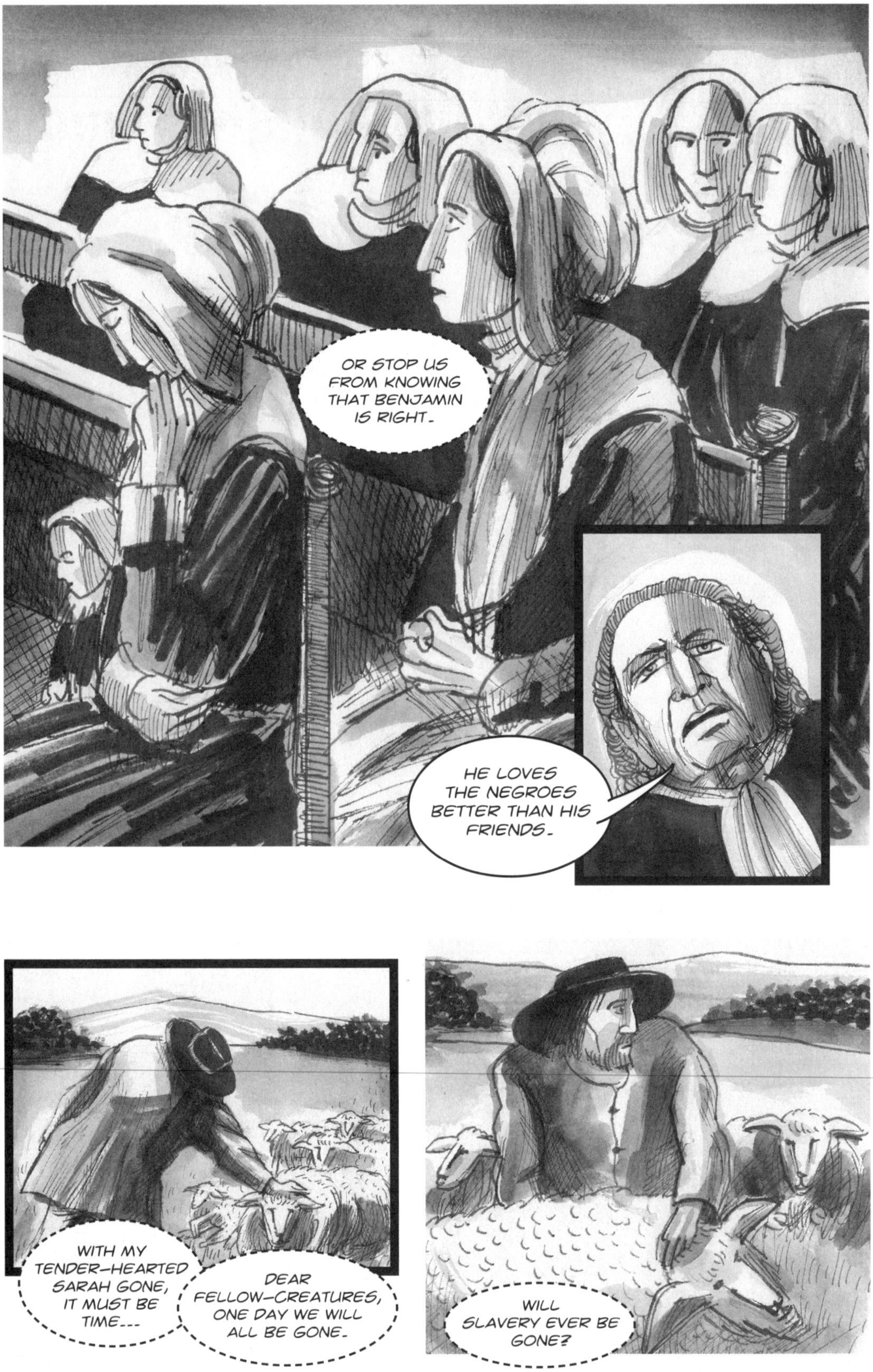
OR STOP US FROM KNOWING THAT BENJAMIN IS RIGHT.
HE LOVES THE NEGROES BETTER THAN HIS FRIENDS.
WITH MY TENDER-HEARTED SARAH GONE, IT MUST BE TIME...
DEAR FELLOW-CREATURES, ONE DAY WE WILL ALL BE GONE.
WILL SLAVERY EVER BE GONE?

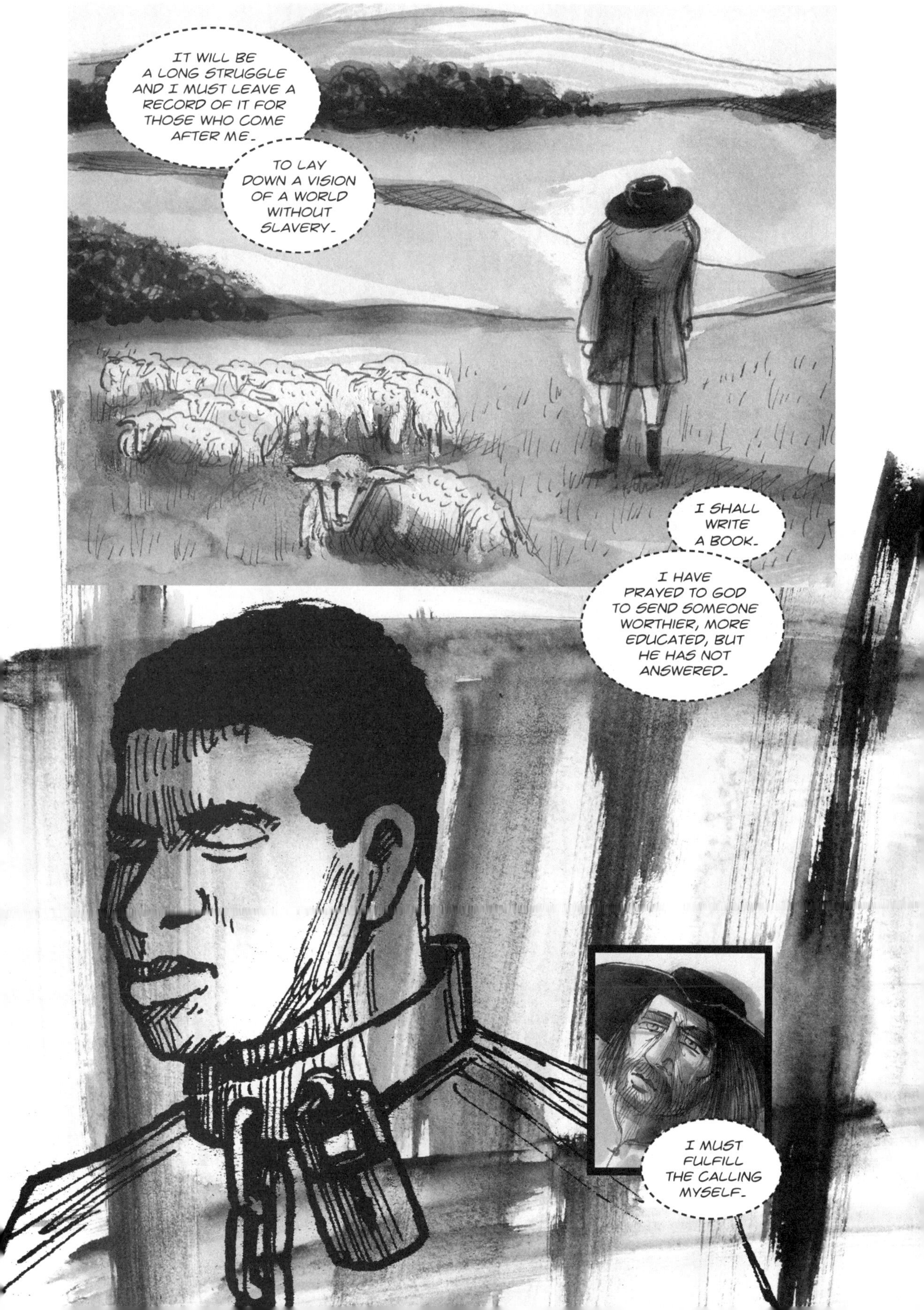
IT WILL BE A LONG STRUGGLE AND I MUST LEAVE A RECORD OF IT FOR THOSE WHO COME AFTER ME.
TO LAY DOWN A VISION OF A WORLD WITHOUT SLAVERY.
I SHALL WRITE A BOOK.
I HAVE PRAYED TO GOD TO SEND SOMEONE WORTHIER, MORE EDUCATED, BUT HE HAS NOT ANSWERED.
I MUST FULFILL THE CALLING MYSELF.

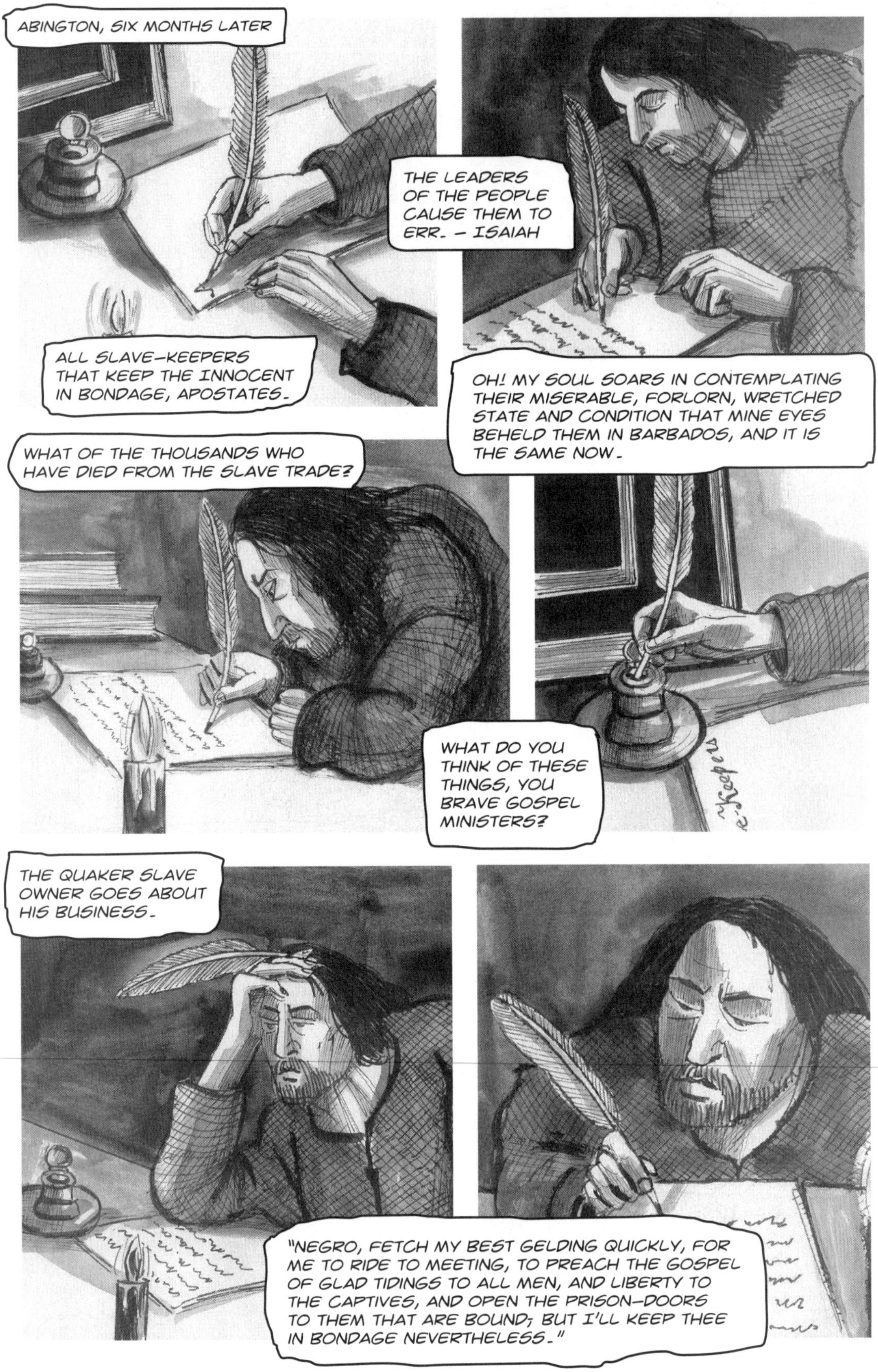
ABINGTON, SIX MONTHS LATER
ALL SLAVE-KEEPERS THAT KEEP THE INNOCENT IN BONDAGE, APOSTATES.
THE LEADERS OF THE PEOPLE CAUSE THEM TO ERR. – ISAIAH
OH! MY SOUL SOARS IN CONTEMPLATING THEIR MISERABLE, FORLORN, WRETCHED STATE AND CONDITION THAT MINE EYES BEHELD THEM IN BARBADOS, AND IT IS THE SAME NOW.
WHAT OF THE THOUSANDS WHO HAVE DIED FROM THE SLAVE TRADE?
WHAT DO YOU THINK OF THESE THINGS, YOU BRAVE GOSPEL MINISTERS?
THE QUAKER SLAVE OWNER GOES ABOUT HIS BUSINESS.
"NEGRO, FETCH MY BEST GELDING QUICKLY, FOR ME TO RIDE TO MEETING, TO PREACH THE GOSPEL OF GLAD TIDINGS TO ALL MEN, AND LIBERTY TO THE CAPTIVES, AND OPEN THE PRISON-DOORS TO THEM THAT ARE BOUND; BUT I'LL KEEP THEE IN BONDAGE NEVERTHELESS."

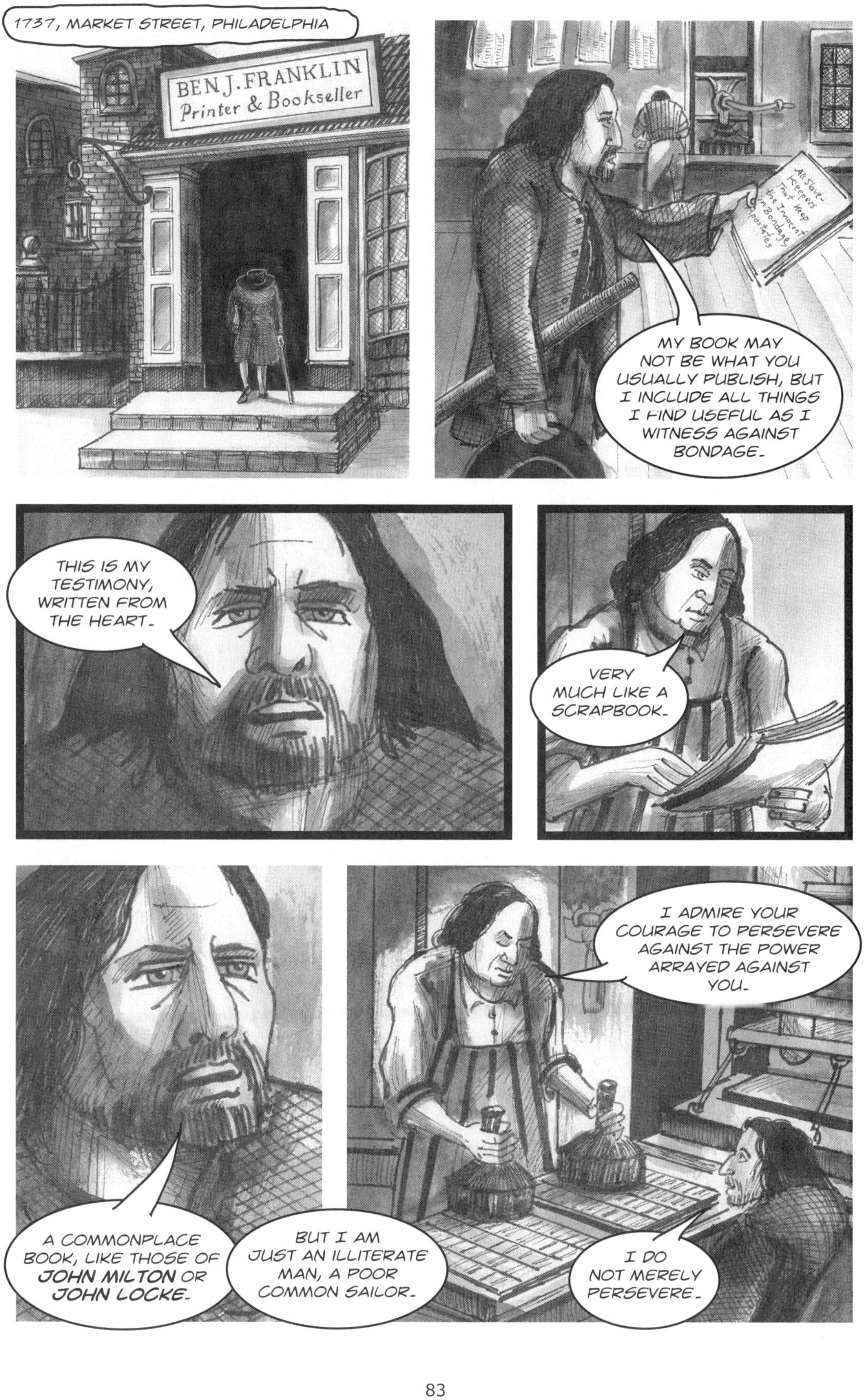
1737, MARKET STREET, PHILADELPHIA
BEN J. FRANKLIN Printer & Bookseller
All Slave-keepers That keep the Innocent in Bondage Apostates
MY BOOK MAY NOT BE WHAT YOU USUALLY PUBLISH, BUT I INCLUDE ALL THINGS I FIND USEFUL AS I WITNESS AGAINST BONDAGE.
THIS IS MY TESTIMONY, WRITTEN FROM THE HEART.
VERY MUCH LIKE A SCRAPBOOK.
A COMMONPLACE BOOK, LIKE THOSE OF **JOHN MILTON** OR **JOHN LOCKE**.
BUT I AM JUST AN ILLITERATE MAN, A POOR COMMON SAILOR.
I ADMIRE YOUR COURAGE TO PERSEVERE AGAINST THE POWER ARRAYED AGAINST YOU.
I DO NOT MERELY PERSEVERE.

YOU WILL BE ATTACKED FOR WRITING THIS BOOK, BENJAMIN.

AND... SO WILL I WHEN I PUBLISH IT.

I SEEK TO ABOLISH SLAVERY AND SAVE QUAKERS FROM THEMSELVES.

WE QUAKERS WERE PERSECUTED FOR OUR BELIEFS IN ENGLAND. NOW A SMALL NUMBER OF US SPEAK OUT AGAINST SLAVERY — AND ARE PERSECUTED BY OUR FELLOW QUAKERS.

WHERE ARE THE LEARNED, LITERATE MEN LIKE YOU, BEN FRANKLIN? **WHY DON'T ALL OF YOU SPEAK OUT?**

HOME OF **JOHN CADWALLADER**, MINISTER

THANK YOU, DEAR FRIEND, FOR INTRODUCING ME TO THE SCHOOL MASTERS, SO THAT I MIGHT TEACH THEIR STUDENTS.

IMPORTANT WORK FOR OUR CAUSE.

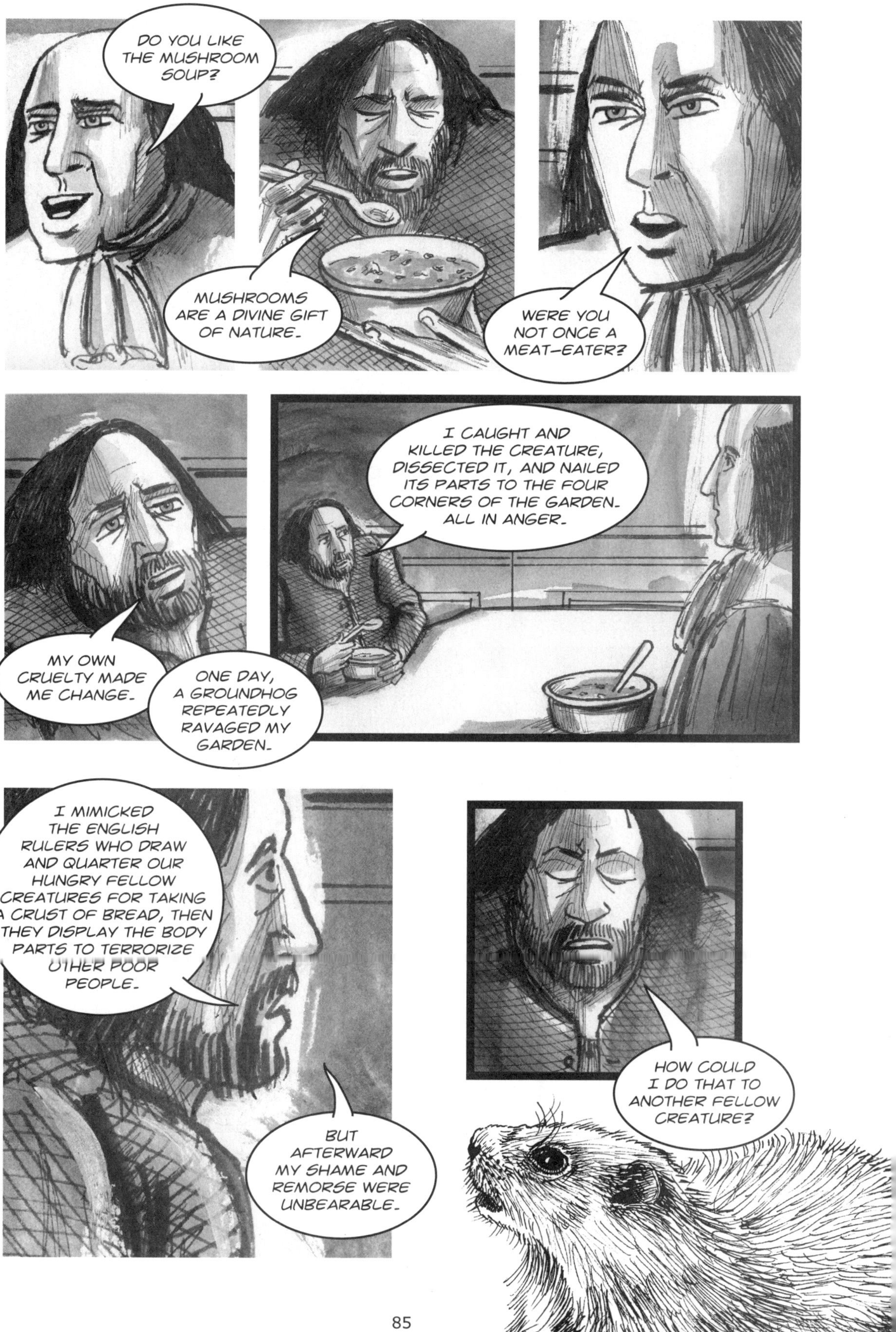
DO YOU LIKE THE MUSHROOM SOUP?
MUSHROOMS ARE A DIVINE GIFT OF NATURE.
WERE YOU NOT ONCE A MEAT-EATER?
MY OWN CRUELTY MADE ME CHANGE.
ONE DAY, A GROUNDHOG REPEATEDLY RAVAGED MY GARDEN.
I CAUGHT AND KILLED THE CREATURE, DISSECTED IT, AND NAILED ITS PARTS TO THE FOUR CORNERS OF THE GARDEN. ALL IN ANGER.
I MIMICKED THE ENGLISH RULERS WHO DRAW AND QUARTER OUR HUNGRY FELLOW CREATURES FOR TAKING A CRUST OF BREAD, THEN THEY DISPLAY THE BODY PARTS TO TERRORIZE OTHER POOR PEOPLE.
BUT AFTERWARD MY SHAME AND REMORSE WERE UNBEARABLE.
HOW COULD I DO THAT TO ANOTHER FELLOW CREATURE?

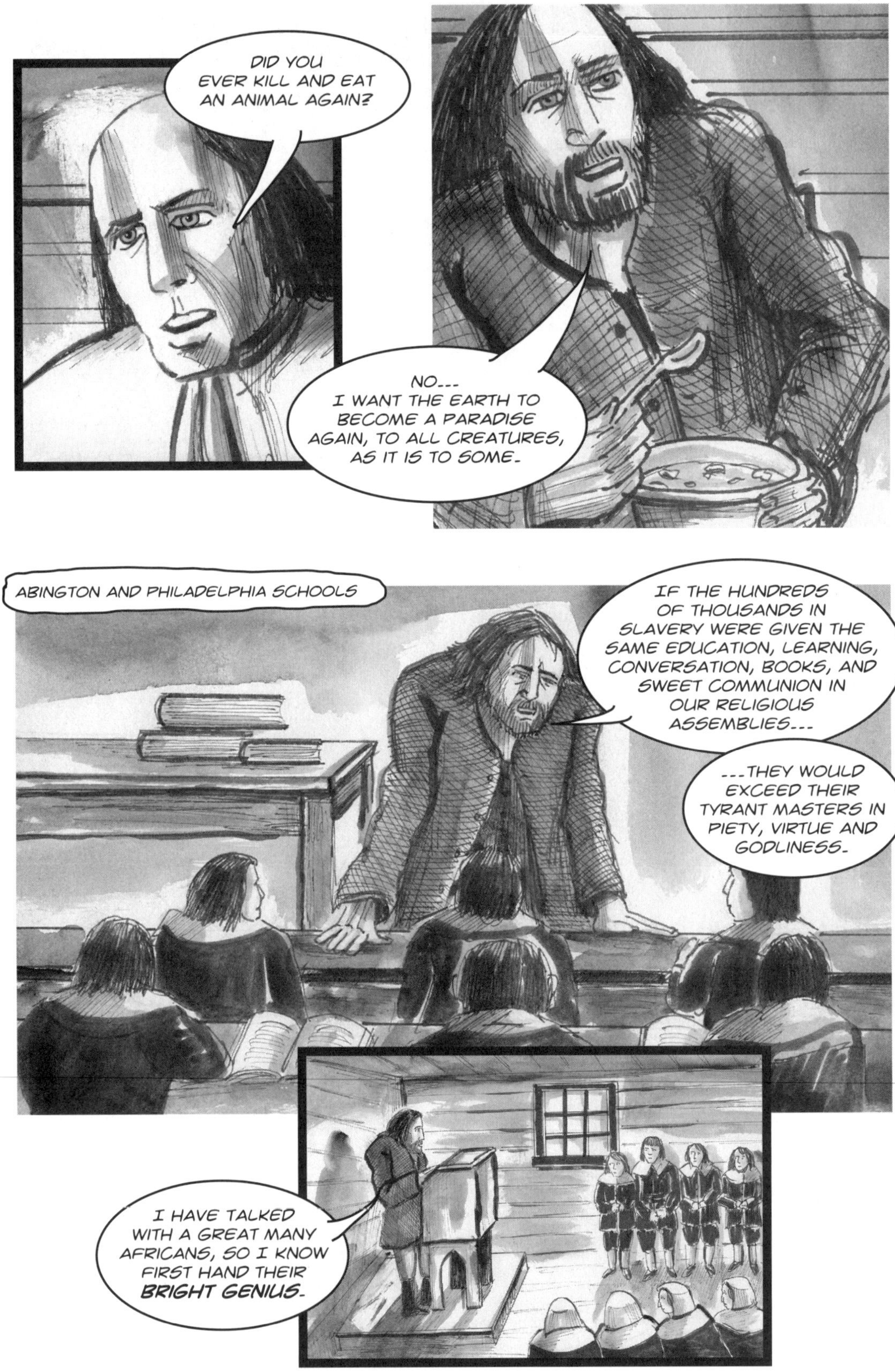
DID YOU EVER KILL AND EAT AN ANIMAL AGAIN?
NO... I WANT THE EARTH TO BECOME A PARADISE AGAIN, TO ALL CREATURES, AS IT IS TO SOME.
ABINGTON AND PHILADELPHIA SCHOOLS
IF THE HUNDREDS OF THOUSANDS IN SLAVERY WERE GIVEN THE SAME EDUCATION, LEARNING, CONVERSATION, BOOKS, AND SWEET COMMUNION IN OUR RELIGIOUS ASSEMBLIES...
...THEY WOULD EXCEED THEIR TYRANT MASTERS IN PIETY, VIRTUE AND GODLINESS.
I HAVE TALKED WITH A GREAT MANY AFRICANS, SO I KNOW FIRST HAND THEIR **BRIGHT GENIUS**.

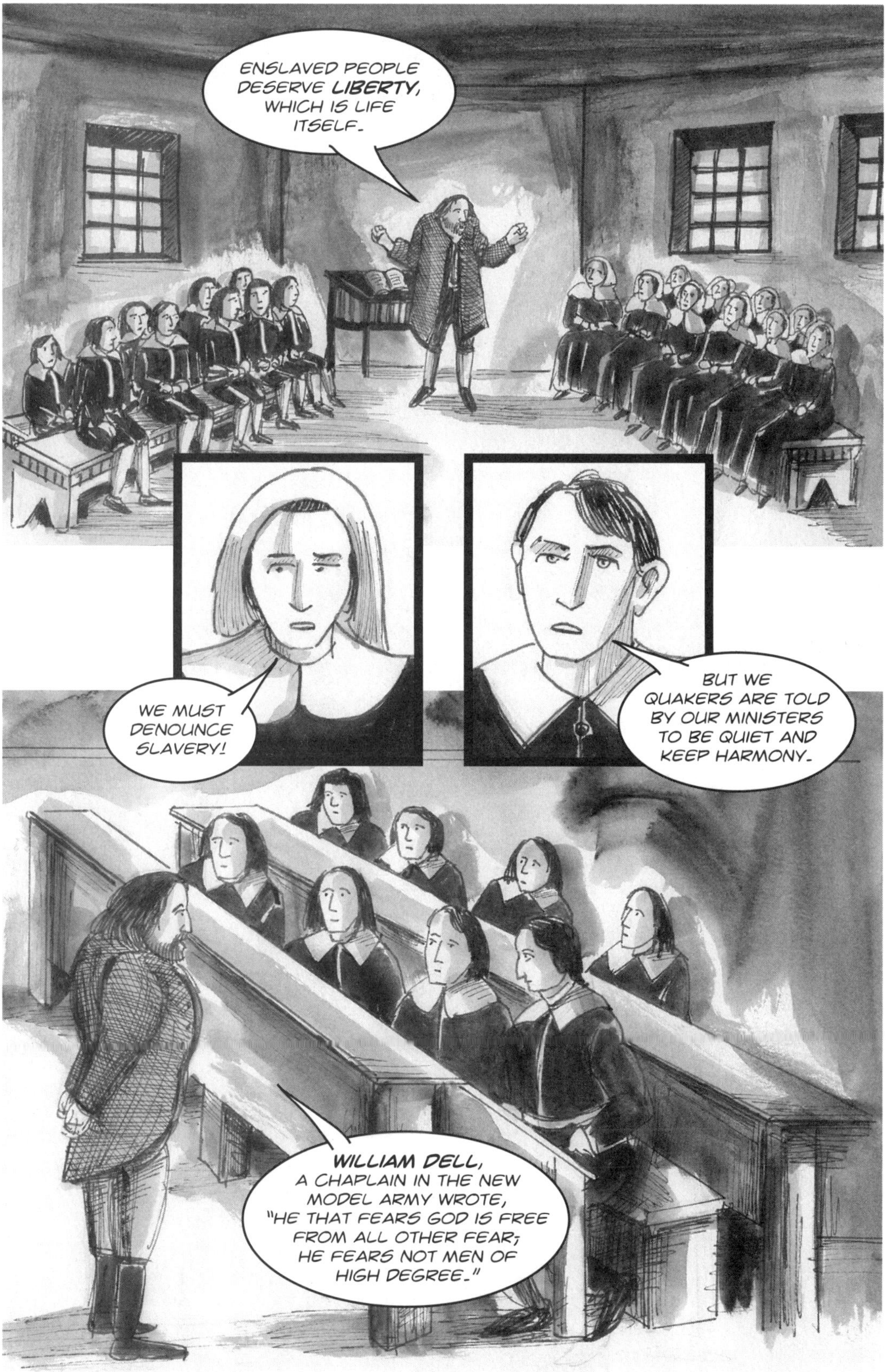
ENSLAVED PEOPLE DESERVE **LIBERTY,** WHICH IS LIFE ITSELF.
WE MUST DENOUNCE SLAVERY!
BUT WE QUAKERS ARE TOLD BY OUR MINISTERS TO BE QUIET AND KEEP HARMONY.
WILLIAM DELL, A CHAPLAIN IN THE NEW MODEL ARMY WROTE, "HE THAT FEARS GOD IS FREE FROM ALL OTHER FEAR; HE FEARS NOT MEN OF HIGH DEGREE."

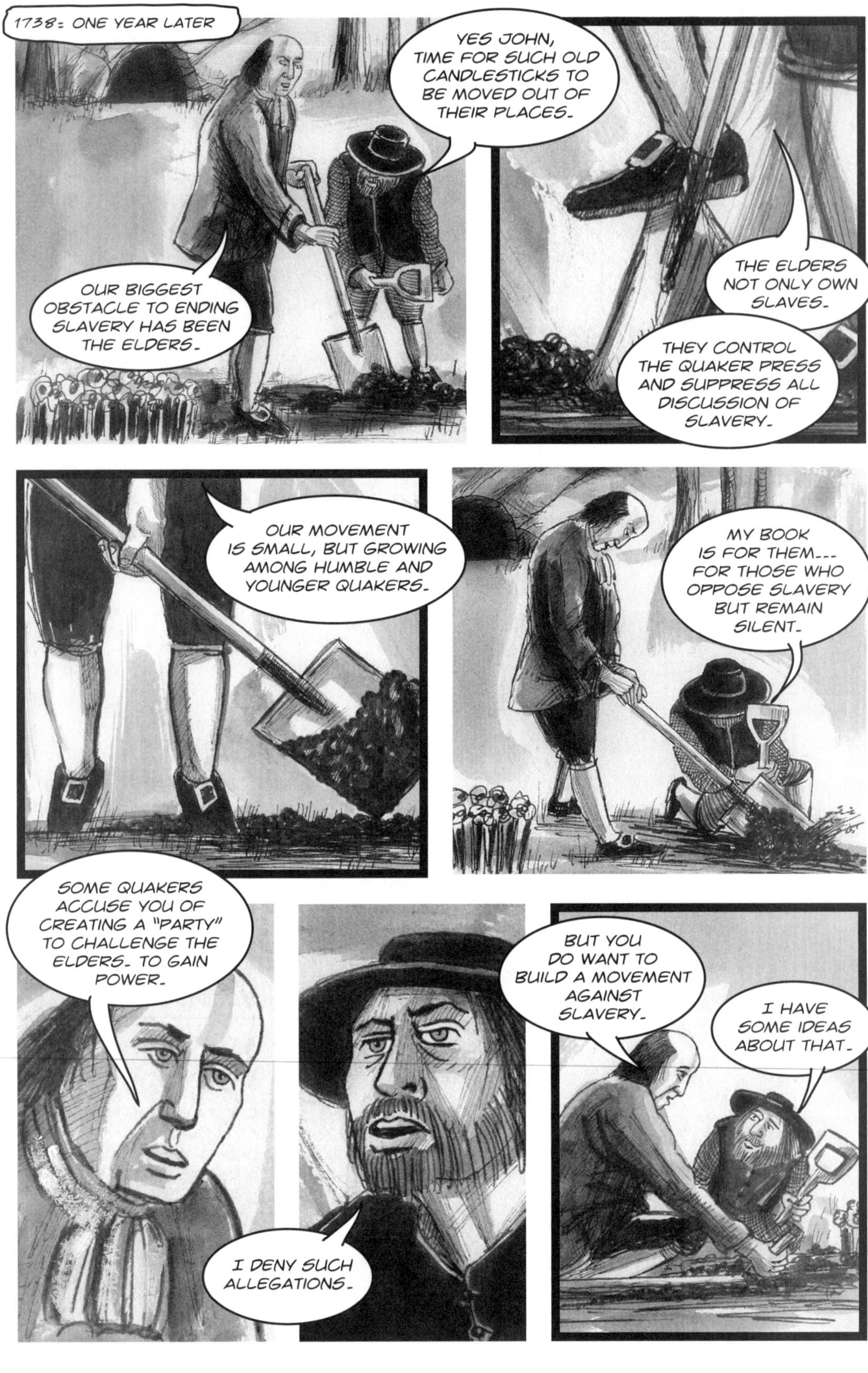
1738: ONE YEAR LATER
YES JOHN, TIME FOR SUCH OLD CANDLESTICKS TO BE MOVED OUT OF THEIR PLACES.
OUR BIGGEST OBSTACLE TO ENDING SLAVERY HAS BEEN THE ELDERS.
THE ELDERS NOT ONLY OWN SLAVES.
THEY CONTROL THE QUAKER PRESS AND SUPPRESS ALL DISCUSSION OF SLAVERY.
OUR MOVEMENT IS SMALL, BUT GROWING AMONG HUMBLE AND YOUNGER QUAKERS.
MY BOOK IS FOR THEM... FOR THOSE WHO OPPOSE SLAVERY BUT REMAIN SILENT.
SOME QUAKERS ACCUSE YOU OF CREATING A "PARTY" TO CHALLENGE THE ELDERS. TO GAIN POWER.
I DENY SUCH ALLEGATIONS.
BUT YOU DO WANT TO BUILD A MOVEMENT AGAINST SLAVERY.
I HAVE SOME IDEAS ABOUT THAT.

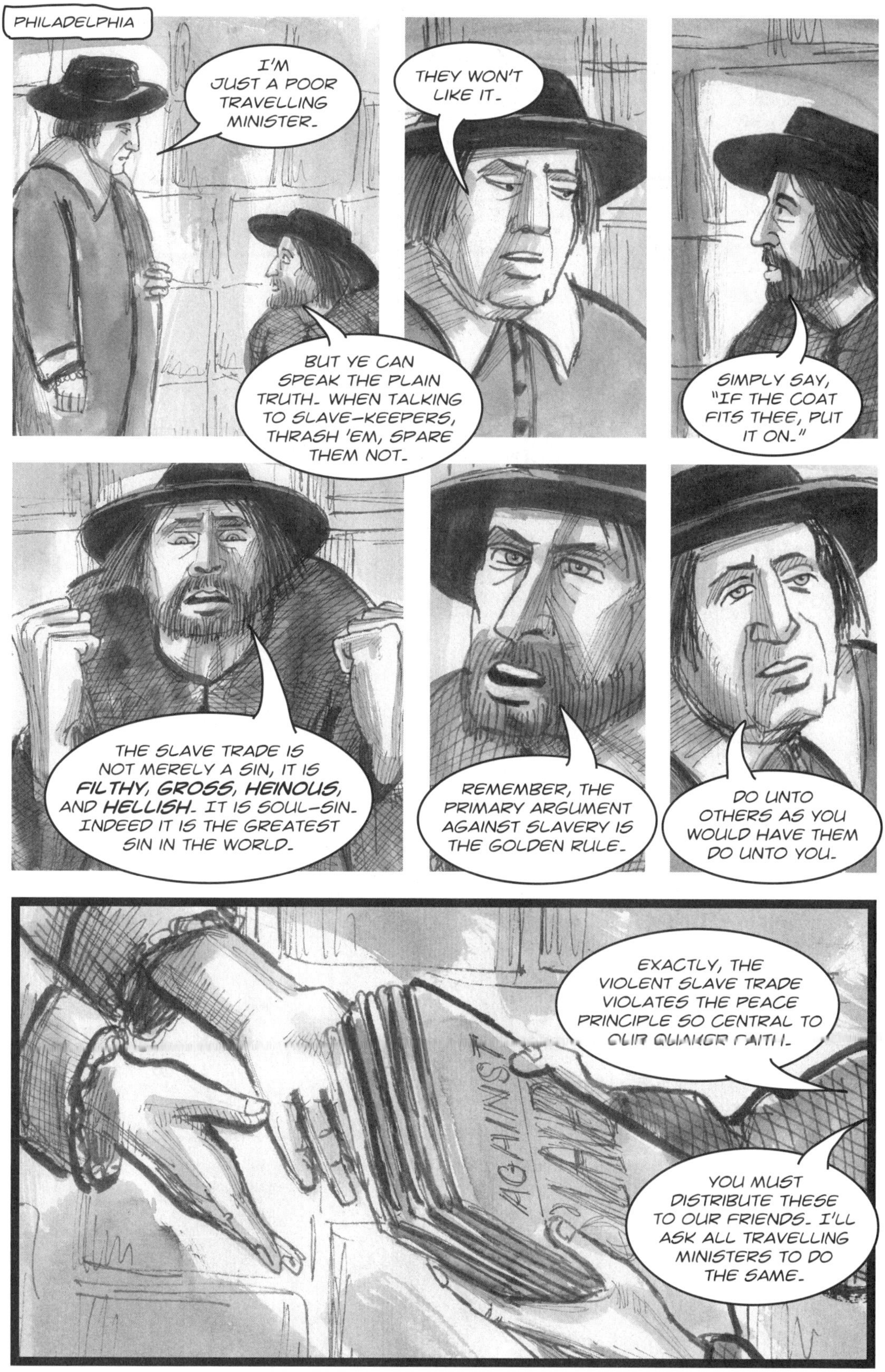
PHILADELPHIA
I'M JUST A POOR TRAVELLING MINISTER.
BUT YE CAN SPEAK THE PLAIN TRUTH. WHEN TALKING TO SLAVE-KEEPERS, THRASH 'EM, SPARE THEM NOT.
THEY WON'T LIKE IT.
SIMPLY SAY, "IF THE COAT FITS THEE, PUT IT ON."
THE SLAVE TRADE IS NOT MERELY A SIN, IT IS FILTHY, GROSS, HEINOUS, AND HELLISH. IT IS SOUL-SIN. INDEED IT IS THE GREATEST SIN IN THE WORLD.
REMEMBER, THE PRIMARY ARGUMENT AGAINST SLAVERY IS THE GOLDEN RULE.
DO UNTO OTHERS AS YOU WOULD HAVE THEM DO UNTO YOU.
EXACTLY, THE VIOLENT SLAVE TRADE VIOLATES THE PEACE PRINCIPLE SO CENTRAL TO OUR QUAKER FAITH.
YOU MUST DISTRIBUTE THESE TO OUR FRIENDS. I'LL ASK ALL TRAVELLING MINISTERS TO DO THE SAME.

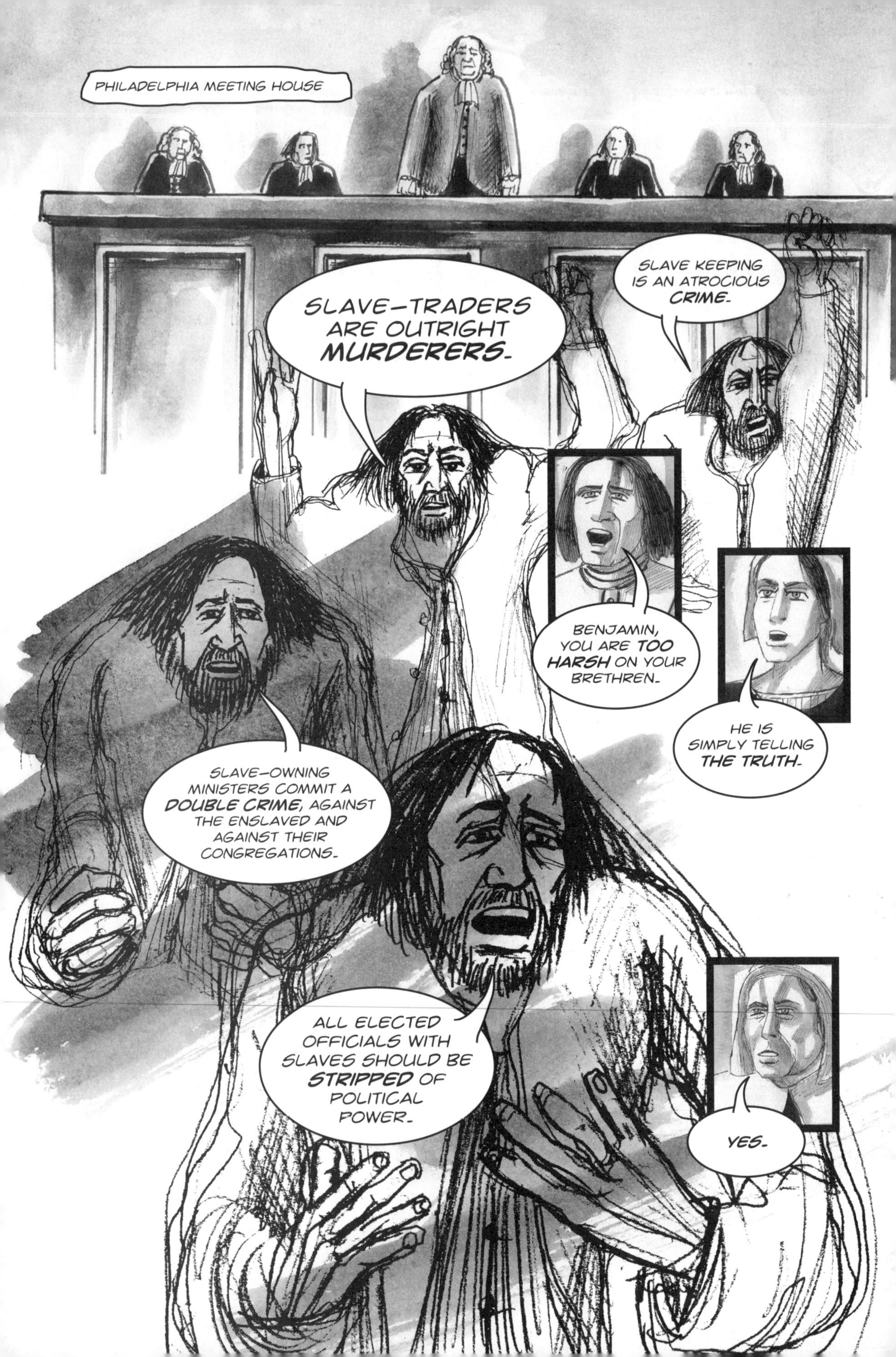
PHILADELPHIA MEETING HOUSE
SLAVE-TRADERS ARE OUTRIGHT MURDERERS.
SLAVE KEEPING IS AN ATROCIOUS CRIME.
BENJAMIN, YOU ARE TOO HARSH ON YOUR BRETHREN.
HE IS SIMPLY TELLING THE TRUTH.
SLAVE-OWNING MINISTERS COMMIT A DOUBLE CRIME, AGAINST THE ENSLAVED AND AGAINST THEIR CONGREGATIONS.
ALL ELECTED OFFICIALS WITH SLAVES SHOULD BE STRIPPED OF POLITICAL POWER.
YES.

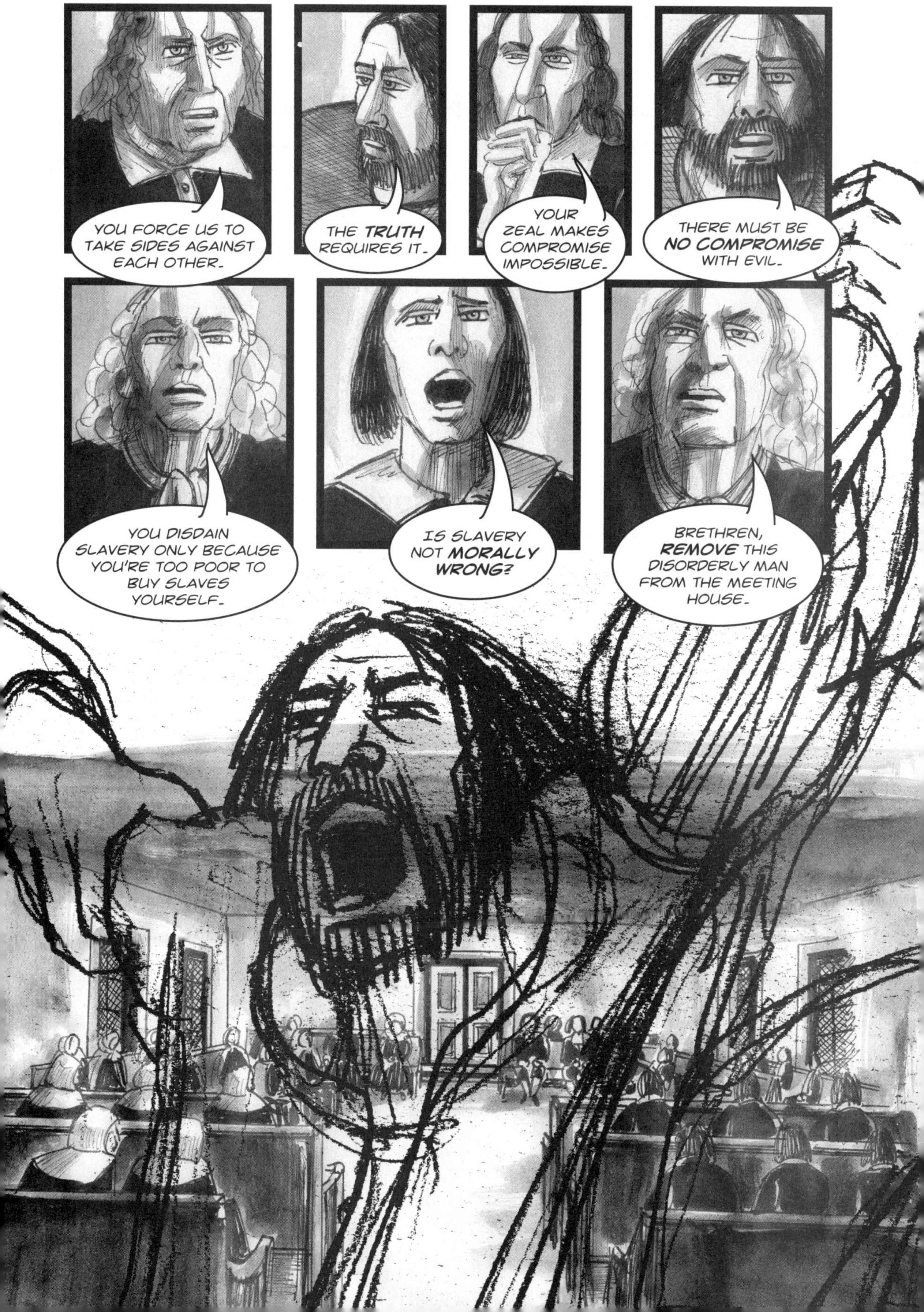
YOU FORCE US TO TAKE SIDES AGAINST EACH OTHER.
THE TRUTH REQUIRES IT.
YOUR ZEAL MAKES COMPROMISE IMPOSSIBLE.
THERE MUST BE NO COMPROMISE WITH EVIL.
YOU DISDAIN SLAVERY ONLY BECAUSE YOU'RE TOO POOR TO BUY SLAVES YOURSELF.
IS SLAVERY NOT MORALLY WRONG?
BRETHREN, REMOVE THIS DISORDERLY MAN FROM THE MEETING HOUSE.

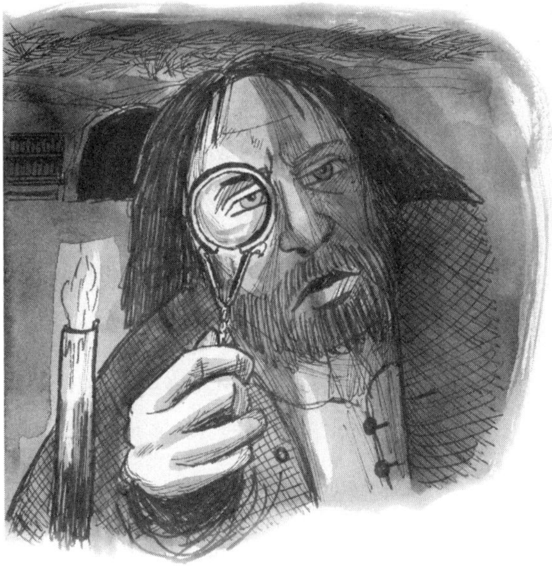

THE

Pennſylvania *GAZETTE.*

By Order of the Yearly Meeting, John Kinsey, Clerk

It is some Months since a Book was published in this City, with the Title, All Slave-Keepers &c. Apostates... Readers may believe the Author was one of the People called Quakers, and that this Book had been printed at their Request... We do hereby give publick Notice, that the Book contains gross Abuses, not only against some of their Members in particular, but against the whole Society: That the Author is not of their religious Community; that they disapprove of his Conduct, the Composition, and Printing of the Book.

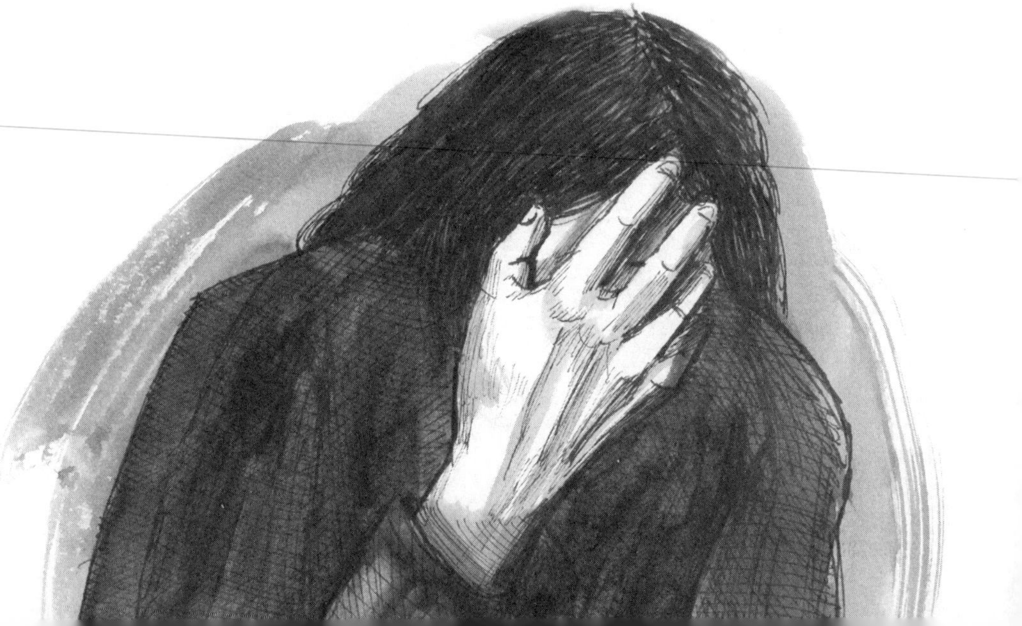

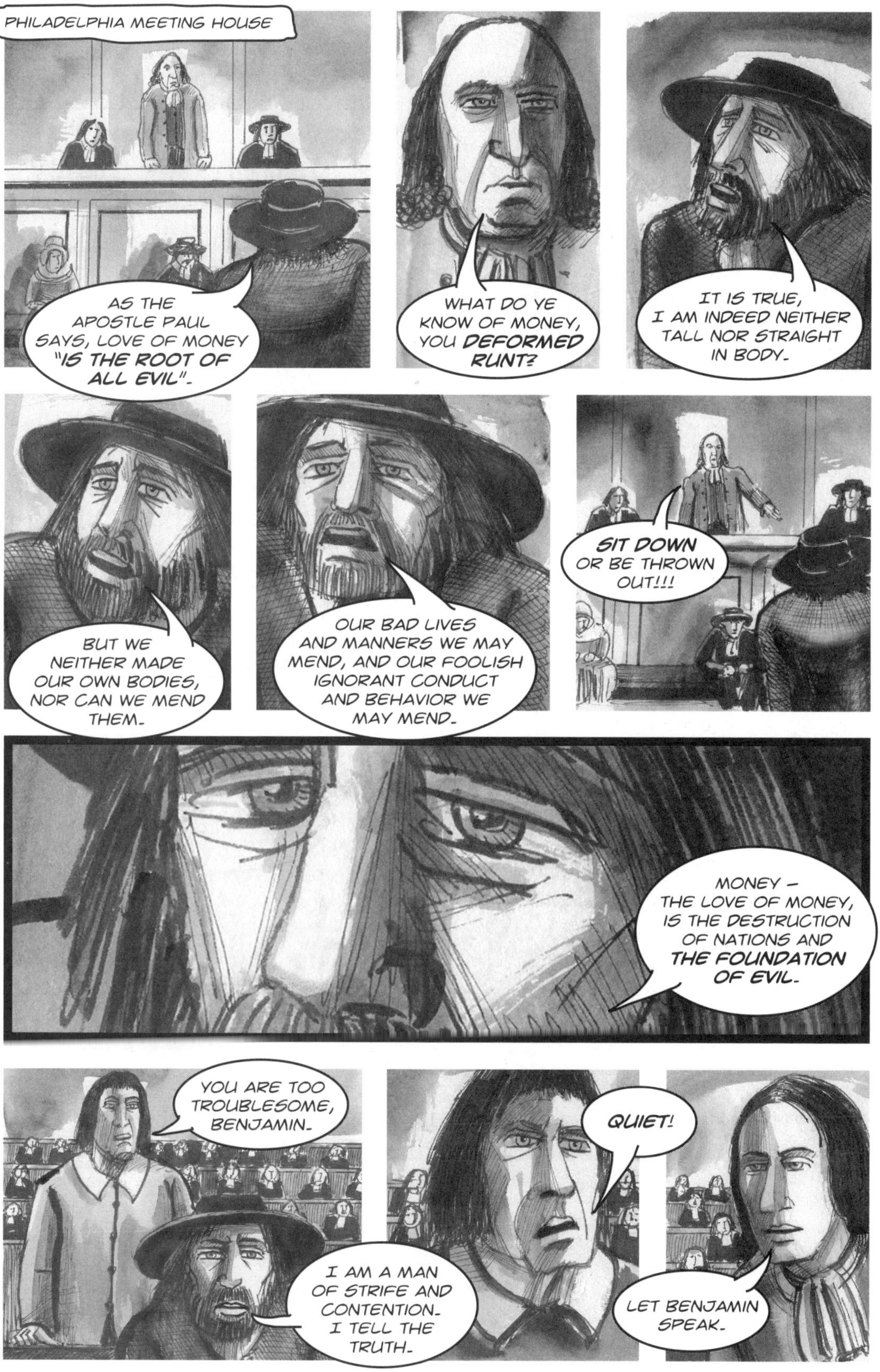
PHILADELPHIA MEETING HOUSE
AS THE APOSTLE PAUL SAYS, LOVE OF MONEY "IS THE ROOT OF ALL EVIL".
WHAT DO YE KNOW OF MONEY, YOU DEFORMED RUNT?
IT IS TRUE, I AM INDEED NEITHER TALL NOR STRAIGHT IN BODY.
BUT WE NEITHER MADE OUR OWN BODIES, NOR CAN WE MEND THEM.
OUR BAD LIVES AND MANNERS WE MAY MEND, AND OUR FOOLISH IGNORANT CONDUCT AND BEHAVIOR WE MAY MEND.
SIT DOWN OR BE THROWN OUT!!!
MONEY – THE LOVE OF MONEY, IS THE DESTRUCTION OF NATIONS AND THE FOUNDATION OF EVIL.
YOU ARE TOO TROUBLESOME, BENJAMIN.
I AM A MAN OF STRIFE AND CONTENTION. I TELL THE TRUTH.
QUIET!
LET BENJAMIN SPEAK.

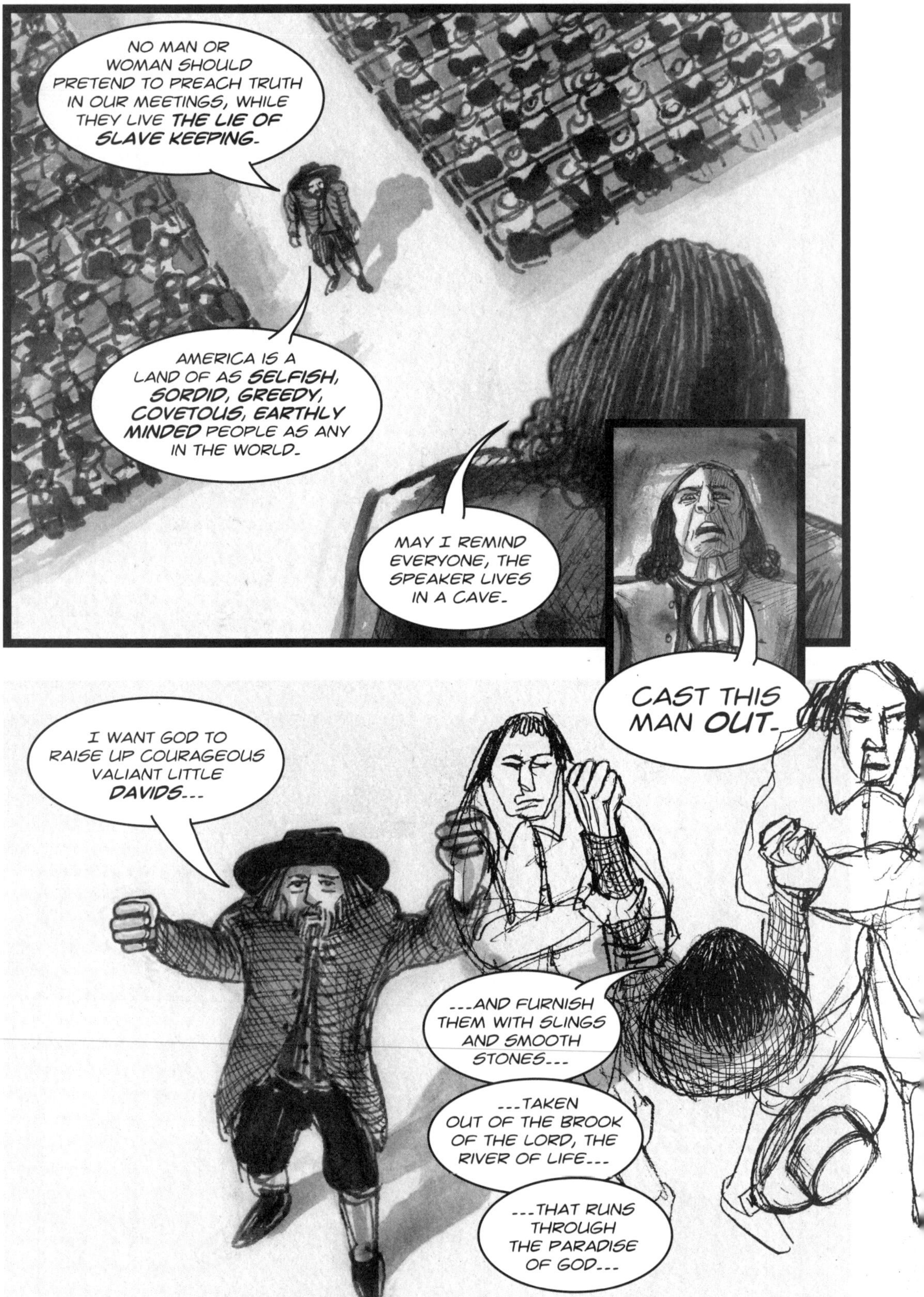
NO MAN OR WOMAN SHOULD PRETEND TO PREACH TRUTH IN OUR MEETINGS, WHILE THEY LIVE THE LIE OF SLAVE KEEPING.
AMERICA IS A LAND OF AS SELFISH, SORDID, GREEDY, COVETOUS, EARTHLY MINDED PEOPLE AS ANY IN THE WORLD.
MAY I REMIND EVERYONE, THE SPEAKER LIVES IN A CAVE.
CAST THIS MAN OUT.
I WANT GOD TO RAISE UP COURAGEOUS VALIANT LITTLE DAVIDS...
...AND FURNISH THEM WITH SLINGS AND SMOOTH STONES...
...TAKEN OUT OF THE BROOK OF THE LORD, THE RIVER OF LIFE...
...THAT RUNS THROUGH THE PARADISE OF GOD...

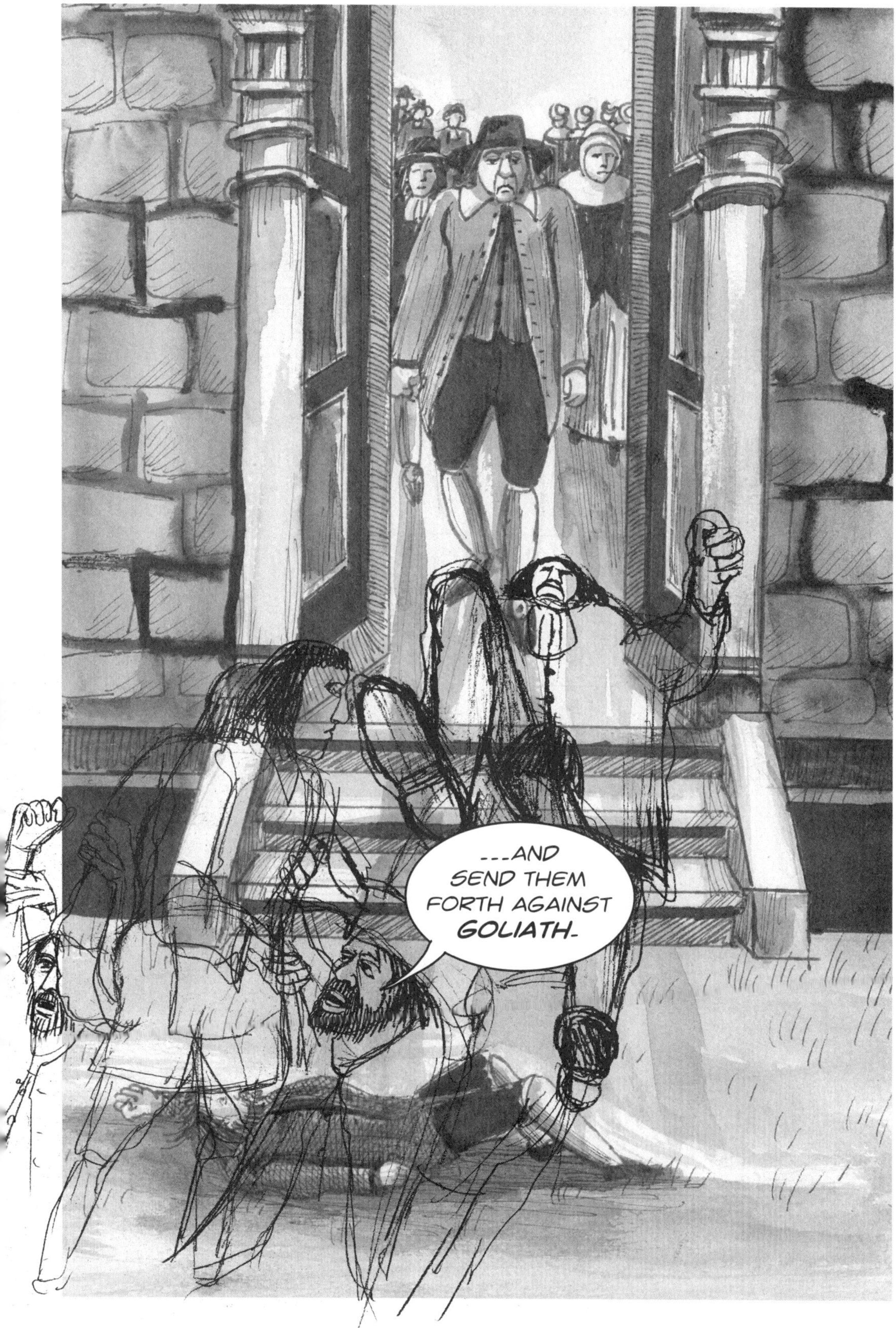
---AND SEND THEM FORTH AGAINST GOLIATH-

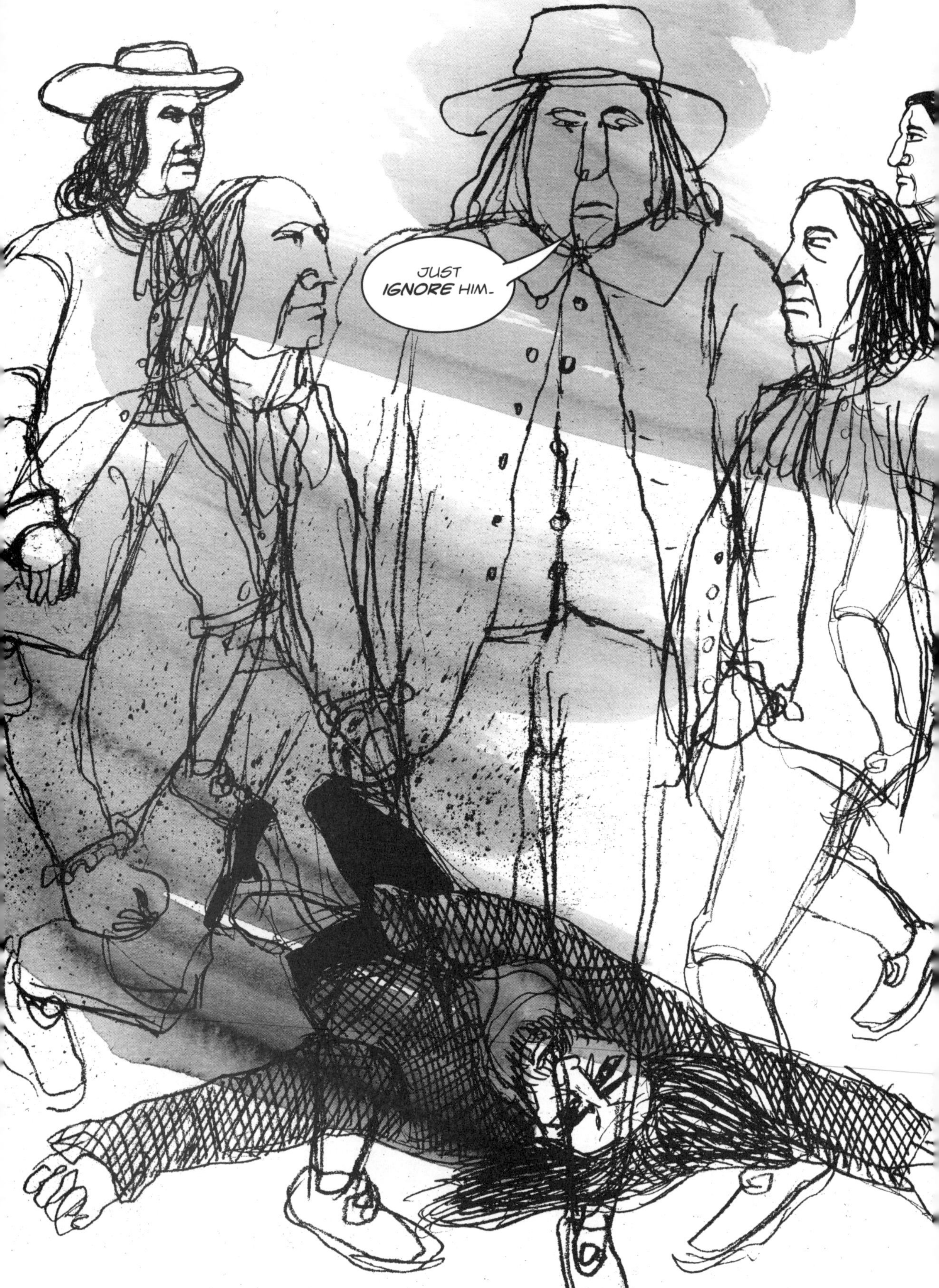
JUST **IGNORE** HIM.

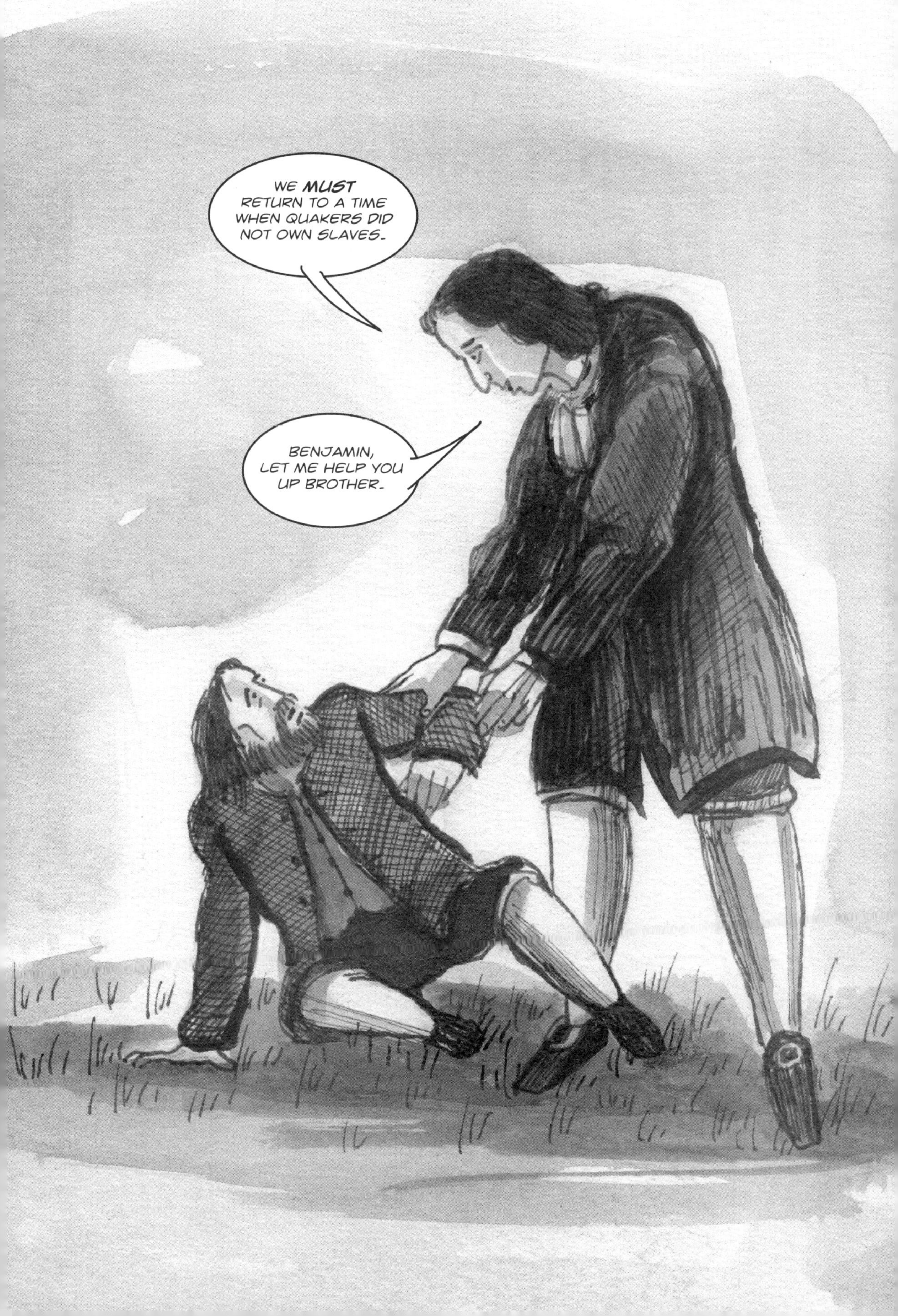
WE MUST RETURN TO A TIME WHEN QUAKERS DID NOT OWN SLAVES.
BENJAMIN, LET ME HELP YOU UP BROTHER.

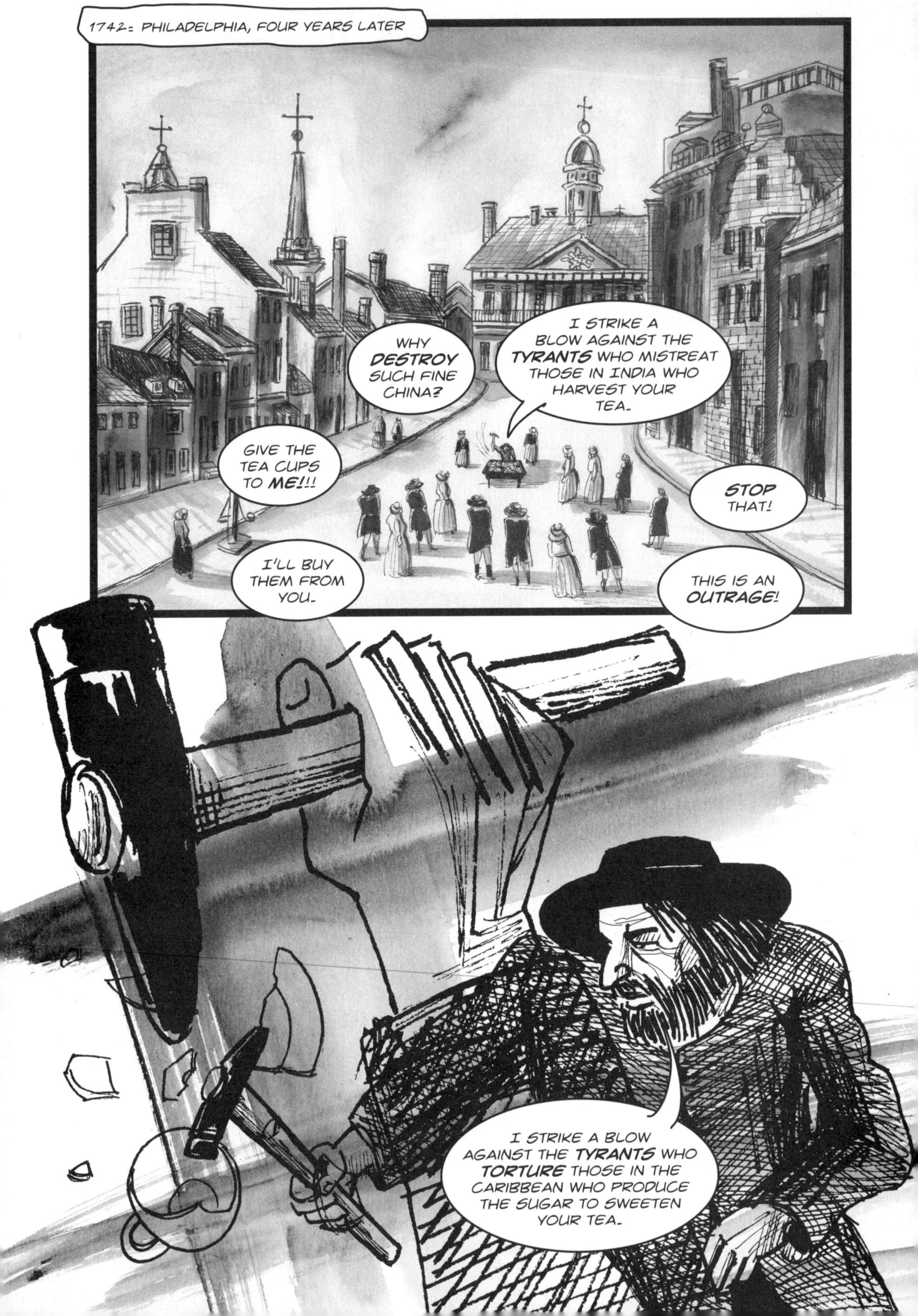
1742: PHILADELPHIA, FOUR YEARS LATER
WHY DESTROY SUCH FINE CHINA?
I STRIKE A BLOW AGAINST THE TYRANTS WHO MISTREAT THOSE IN INDIA WHO HARVEST YOUR TEA.
GIVE THE TEA CUPS TO ME!!!
STOP THAT!
I'LL BUY THEM FROM YOU.
THIS IS AN OUTRAGE!
I STRIKE A BLOW AGAINST THE TYRANTS WHO TORTURE THOSE IN THE CARIBBEAN WHO PRODUCE THE SUGAR TO SWEETEN YOUR TEA.

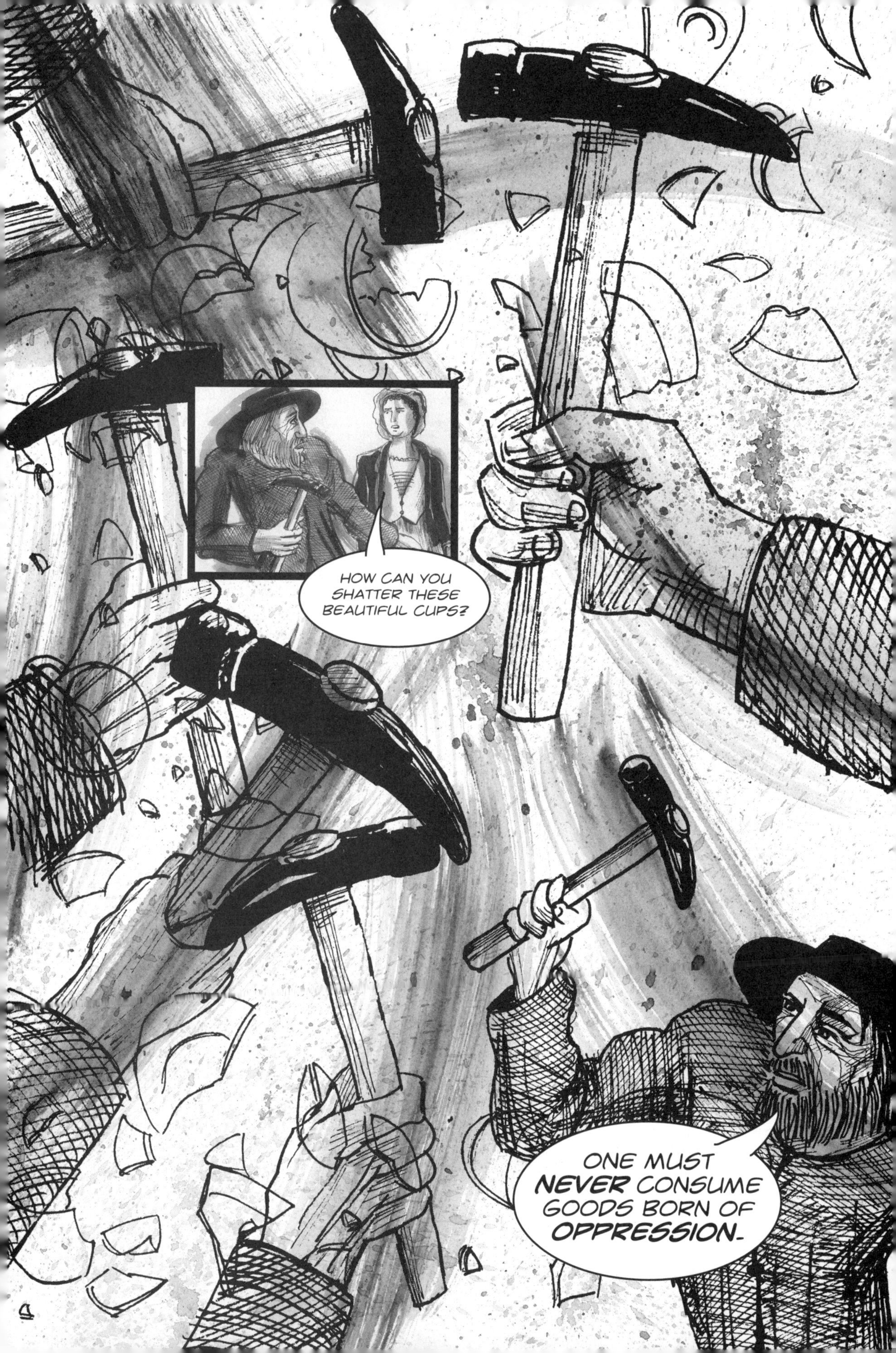
HOW CAN YOU SHATTER THESE BEAUTIFUL CUPS?
ONE MUST NEVER CONSUME GOODS BORN OF OPPRESSION.

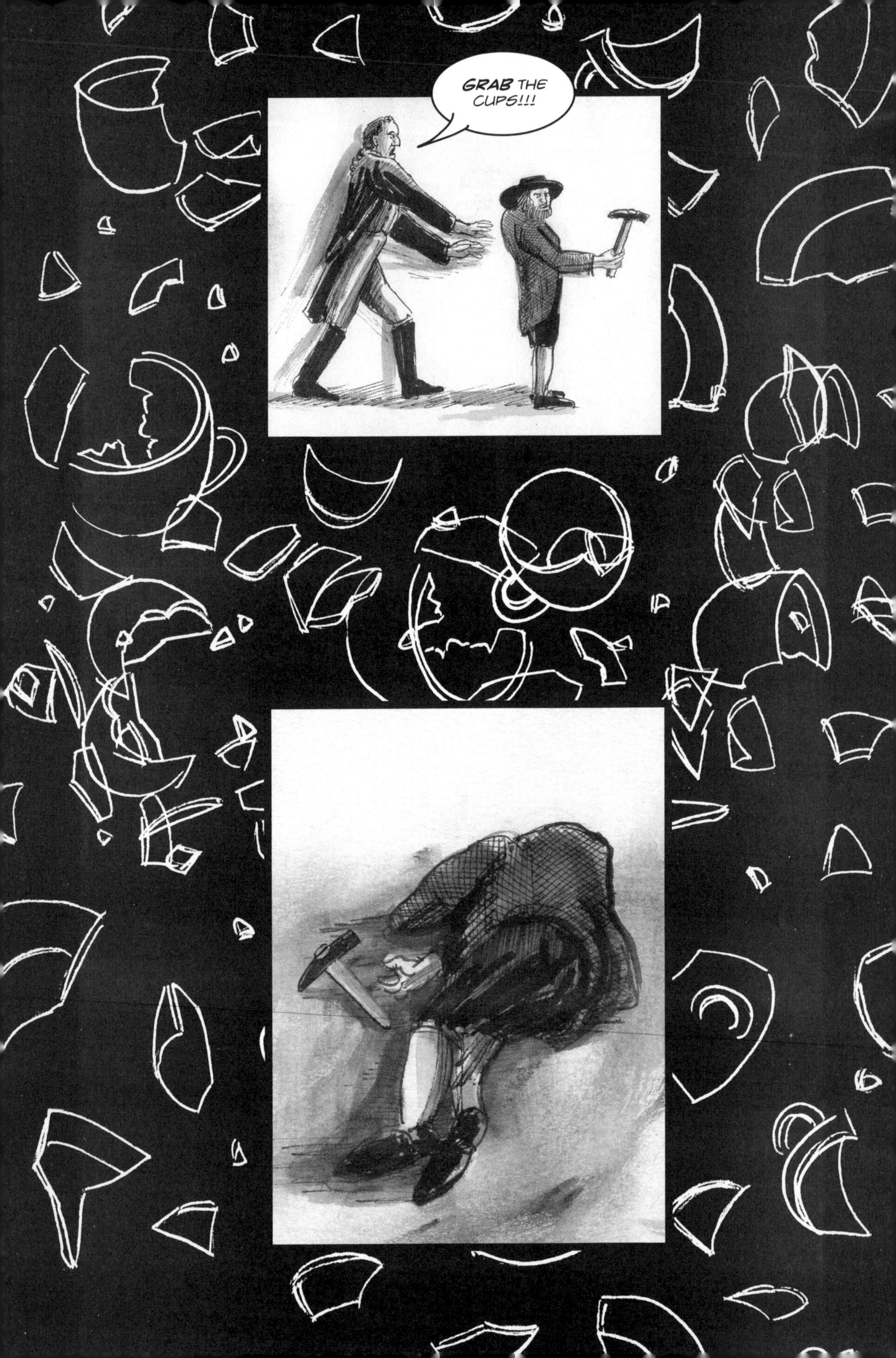
GRAB THE CUPS!!!

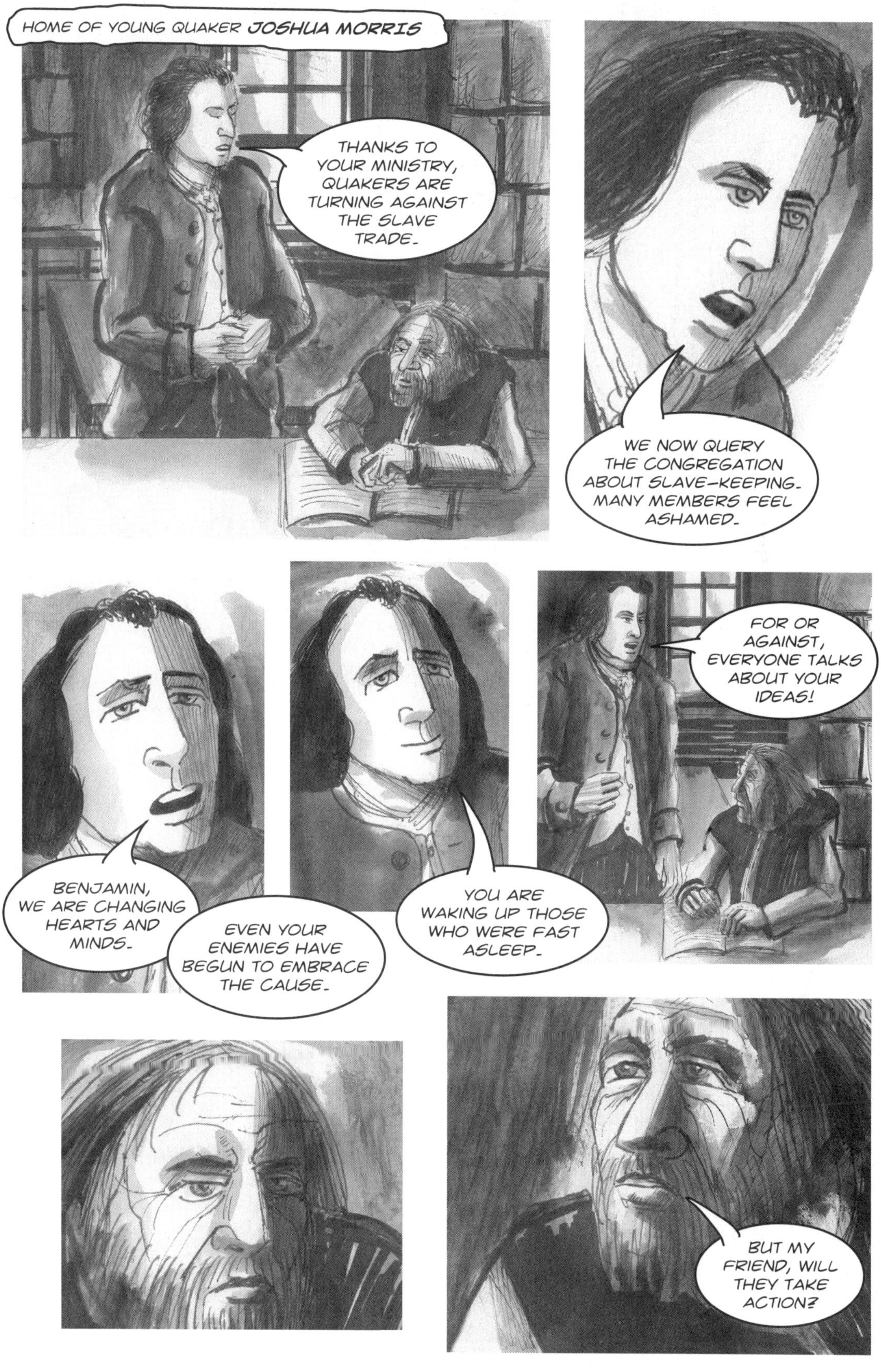
HOME OF YOUNG QUAKER JOSHUA MORRIS
THANKS TO YOUR MINISTRY, QUAKERS ARE TURNING AGAINST THE SLAVE TRADE.
WE NOW QUERY THE CONGREGATION ABOUT SLAVE-KEEPING. MANY MEMBERS FEEL ASHAMED.
BENJAMIN, WE ARE CHANGING HEARTS AND MINDS.
EVEN YOUR ENEMIES HAVE BEGUN TO EMBRACE THE CAUSE.
YOU ARE WAKING UP THOSE WHO WERE FAST ASLEEP.
FOR OR AGAINST, EVERYONE TALKS ABOUT YOUR IDEAS!
BUT MY FRIEND, WILL THEY TAKE ACTION?

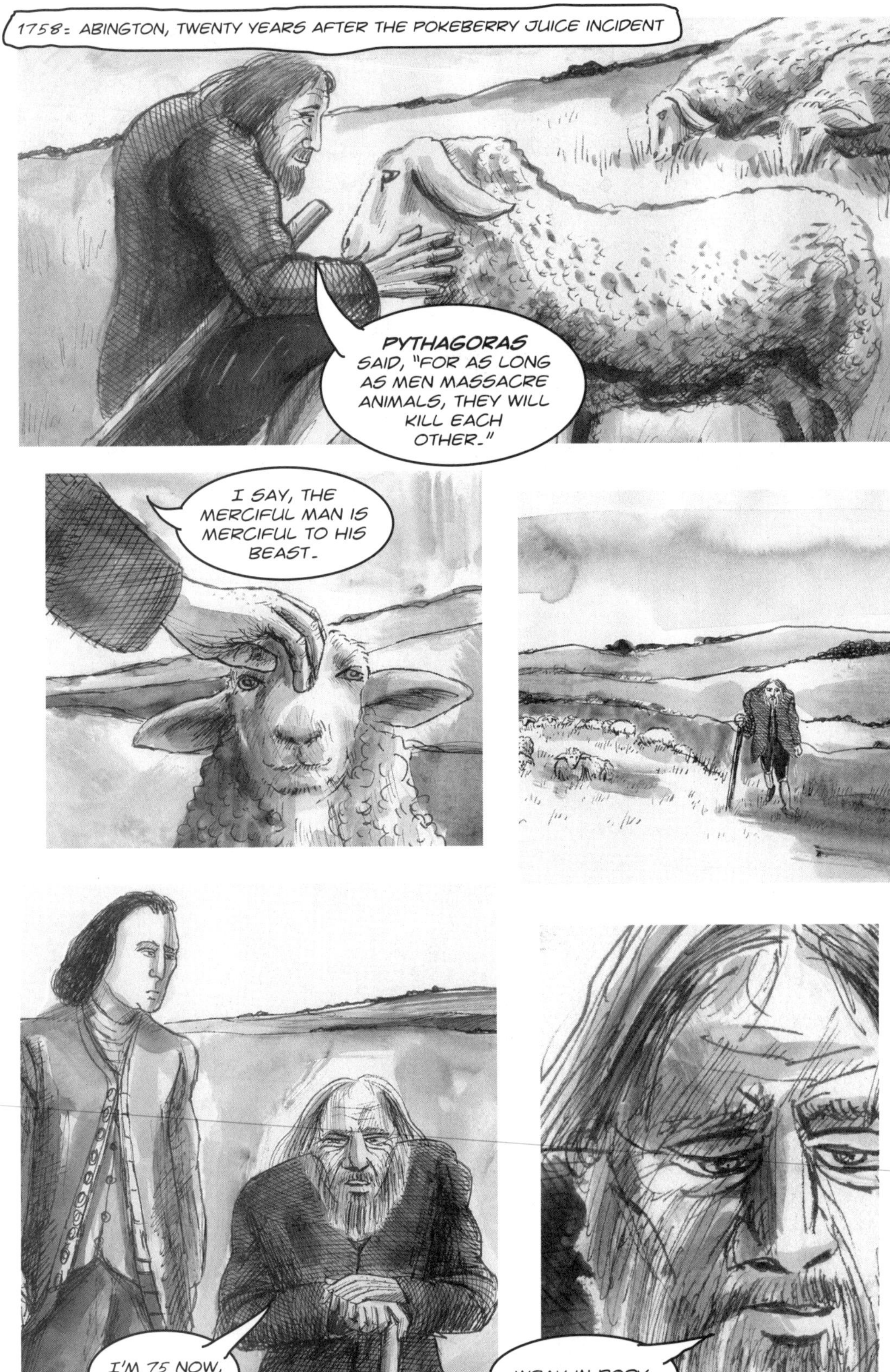
1758: ABINGTON, TWENTY YEARS AFTER THE POKEBERRY JUICE INCIDENT
PYTHAGORAS SAID, "FOR AS LONG AS MEN MASSACRE ANIMALS, THEY WILL KILL EACH OTHER."
I SAY, THE MERCIFUL MAN IS MERCIFUL TO HIS BEAST.
I'M 75 NOW, JOSHUA.
WEAK IN BODY.

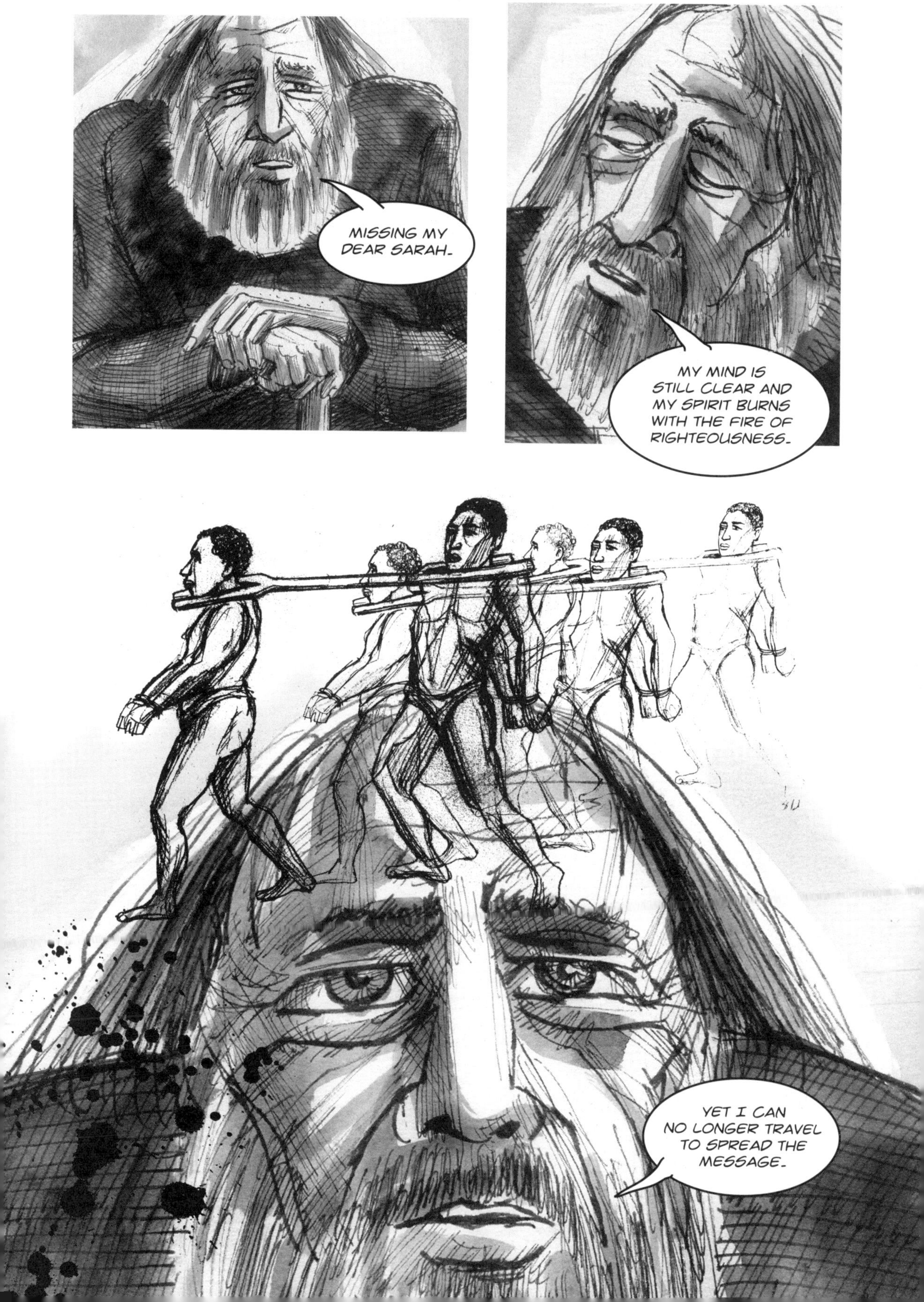
MISSING MY DEAR SARAH.
MY MIND IS STILL CLEAR AND MY SPIRIT BURNS WITH THE FIRE OF RIGHTEOUSNESS.
YET I CAN NO LONGER TRAVEL TO SPREAD THE MESSAGE.

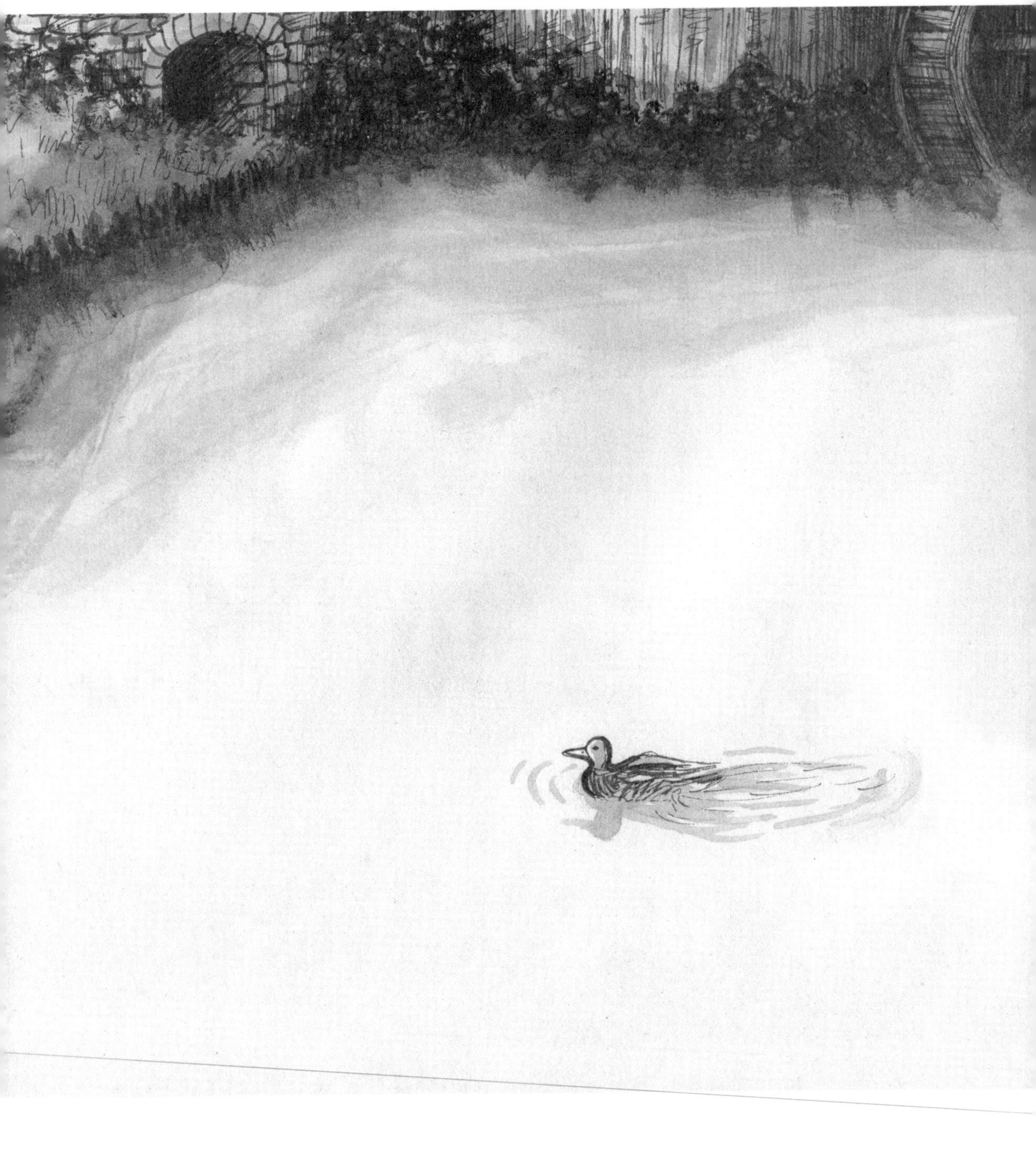

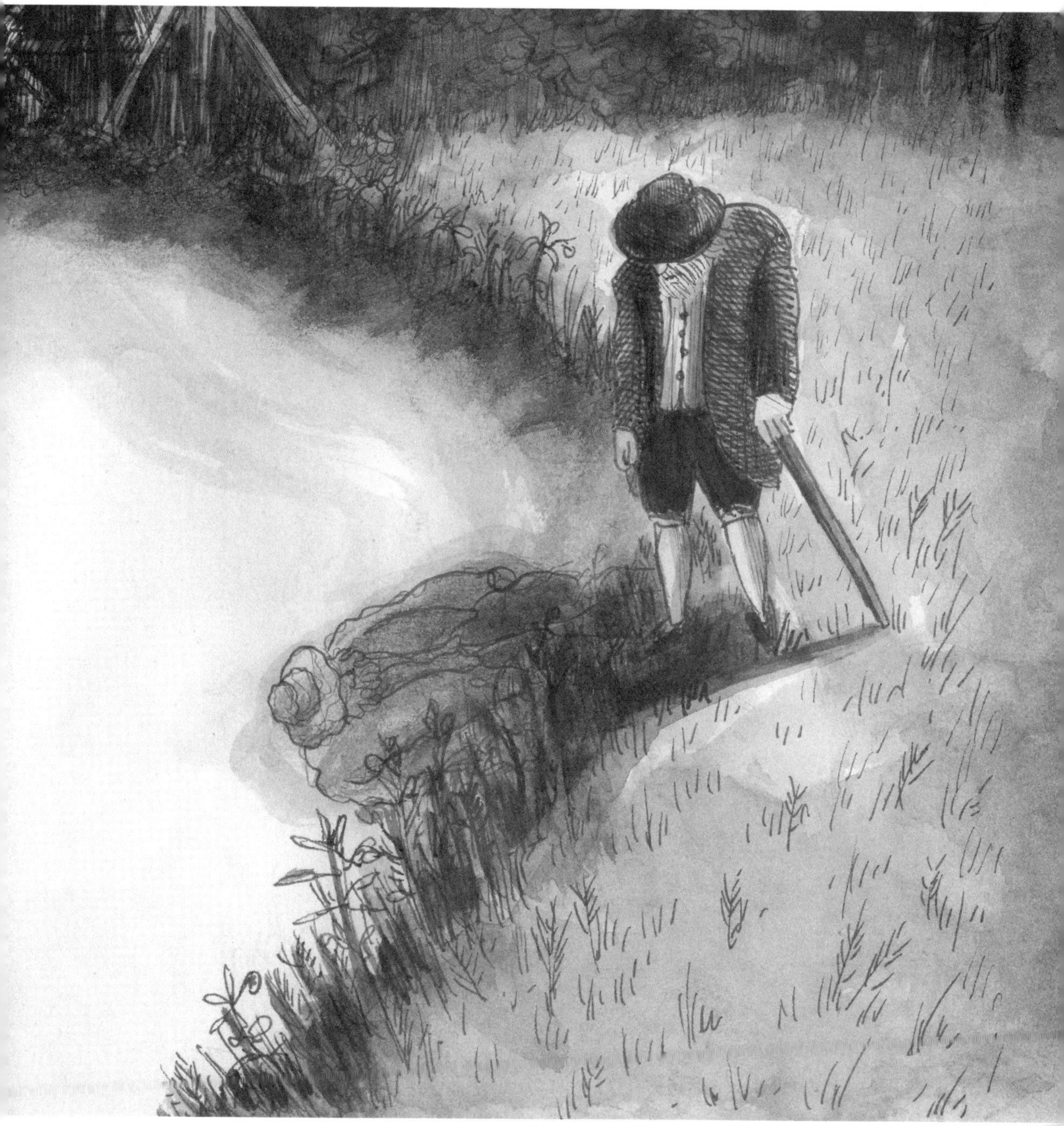

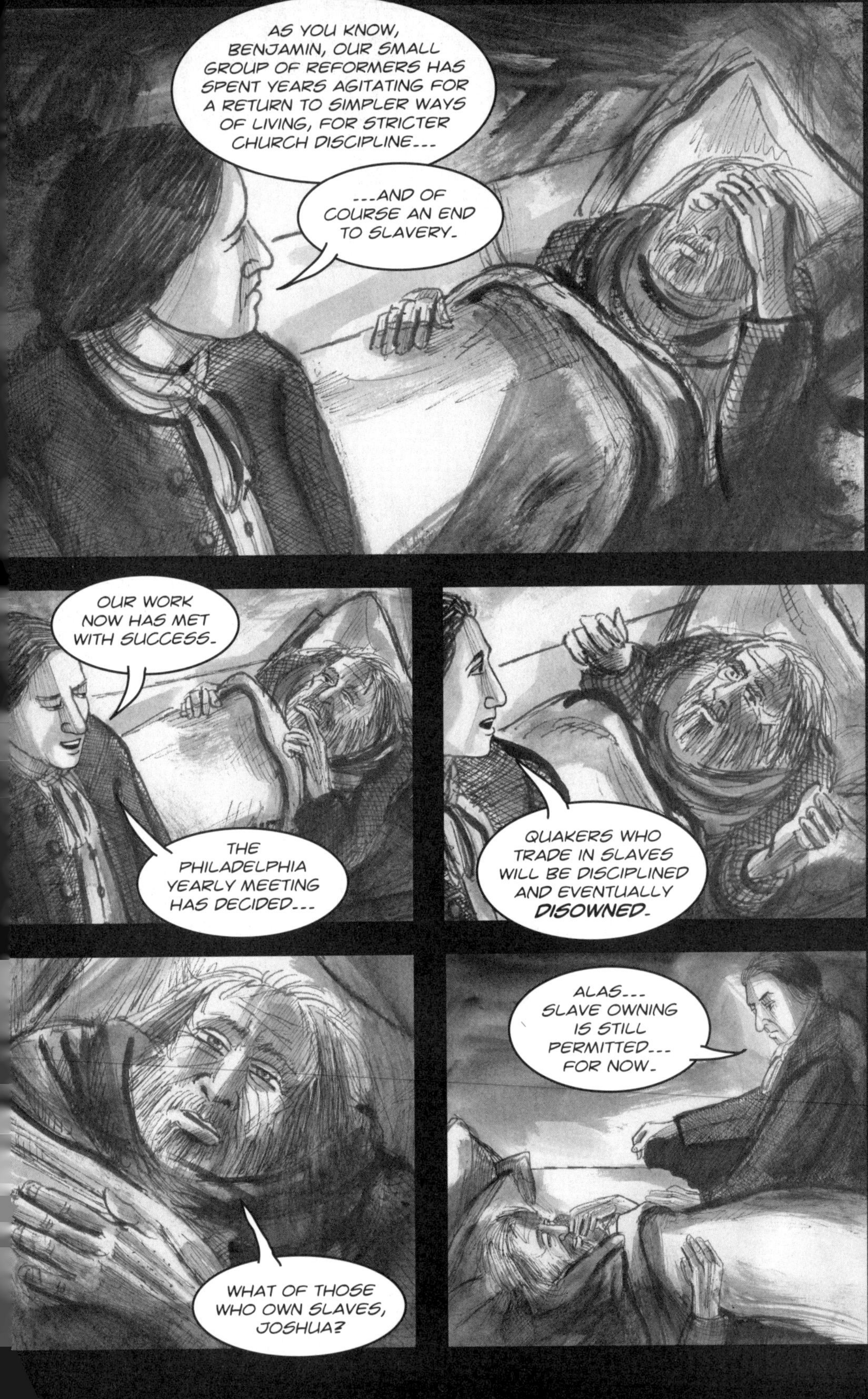
AS YOU KNOW, BENJAMIN, OUR SMALL GROUP OF REFORMERS HAS SPENT YEARS AGITATING FOR A RETURN TO SIMPLER WAYS OF LIVING, FOR STRICTER CHURCH DISCIPLINE...
...AND OF COURSE AN END TO SLAVERY.
OUR WORK NOW HAS MET WITH SUCCESS.
THE PHILADELPHIA YEARLY MEETING HAS DECIDED...
QUAKERS WHO TRADE IN SLAVES WILL BE DISCIPLINED AND EVENTUALLY **DISOWNED**.
WHAT OF THOSE WHO OWN SLAVES, JOSHUA?
ALAS... SLAVE OWNING IS STILL PERMITTED... FOR NOW.

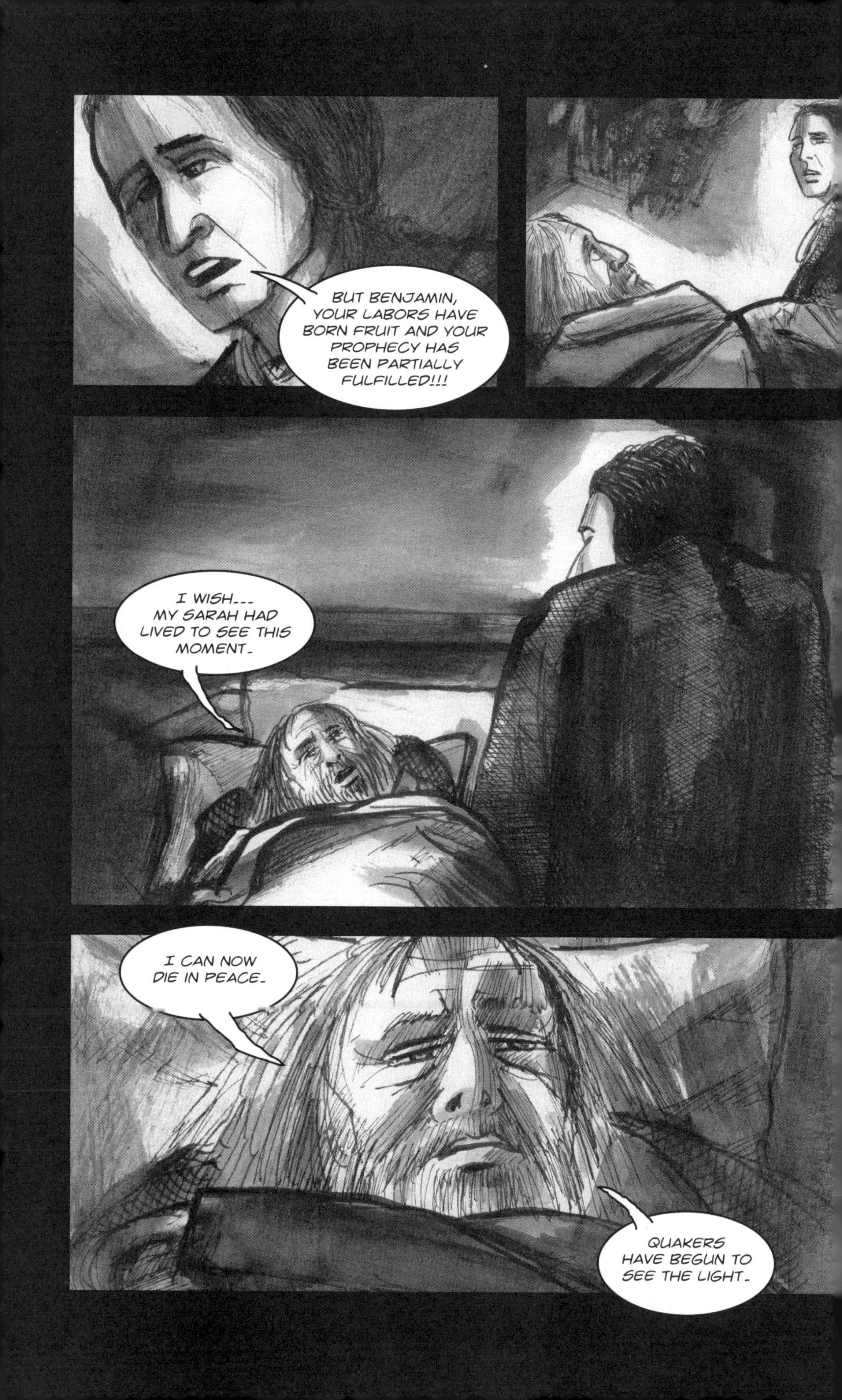
BUT BENJAMIN, YOUR LABORS HAVE BORN FRUIT AND YOUR PROPHECY HAS BEEN PARTIALLY FULFILLED!!!
I WISH... MY SARAH HAD LIVED TO SEE THIS MOMENT.
I CAN NOW DIE IN PEACE.
QUAKERS HAVE BEGUN TO SEE THE LIGHT.

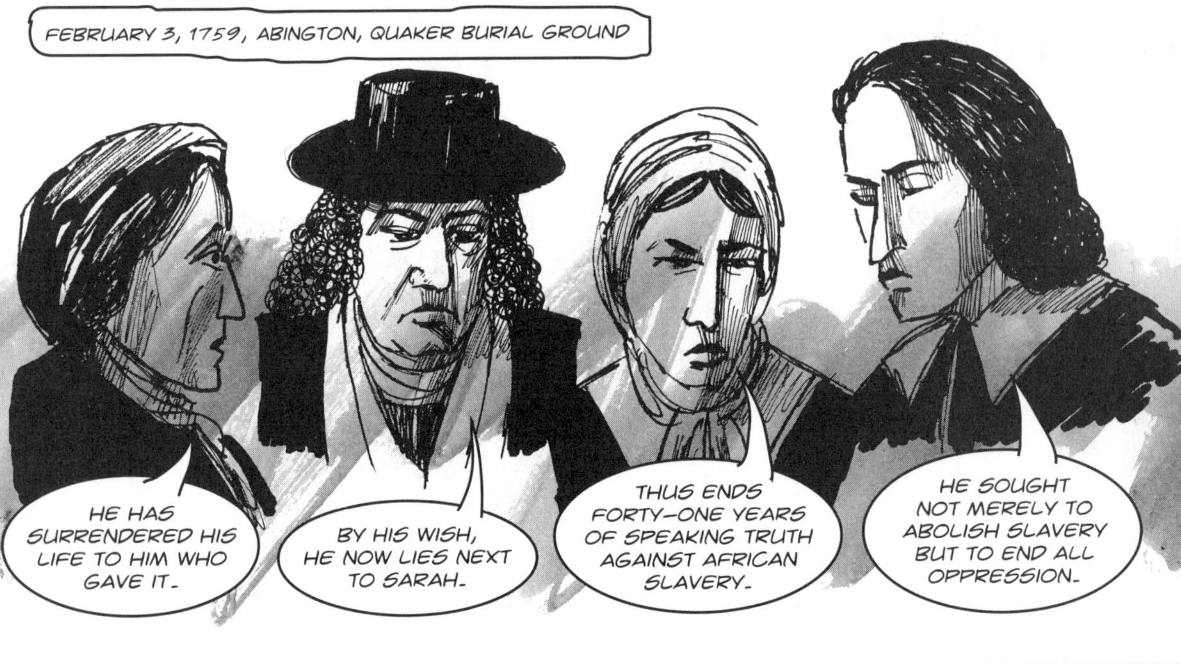
FEBRUARY 3, 1759, ABINGTON, QUAKER BURIAL GROUND
HE HAS SURRENDERED HIS LIFE TO HIM WHO GAVE IT.
BY HIS WISH, HE NOW LIES NEXT TO SARAH.
THUS ENDS FORTY-ONE YEARS OF SPEAKING TRUTH AGAINST AFRICAN SLAVERY.
HE SOUGHT NOT MERELY TO ABOLISH SLAVERY BUT TO END ALL OPPRESSION.
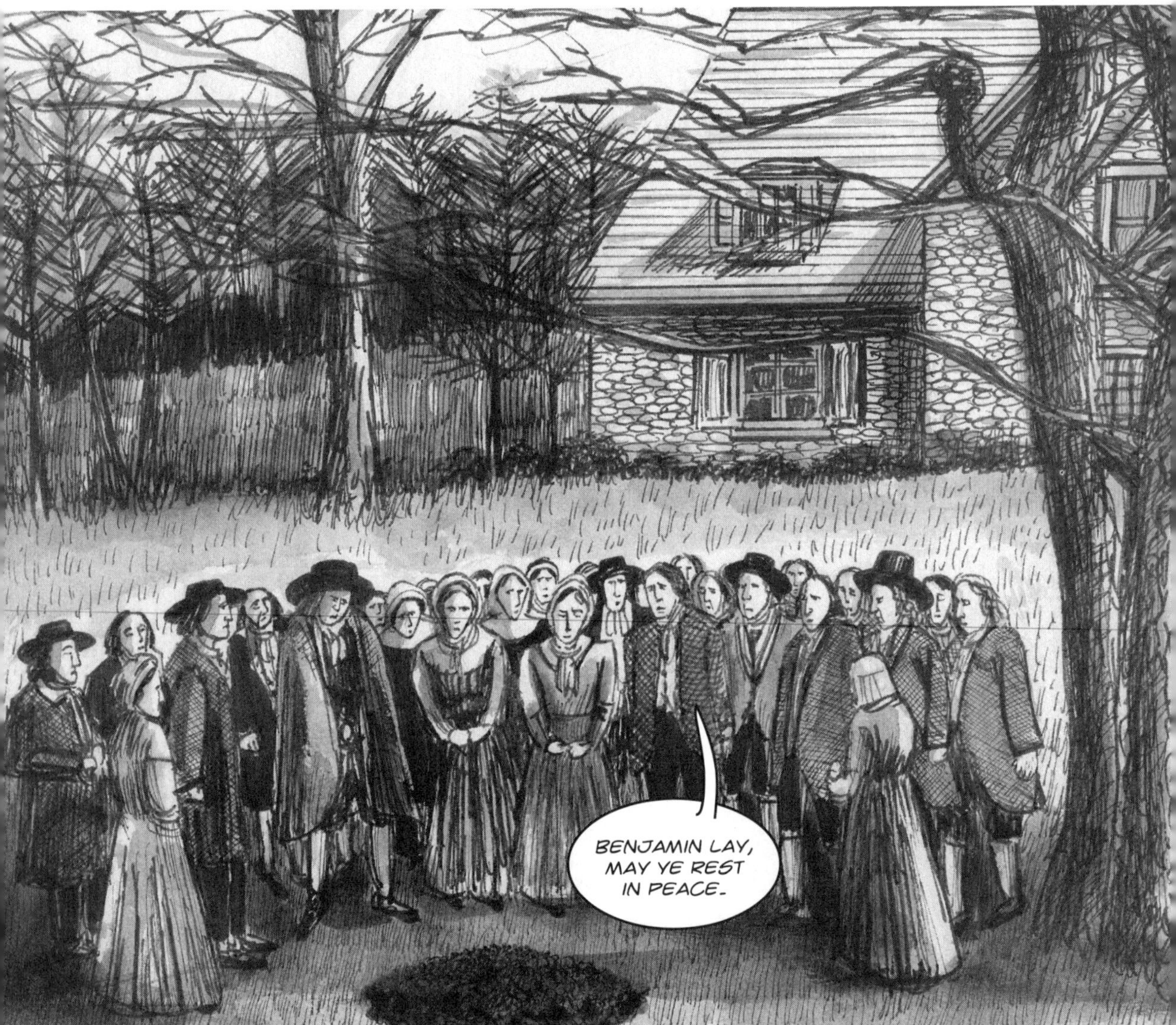
BENJAMIN LAY, MAY YE REST IN PEACE.

POSTSCRIPT

Quakers would continue to own slaves for another 17 years, until 1776. Slavery continued in America for another 103 years, until Abraham Lincoln signed the Emancipation Proclamation in 1862. Lay prophesied that slavery and racism would haunt America for centuries afterward: they "will be as the Poison of Dragons, and the cruel Venom of Asps, in the end, or I am mistaken."

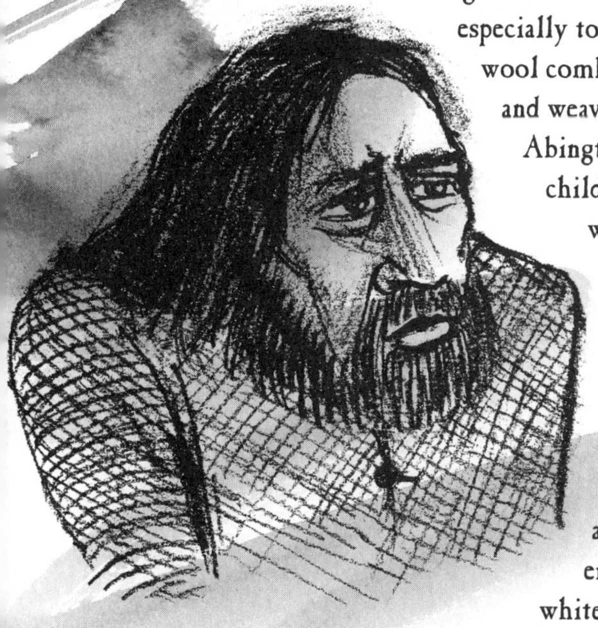

At his death Benjamin Lay had an estate valued at 586 pounds, distributed according to his will among family members in England and especially to "poor Friends," including fellow workers – wool combers, gardeners, sawyers, thatchers, millers, and weavers. Forty pounds went to the school of the Abington Monthly Meeting for the education of poor children. More than half of the recipients were women, mostly widows, but the largest amount of money went to pay the travel costs of Quakers who wanted to come to America without having to indenture themselves as unfree servants.

Abolitionism became the first great social movement in North America. Lay played an important role in founding it, but he was erased from history after the Civil War, when white supremacy was reestablished and public memory of the struggle against slavery faded.

"Perhaps the turbulence and severity of his temper were necessary to rouse the torpor of the human mind .... The meekness and gentleness of Anthony Benezet, who completed what Mr. Lay began, would probably have been as insufficient [but] for the work performed by Mr. Lay."

Benjamin Rush, 1790, signer of the U.S. Declaration of Independence

"Those who profess to favor freedom and yet depreciate agitation, are people who want crops without ploughing the ground; they want rain without thunder and lightning; they want the ocean without the roar of its many waters. The struggle may be a moral one, or it may be a physical one, or it may be both. But it must be a struggle. Power concedes nothing without a demand. It never did and it never will."

– Frederick Douglas, 1857, African American abolitionist

"Let your lives speak." – old Quaker motto

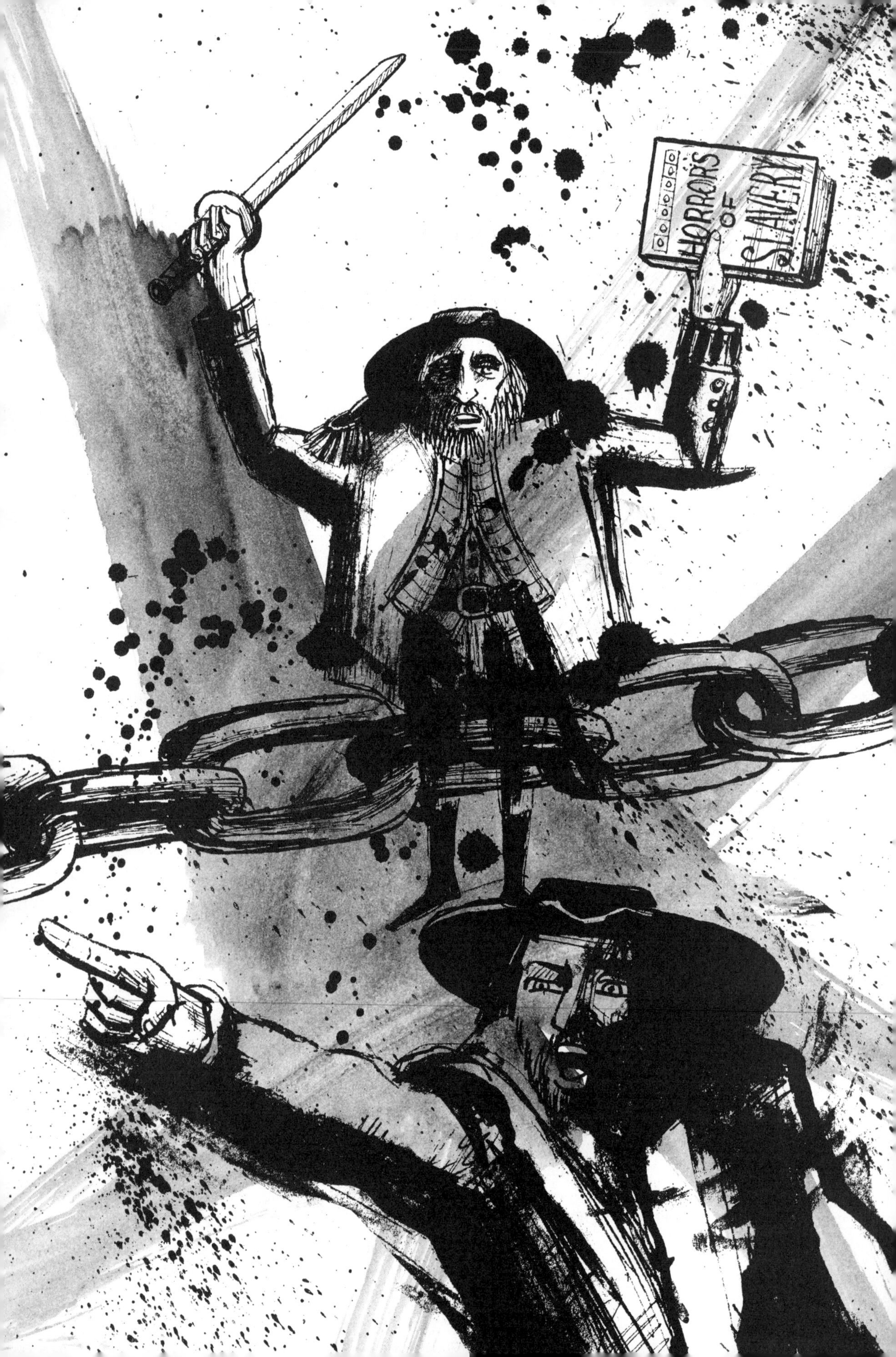
HORRORS OF SLAVERY

AFTERWORD

Why We Need Benjamin Lay

Marcus Rediker

David Lester has brought to life an unusual historical figure, the radical eighteenth-century Quaker Benjamin Lay, one of the first people to demand the worldwide abolition of slavery. Benjamin happened to have dwarfism; he stood around four feet tall. He enacted guerrilla theater against rich Quaker slaveowners, spattering them with fake blood to humiliate them in public. He drew their wrath and was punished for his direct action. Four different Quaker meetings, two in England, two in the United States, excommunicated him; he was the most disowned Quaker of his era. Even though Benjamin was well known in his own day—despised by many, loved by some—he disappeared from public memory in the late nineteenth century and has only recently begun to return. David Lester, Paul Buhle, and I created this graphic novel to recover his inspiring life for our tumultuous times.

As the foregoing pages make vividly clear, Benjamin was a revolutionary. He wanted to "turn the world upside down"—a Biblical phrase often used during the English Revolution to signal the overthrow of the rule of monarchy, gentlemen, slaveowners, patriarchs, and all other kinds of oppressors. This ordinary worker wrote a blistering attack on rich men who "poison the earth for gain." He insisted that slave masters were literally the spawn of Satan and must be crushed, their victims emancipated. He believed that men and women were equal, and indeed he subverted the Quaker gender hierarchy by sitting in the women's section during worship services. He agreed with Pythagoras that people who kill animals will always kill each other. He was committed to animal rights and

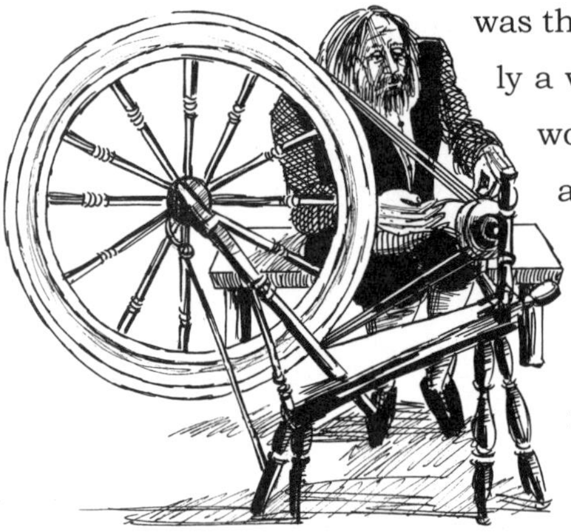

was therefore a vegetarian, more specifically a vegan, two hundred years before the word was invented. He abjured luxury as corruption and lived in a cave (with a big library). He grew his own food and made his own clothes to avoid exploiting the labor of others. He refused to consume any commodity that oppressed people were forced to produce. He rejected the tea manufactured on plantations in India and likewise the sugar made with the blood of enslaved Africans in the Caribbean. Benjamin was a class-conscious, race-conscious, gender-conscious, environmentally conscious man with a fully integrated radical worldview; he was "intersectional" almost three centuries ago!

What can we learn from the life of Benjamin Lay? We can learn about the traps and perils of *complicity*, the ways large and small by which people often unwittingly participate in and perpetuate systems of injustice. By pioneering the boycott of slave-produced commodities, Benjamin created the principle that animates current global struggles against sweatshops operated by Nike and other multinational corporations. Benjamin also made clear that we must not let the markets of capitalism govern our lives, because all commodities disguise their origins in human labor and implicate us in oppressing others. He recognized before almost anyone else that every consumption choice was political and ethical, from smoking Virginia tobacco to eating beef. This tenderhearted man refused to ride horses in order to lessen their exploitation by humans.

Benjamin Lay also teaches us about the power of *solidarity* and *agitation*. He considered all of the natural world, human beings as well as animals, to be his "fellow creatures," a phrase often used among those who sought to turn the world upside down in England in the 1640s and 1650s. Much of what Benjamin knew about solidarity he learned during the twelve years he worked at sea as a common sailor. Seamen entrusted each other with their lives every day at sea and developed strong bonds among themselves amid the danger; they created fictive kinship and called each other "Brother Tars." Benjamin took solidarity further by offering compassion and practical assistance to all who worked under hard conditions, especially the enslaved Africans he met in Barbados and Pennsylvania. But Benjamin made it clear that solidarity was not enough to achieve justice. One also had to "speak truth to power." This self-educated philosopher had read the radical thinker of ancient Greece, Diogenes, who was committed to *parrhesia*, radical free speech. Benjamin spoke fearlessly to the rich and the mighty throughout his life. He advanced his causes through direct confrontation and productive controversy. For or against, all those who knew Benjamin discussed his ideas.

Like an Old Testament prophet, Benjamin warned Americans that if they did not follow his demand to abolish bondage immediately, the legacy of slavery and racism would be profound and lasting. He wrote in 1738, in his scorching book *All Slave-Keepers That Keep the Innocent in Bondage, Apostates*, slavery "will be as the Poison of Dragons, and the cruel Venom of Asps, in the end, or I am mistaken."

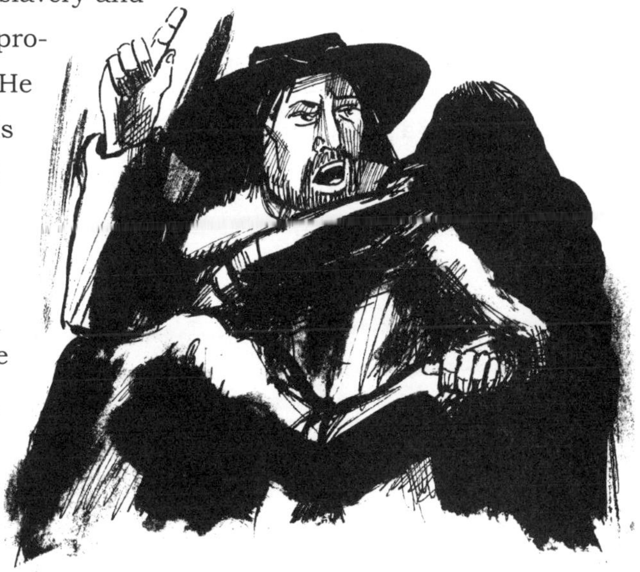

Almost three centuries later, we are still trying to get the poison and the venom—structural racism and its many injustices—out of the body politic.

Benjamin imagined a world without slavery at a time when most people of European descent considered the so-called peculiar institution to be as natural and as eternal as the sun, the stars, and the moon in the heavens. Since Benjamin fashioned his critique of slavery two full generations before antislavery movements developed in the 1780s, it took time for people to catch up to his progressive ideals. His fellow Quakers, who had repeatedly disowned him, finally, in 1776, became the first group to abolish slavery in their own midst: it was no longer possible to be a Quaker and own a slave. Energized by Lay's radicalism, Quaker abolitionists influenced Thomas Clarkson and the early abolitionist movement in England, as well as the Société des Amis des Noirs in France. Benjamin was a transatlantic vector of revolution, a line of force. He should be remembered as a major contributor to the struggle against slavery.

And yet he was, for many years, almost entirely forgotten: Benjamin came from the wrong class; he had the wrong kind of body; he used the wrong methods of protest; he espoused ideas considered too radical. With this graphic novel, David Lester has helped bring him back for a new generation of readers, who might just see in Benjamin's story creative possibilities for a better future, in which we can all live together on "the innocent fruits of the earth" in genuine, abiding peace and equality.

Comic Art and the Artist

Paul Buhle

David Lester is a most unusual artist, perfectly suited for the unique storytelling demands of this book. The pages of many graphic novels today are generally filled with action (the superhero must act) or dialogue (often the very real angst of today's subject). Lester discovered for himself, some years ago, that "wordless" or purely visual pages slow down the action and focus the reader's thoughts. This choice fits Benjamin Lay, the idealist and activist, because Lay spent long periods of his life in contemplation, staring at the sea from aboard ship or at the landscapes of rural England and Pennsylvania.

Historical comics, as Lester notes, can present more than facts. They can impart a "feeling of events unfolding," a process that

involves the artist in "the silence of drawing without words" and engages the reader in the same way.

If we are concerned with predecessor artists and influences, we might look to Lynd Ward's wordless woodcut novels of the 1930s. Ward was inspired in his time by the remarkable and highly lauded works of the Flemish modernist Frans Masereel, so popular in Europe between the world wars. The work of these two twentieth-century giants anticipated the graphic novel by several generations and also established the humane, contemplative quality so marked in this corner of comic art.

Lester looks back, also, to the inspiration he has taken from the drawings and prints of William Hogarth (1697–1764), Albrecht Dürer (1471–1528), and James Gillray (1756–1815), as well as contemporary comic artists Jason Lutes, Kate Evans, Nate Powell, and Joe Sacco.

He goes on to say that "Benjamin Lay's height became a visual dynamic of this book, even though it is only directly referenced in the text a few times. I wanted his height and hump to be depicted in a matter-of-fact way in scenes with his wife, Sarah, and other colleagues, as I imagined that, to these people, his looks would not have aroused any special concern."

In Benjamin's "confrontations with the Quaker establishment, I wanted to depict him as very small at first, but as the story unfolds, Benjamin's arguments gain the moral and political high ground. Tight close-ups of his face also indicate that the dynamic has shifted (his vision cannot be contained). By using close-ups and tilting the angle of his head, metaphorically, it becomes Benjamin who is looking down upon the moral failings and hypocrisy of the Quaker slave-owners, who now must look up. At times, I think Benjamin viewed his height metaphorically, in a David and Goliath battle against slavery. In one scene, I exaggerated that dynamic completely."

These passages of explanation tell us much of what we need to know. Lay is seen, early in the book, as practicing a kind of "guerrilla theater" of the seemingly powerless and, for that time, the aged (at fifty-five) against the powerful, in that sense serving as an inspiration to every reader. This, for Lester, would set the tone properly.

Lester has seized upon visual details in ways that might remind us of the art historian explaining to a rapt audience the nature of a medieval masterpiece. Hands are expressive, as we need to be reminded, and Lester says, "I repeatedly used a visual motif of clasped or touching hands . . . such as when Ben meets a black sailor; his wife; Ralph Sandiford; [and upon] the death of his wife—as ways of showing friendship, love, solidarity, comradeship, and working collectively for a greater good." Visual repetition is, for Lester, at once a mirror and a reflection upon the nature of political activism. The process of social change demands that the same or similar things be done again and again.

Lester is keen, perhaps too keen, on the limits of comic art. Artists drawing "movement" cannot really create a sense of movement with finished work, and in that sense, a rough drawing can be superior (he cites Matisse's *La Danse*, 1910) to one more apparently finished. Having quick sketches overlaid upon each other, such as those showing Benjamin being dragged out of the Quaker meetings, creates that sense of movement and disarray. Likewise, Lester seeks in his drawing of enslaved people to create an unfinished sense, their lives in suspension, while they perform forced labour that creates profit for slave masters.

So far, few historical graphic novels have reached back further than the nineteenth century, and the treatment of slavery and the struggles against slavery have rarely reached the artist's hand. *Prophet Against Slavery* establishes a precedent and lifts comic art upward to a new level.

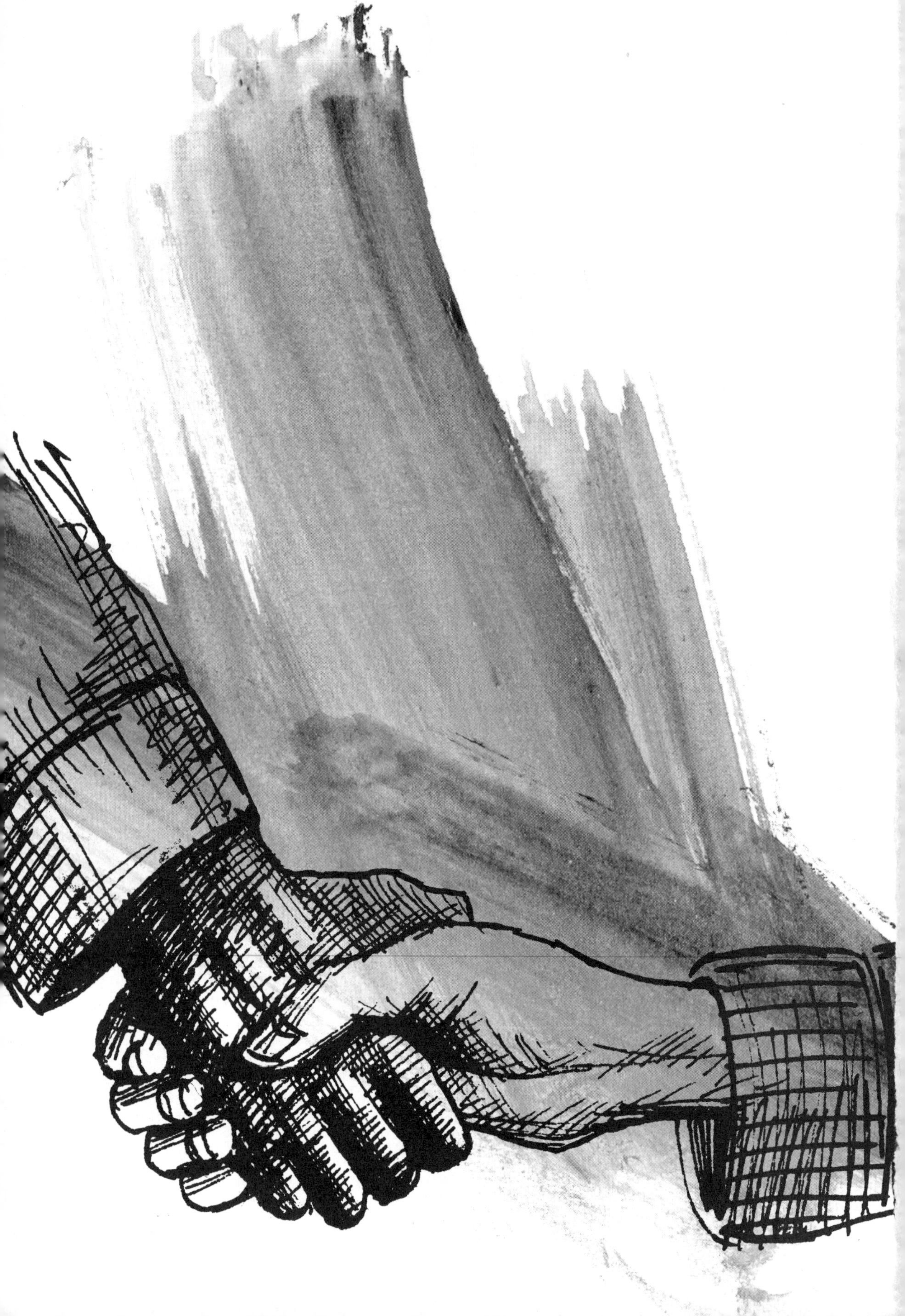